International Marketing Strategy
2002–2003

International Marketing Strategy 2002–2003

Steve Carter

OXFORD AMSTERDAM BOSTON LONDON NEW YORK PARIS
SAN DIEGO SAN FRANCISCO SINGAPORE SYDNEY TOKYO

Butterworth-Heinemann
An imprint of Elsevier Science
Linacre House, Jordan Hill, Oxford OX2 8DP
225 Wildwood Avenue, Woburn MA 01801-2041

First published 2002

British Library Cataloguing in Publication Data
A catalogue record for this book is available from the British Library

ISBN 0 7506 5709 X

For information on all Butterworth-Heinemann publications
visit our website at www.bh.com

Typeset by Integra Software Services Pvt. Ltd, Pondicherry, India
www.integra-india.com
Printed and bound in Italy

Contents

An introduction from the academic development advisor

This year has seen the continuation of our commitment to ensure that the CIM Coursebooks are kept up to date and relevant for the forthcoming session. This is deemed as essential as the dynamics of the global market are forever changing, often in a way most unexpected and indeed not anticipated – as no doubt you will have all experienced, especially in the wake of September 11th.

Over the past few years there have been a series of syllabus changes initiated by the Chartered Institute of Marketing to ensure that their qualifications continue to be relevant and of significant consequence in the world of marketing, both within industry and academia. As a result Butterworth-Heinemann and I are continuing to rigorously revise and update the Coursebook series in order to make sure that every title is the best possible study aid and accurately reflects the latest CIM syllabus.

The ongoing updates and revisions to the series include both restructuring and the inclusion of many new mini cases and examples to support the learning and assessment process. The authors are accomplished writers and have been commissioned both for their CIM course teaching and examining experience and their wide general knowledge of the latest marketing thinking.

We are certain that the coursebooks will be highly beneficial to your study, providing you with structure, direction, relevant examples and assessment opportunities that will enable you to focus on acquiring the broad range of theory and concepts required to underpin the examination and continuous assessment process.

The editorial team and authors wish you every success as you embark upon your studies.

Karen Beamish

Academic Development Advisor

How to use these coursebooks

Everyone who has contributed to this series has been careful to structure the books with the exams in mind. Each unit, therefore, covers an essential part of the syllabus. You need to work through the complete coursebook systematically to ensure that you have covered everything you need to know.

This coursebook is divided into units each containing a selection of the following standard elements:

- **Objectives** tell you what part of the syllabus you will be covering and what you will be expected to know, having read the unit.
- **Study guides** tell you how long the unit is and how long its activities take to do.
- **Questions** are designed to give you practice – they will be similar to those you get in the exam.
- **Answers** (at the end of the book) give you a suggested format for answering exam questions. *Remember* there is no such thing as a model answer – you should use these examples only as guidelines.
- **Activities** give you a chance to put what you have learned into practice.
- **Debriefings** (at the end of the book) shed light on the methodologies involved in the activities.

- **Exam hints** are tips from the senior examiner or examiner which are designed to help you avoid common mistakes made by previous candidates.
- **Study tips** give you guidance on improving your knowledge base.
- **Insights** encourage you to contextualize your academic knowledge by reference to real-life experience.
- **Definitions** may be used for words you must know to pass the exam.
- **Summaries** cover what you should have picked up from reading the unit.

While you will find that each section of the syllabus has been covered within this text, you might find that the order of some of the topics has been changed. This is because it sometimes makes more sense to put certain topics together when you are studying, even though they might appear in different sections of the syllabus itself. If you are following the reading and other activities, your coverage of the syllabus will be just fine, but don't forget to follow up with trade press reading!

The coursebook in a glance

Unit	Objectives	Syllabus	Summary
Unit 1 Introduction	International marketing strategy has always been a major factor in the success of important trading nations such as Britain. Now that membership of the EU has been secured, international marketing skills are becoming even more important to marketers. In this unit you will: • Understand the range of tasks involved in international marketing strategy • Review the strategic process See syllabus sections 2.1.1, 2.1.2, 2.2.1, 2.2.2, 2.2.3, 2.2.8 and 2.2.10 • Understand the Diploma International Marketing syllabus • Understand what is meant by international marketing See syllabus section 2.1.2 • Understand the reasons why organizations 'go international' See syllabus sections 2.1.1 and 2.1.2	2.1.1, 2.1.2, 2.1.4, 2.1.5, 2.1.6, 2.1.7, 2.2.1, 2.2.2, 2.2.3, 2.2.8, 2.2.10	In this introductory unit we have considered the format and approach that this book will take in addressing the international marketing strategy syllabus and the importance of using this book in conjunction with other international marketing texts recommended for the examination. We have also considered the detailed analysis of the syllabus as well as the all-important learning objectives and outcomes required for a successful attempt at the examination itself. Finally, we considered the overall nature of the international marketing strategy tasks and we concluded that: • There is little conceptual difference between international marketing and domestic marketing. • The focus of the international marketer's activity is the customer (as in the domestic situation), but the customer happens to be in a foreign market with all that that entails.

Unit	Objectives	Syllabus	Summary

Objectives

- Review the principal forms of financial risk for the international organization

  See syllabus sections 2.1.4 and 2.1.5
- Consider the role of the marketing information system in reducing the risk of international expansion

  See syllabus sections 2.1 6 and 2.1.7
- Review the range of models that may be of use in assessing foreign market opportunities.

  See syllabus sections 2.1.4, 2.1.5 to 2.1.8

Having completed this unit you will be able to:

- Explain how to avoid problems in international marketing
- Appreciate the key questions involved in 'going international'
- Advise an organization on whether to go international and the key questions involved in this strategic decision
- Explain the role of international marketing in the overall international business process
- Identify the key drivers behind an organization's international strategy
- Evaluate the main areas of risk in international operations
- Establish ways of reducing risk in planning an organization's international marketing strategy.

Syllabus Summary

- A primary problem in successful international business is the social/cultural conditioning of the international marketer (remember the SRC).
- International marketing consists of four interrelated questions: Whether to? Where to? What to? How to?
- The international marketing strategic process can be seen as a logical series of steps which will take the business from a domestic organization to an international organization and possibly to a global organization.

In this unit we have seen that there are a number of very good reasons why organizations may decide to 'go international'. The opportunities and potential profits for an organization can often be quite sizeable. At the same time, there are some significant risks in such operations, particularly foreign exchange risk and political risk. In any event, some detailed market research and analysis is required in order to uncover likely marketplace opportunities for the organization and a range of models exist to help you in this evaluation process.

One final word of warning is that you should bring some common sense to bear on the market research data when available. The data analysis and scanning may identify gaps in the marketplace – the international marketer has to decide whether there is a market in the g!

Unit	Objectives	Syllabus	Summary

Unit 2
The importance
of international
marketing

In this unit we highlight the growing importance of international marketing and the changes that are accelerating its importance. Understanding the changes that are underpinning the development of world trade – events that are shaping everyone's life wherever they might live and work. In this unit you will:

- Appreciate the growth and scale of world trade
- Consider just how 'international' our everyday lives are

  See syllabus sections 2.1.1 and 2.1.3
- Understand the macro forces at work shaping the business world of today and the future

  See syllabus section 2.1.3
- Study the factors that are increasingly important in defining success

  See syllabus sections 2.2.2 and 2.1.3

Having completed the unit you will be able to:

- Identify the key drivers in world trade
- Appreciate what is creating convergence in consumer behaviour
- Understand the changes in international business
- Recognize that domestic horizons are increasingly meaningless in the fast-changing 'global village'
- Explain the essential balance of trade between the key trading nations
- Discuss potential future developments and the impact of the emergence of new giant economies

2.1.1,
2.1.3,
2.2.2

Having read this unit you should be in no doubt that international marketing is a driving force in developing world trade. Fewer firms can restrict their thinking to the narrow confines of domestic marketing. International influences are affecting everyone's behaviour. Reliance on the 'home' market can only be sustainable where government protection prevails – and that is in decline. Facing up to international trends in planning for inward competition is an essential prerequisite of every organization.

Trade between nations is the engine that drives the world economy. It needs supporting otherwise the alternative (i.e. a breakdown in international trade) will result in misery for everyone. Yet unfettered trading can also create a perilous scenario. Of crucial importance is balance – equilibrium with openness and liberalization held in perspective by world forces. But this balance is constantly under threat as individual nations protect and encourage home industries. Tensions are forever arising as nations expand or decline on the world scene. World trade is not static, it is forever changing.

Unit	Objectives	Syllabus	Summary

- Debate whether regionalism will be a force for good or bad
- Understand barriers to trade and their impact
- Initiate discussion on the role of the key facilitating agencies (e.g. GATT/WTO) and relate their relevance to the nation state and the individual firm.

Unit 3 Customers

Customers and an understanding of customer needs and motivations are key to any successful marketing strategy – domestic or international. In international marketing strategy the problem is made more complex for two reasons. First, customers tend to be in different countries and different markets with different environmental effects acting upon them. Second, the self-reference criterion makes it difficult for marketers of a different culture to understand fully how and why a given customer in an overseas market may act differently to the same marketing stimulus. In this unit we will look at the key factors which impinge upon customer behaviour in overseas markets and we will attempt to build a picture of how the international marketer might go about trying to understand the nature and complexities of the foreign market selected.

The best way to understand customers (or to attempt to!) is to analyse and identify those factors of the environment that affect the way that they think and behave. In this unit you will:

- Review the factors that affect buyer behaviour
- Evaluate the key elements of culture

2.1.4, 2.1.5, 2.1.6, 2.1.8

In this unit we have considered the various environmental factors which act upon the customer in a given or prospective foreign marketplace. We have seen the heavy impact of culture on buyer behaviour and perceptions as well as the infrastructure constraints delivered by legal, economic and political systems.

Technology, competition and currency are all moving to global stages and are having serious effects on international business worldwide. Although often difficult to predict, these effects cannot be ignored or international profitability will suffer badly.

Finally we considered how to select target markets on the basis of this analysis and the broad parameters required for successful marketing strategy implementation which follows.

| | • Consider the main aspects of the international legal environment
• Consider the main aspects of the international political environment
• Consider the main aspects of the international economic environment

See syllabus sections 2.1.4, 2.1.5 and 2.1.6
• Review the process of international market selection

See syllabus sections 2.1.4, 2.1.5 and 2.1.8
Having completed this unit you will be able to:
• Understand the differences in business and social/cultural conventions which affect buying behaviours in international markets
• Understand how different stages of economic growth affect buying behaviours
• Appreciate how marketing approaches for different foreign markets are driven by local needs and environmental conditions
• Prioritize and select foreign markets. | | |
| Unit 4
The search for information | Knowledge is power. In this unit you will study the key issues relating to gathering information on the international front. The scale of the task is wider and the problems in collecting data multiply as markets and | 2.1.6, 2.1.7 | All too frequently organizations fall back on one of two strategies when dealing with information issues on the international front. Self-reference criteria, i.e. foreigners are just like us and if we licked the problem 'here' we can do it |

Unit	Objectives	Syllabus	Summary

customers differ. The major thrust of the unit is not concerned with the specifics and technical details of gathering information but discusses the management perspective. You will:

- Understand issues relating to scanning international markets to decide initially where we should go in the broadest terms
- Examine models of how to approach the broad tasks of identifying market/product combinations and on to prioritize opportunities
- Study the sources of international data and how to deal with such issues as researching within numerous markets
- Understand the difficulties involved in comparing data across countries/markets, i.e. cross-country research.
- Have a knowledge of the problems and pitfalls of international primary and secondary research.
- Know the basic principles of appointing an international market research agency
- Be aware of technology and its impact on information gathering, i.e. the internet.

See syllabus sections 2.1.6 and 2.1.7.

Having completed the unit you will be able to:

- Explain the difference between gathering data from an international market(s) and a domestic one

overseas or, alternatively, use guesswork. Both approaches invariably result in grief. It is clear that if information = knowledge = power then it is even more important that we have the facts in dealing with environments beyond our normal range of experience. Knowing where to start and how to go about gathering information on overseas nations and customers must be the fundamental benchwork that underpins all our thinking.

Unit	Objectives	Syllabus	Summary
	• Apply the process of narrowing down broad-scale international opportunities and identify specific countries for further more detailed examination • Match sources of data to specific problems • Identify the resource implications of international market research. NB: A lot of the fine detail concerning management information and subsequent market decisions is covered in the module 'Management Information and Market Decisions' at Advanced Certificate Level.		
Unit 5 Planning for international marketing	This unit is concerned with the ways in which the firm can exploit defined marketing opportunities in international markets and how best it can organize itself. In studying the unit you will: • Understand the concepts of international marketing planning • Come to terms with the importance of planning and the changing frameworks as companies deepen their involvement See syllabus section 2.2.1 and 2.2.2 • Review the key planning models and match marketing variables to strategic international decisions See syllabus sections 2.2.3, 2.2.4 and 2.2.6 • Understand the basic options in determining	2.2.1, 2.2.2, 2.2.3, 2.2.4, 2.2.6, 2.2.7, 2.2.10, 2.2.11	This unit has covered two strategic aspects of international marketing: first, the line of marketing planning and second the organizational implications. Both involved a high degree of personnel issues. The unit discussed briefly the importance of models in developing strategy and also considered the marketing planning variables set against the key international decision areas. This particular matrix is of considerable help in defining quickly your options (from the perspective of the examination) and the issues revolving around control. Likewise, the manner in which the company organizes itself to best deal with its international development establishes the level of involvement and the intensity of its competitive impact. There is a wide variety of choice. Finally, the unit discussed developments that will shape the competitive

the international market entry plan

See syllabus section 2.2.10

- Recognize that control systems are even more important internationally than domestically
- Identify the key organizational issues that concern international development and the employment decision.

See syllabus sections 2.2.7 and 2.2.11

See also the Planning and Control syllabus of the Diploma in Marketing for further detail of the planning process relevant to this section.

Having completed the unit you will be able to:

- Cross-reference planning with strategic issues
- Evaluate the suitability of specific market entry strategies
- Identify the elements of an international marketing plan
- List the stages of the control process and establish key principles of a control system
- Explain the different methods a firm might employ in creating and developing its international organization
- Explain the variables that affect organizational structure
- Evaluate the roles and conflicts of HQ versus local management structures.

challenges in the future.

Choosing the appropriate entry strategy is probably the most perplexing decision that companies have to make. A survey among CEOs of American companies suggested that they spent more time deliberating this question than any other in international business. Once the decision is taken it determines the rest of your strategy – financial, managerial as well as marketing. Moreover, it establishes the terms of engagement in the war for sales in a chosen marketplace. Such decisions are not taken lightly. But success in the future is not for the slow or the timid. Companies are going to have to become more ambitious and radical in their approach to the question – joint ventures, strategic alliances, complex partnerships between firms and governments are becoming the order of the day. The pace of advancement, customer demand and technology are forcing developments. Yet exit strategies are also important considerations. So the final thought is that flexibility will prevail over rigidity in the future.

Unit	Objectives	Syllabus	Summary
Unit 6 Globalization	Globalization as a strategic option open to the international organization has been a major topic of discussion since Theodore Levitt wrote his mould-breaking article in 1983 (*Harvard Business Review*). Globalization, in essence, is about treating the world as one market both for marketing and for production purposes. In this unit you will: • Understand what globalization means • Consider the factors which drive an organization towards a globalized strategy • Understand the factors which may affect or inhibit a drive towards globalization • Be aware of when a globalized strategy is appropriate for an organization and when it is not See syllabus sections 2.2.2 and 2.2.5 Having completed this unit you will be able to: • Consider the viability or otherwise of globalization as a strategy for the international organization • Understand the implications of a globalization strategy upon the organization, its marketing, its production and organizational structure • Understand the effects of a globalization strategy upon the international marketing mix.	2.2.2, 2.2.5	In this unit we have seen that globalization is a major force in international marketing strategy. The benefits from a globalized marketing approach are significant and offer major economies from a standardized approach to foreign markets. There are a number of reasons globalization is coming to the fore and many international marketing variables are stimulating interest in this area. There are also a number of factors which may stand in the way of an organization successfully globalizing its operations, and most of these are concerned with local tastes, requirements and perceptions. In any event, the organization considering globalization should: 1 Not be dazzled by the rare instances of successful pure globalization 2 Carefully research and understand overseas markets before moving to globalization 3 Look for similarities as well as differences in overseas markets before planning 4 Carefully evaluate the savings to be made from a globalized/ standardized approach against the likely loss of sales from not fully meeting local market requirements.

Unit	Objectives	Syllabus	Summary
Unit 7 Managing international marketing	This unit is concerned with issues pertaining to managing international business/marketing. The issues covered straddle other complementary ones which are mentioned in a variety of areas in the study guide. In studying the unit you will:	2.2.4, 2.2.6, 2.2.7, 2.3.6, 2.3.7	Successful firms of tomorrow will have to leapfrog the mindset of the domestic organization. Literally thinking global will be one of the crucial management skills. Leadership, vision, flexibility and cross-cultural diversity are prerequisites. The day of the manager with a lifetime's experience in one country only may soon be a thing of the past.

- Recognize that, with the changing nature of international business and customers, the successful company must develop a learning culture.

  See syllabus section 2.2.4.

- Recognize that economic transience affects all firms and that strategies need to be developed to cope with change and uncertainty.

  See syllabus section 2.2.6.

- Understand the principles involved in controlling in-house and external resources.

  See syllabus section 2.2.7.

- Understand that the management and development of global human resource management, planning, training and creating a global mindset are essential prerequisites for success.

  See syllabus sections 2.3.6 and 2.3.7. This element is developed in detail in the next unit, 'Managing the International Mix'.

Unit	Objectives	Syllabus	Summary
Unit 8 Managing the international mix	International marketing, like domestic marketing, ultimately depends on satisfying customer needs and wants. To do this the organization must use the full range of the marketing mix. Using the 7Ps* mix, this unit, and the next unit, will consider: * Note: The international place policy is dealt with separately in Unit 10, embracing distribution, operational and implementation issues. • The international product mix See syllabus sections 2.2.8 and 2.3.1. • The international pricing mix See syllabus section 2.3.2. • The international promotion and physical evidence mix See syllabus section 2.3.3 and 2.3.6. • The international people mix • The international process mix. See also section 3.4 of the Planning and Control syllabus Diploma paper and the Integrated Marketing Communications syllabus Diploma paper. Having completed this unit you will be able to: • Evaluate the factors which drive decisions in the international mix • Identify the optimum product range through international portfolio analysis • Apply the tools of international marketing communications to a	2.2.8, 2.3.1, 2.3.2, 2.3.3, 2.3.6	In this unit we have seen that the primary question in international product policy is that of product standardization. The argument over standardization-adaptation is a very important one because: • The economies of scale which can be obtained through a standardized approach to international markets are considerable. • The reasons for an organization to adapt or modify its product/service offering to each separate international market are also compelling. At the end of the day, the primary consideration must be for long-term profitability and the candidate will be required to assess this objective against any situations presented in the questions or the case study. Remember also that profitability is not the same thing as sales maximization, nor is it driven out by economies of scale on their own. A balance needs to be struck between the needs of the organization and those of the marketplace. • Product policy is a key area in international marketing and decisions here will affect the entire marketing mix which follows. Customer considerations must always be top of mind for the marketer – domestic or international, and the

given set of circumstances
- Develop the physical evidence of international operations
- Discuss the debate on international branding
- Integrate pricing into the other elements of the international marketing mix.

role of market research in uncovering market needs cannot be overestimated in the international market situation.
- In this section we have considered the array of factors which influence and should help the international marketer to determine international pricing policy. Pricing is probably one of the most complicated areas of international marketing strategy but has major impact upon the financial performance of the organization. Pricing also plays a major role in supporting product strategy (differentiation and positioning) as well as communication strategy where it has a major impact on perceived quality.
- We have seen that in order to arrive at sensible prices the international marketer needs to understand the objectives behind the pricing approach as well as the factors which are often different from market to market. Standardized pricing approaches for international markets are not always necessary although some degree of coordination between markets may be desirable if only to stop the possibility of parallel importing.
- Pricing is treated by many marketers as a

tactical activity. In this unit you should have understood that pricing policy has a major strategic influence on the organization and should not be relegated to purely tactical decision making at a lower level.

- Marketing communication is probably the most discussed area of international marketing. Not only is it rarely out of the news (it invites controversy) but the majority of us have exposure to it. What makes it so interesting is that it is culturally loaded. Everyone has a view. The challenge for the future is increasingly to internationalize the communicative mix. World consumers, world competitors, world advertising agencies lead to a consolidation in strategic terms of the marketing effort. Yet the paradox exists. Consumers though seeking global benefits remain doggedly local in their outlook. While strategy can take the global view, marketing must balance the benefits of 'one sight, one sound, one sell' with local needs. Issues such as cost, coordination and control also require careful consideration before any decisions are taken.

Unit	Objectives	Syllabus	Summary
Unit 9 International people and process	This unit is a continuing discussion of the international marketing mix stated in the previous unit. A long-held traditional approach to the marketing mix has been that of the '4Ps', however, in recent years, the mix has been extended to include the vital '3Ps', physical evidence, people and process. We have already dealt with physical evidence in the last unit so this unit concerns itself with people and process. Without people to plan, implement and control the international marketing plan then nothing will happen. This means that they need good human resource management also, for without proper motivation as well as control, staff will be ineffective and inefficient. Staffing issues concern the use of both internal, expatriate and local staff. Similarly, process management is all about production, maketing and operations management. This involves issues of customer contact and quality control standards. It must always be remembered that international operations are all about people engaging with people, hence the importance of people and process. In this unit you will study: • The international people mix See syllabus section 2.3.7 • The international process mix See syllabus section 2.3.6.	2.3.6, 2.3.7	In this unit we have considered the vital marketing mix elements of people and process and looked at a case study of a global operator, utilizing the international marketing mix. International operations would not take place without either of these elements. In considering people we have to look closely at the engagement of local people versus expatriates. Equally we have to carefully manage our own employees both effectively and efficiently. The degree of customer contact and quality control standards are other vital issues. It is the whole essence of marketing that customers are delighted every time that they come in contact with an organization. On a global scale this is extremely important but difficult to accomplish. People are a vital part of this process. Product policy is a key area in international marketing and decisions here will affect the entire marketing mix which follows. Customer considerations must always be paramount in the mind of the marketer – domestic or international, and the role of market research in uncovering market needs cannot be overestimated in the international market situation. In this section we have considered the array of factors which influence and should help the international marketer to determine international pricing policy. Pricing is probably one of the most complicated areas of international marketing strategy but has major impact upon the financial performance of the organization. Pricing also

Unit	Objectives	Syllabus	Summary

On completing the unit you will be able to:

- Understand the importance of people and process in international operations
- Develop the people and process elements of international operations.

plays a major role in supporting product strategy (differentiation and positioning) as well as communication strategy where it has a major impact on perceived quality.

We have seen that in order to arrive at sensible prices the international marketer needs to understand the objectives behind the pricing approach as well as the factors which are often different from market to market. Standardized pricing approaches for international markets are not always necessary although some degree of coordination between markets may be desirable if only to stop the possibility of parallel importing.

Pricing is treated by many marketers as a tactical activity. In this unit you should have understood that pricing policy has a major strategic influence on the organization and should not be relegated to purely tactical decision making at a lower level.

Marketing communication is probably the most discussed area of international marketing. Not only is it rarely out of the news (it invites controversy) but the majority of us have exposure to it. What makes it so interesting is that it is culturally loaded. Everyone has a view. The challenge for the future is increasingly to internationalize the communicative mix. World consumers, world competitors, world advertising agencies lead to a consolidation in strategic terms of the marketing effort. Yet the paradox exists. Consumers though seeking global benefits remain doggedly local in their outlook. While

Unit	Objectives	Syllabus	Summary
			strategy can take the global view, marketing must balance the benefits of 'one sight, one sound, one sell' with local needs. Issues such as cost, coordination and control also require careful consideration before any decisions are taken.
Unit 10 Operational and implementation issues	Distribution and logistics are fast becoming critical factors in international marketing. Speed or time is increasingly the critical differential linked to costs. Getting the product or service delivered to the customer when it is needed and responding flexibly to marketplace demands has now assumed paramount importance. Federal Express is the world's sixth largest airline, succeeding by fast delivery worldwide. Customerization and groupage are again logistic advances. In the field of distribution things are equally dynamic with technology and modernity changing old-established routes to the customer (e.g. garage forecourts have become a major competitor in grocery retailing terms in the past five years). The financial implications of international marketing are too often ignored or are placed in a less important role by modern marketers. Finance and marketing are inextricably linked. Marketing is the primary source of revenue to any organization (interfacing as it does with the customer). Whether revenue produces profits, the lifeblood of the organization, depends on the ability of marketing and finance to work together. In this unit you will: • Study the factors important in developing	2.3.4, 2.3.5	Distribution and logistics are the fastest-changing areas in international marketing. It is essential that companies monitor trends in international trade. Yesterday's methods can and are being outdated virtually overnight. Think how companies such as Direct Line have revolutionized the marketing of motor insurance in the UK and are now moving on to household insurance and mortgages. Ideally, firms would like to deal direct with customers. It may happen in the UK but in overseas markets it may not be feasible. Political and other numerous factors prevent this. The firm would also like to use a similar distribution chain to its home market. Again it is extremely rare that distribution and logistical systems in one country is replicated elsewhere. There are too many variables. Whatever route(s) is chosen, care must be taken to plan and control the effort. Inefficiencies have to be minimized in order to succeed. In this unit we have seen that every marketing strategy activity in foreign markets has financial implication for the organization. The international marketer must understand the financial implications of any proposed strategy and given a choice between alternative strategic choices the marketer

distribution strategies
- Recognize the cost implications of logistics
- Be aware that service levels are a very important marketing tool
- Consider the management aspects of distribution
- Study new trends for the future.
- Review the role of capital in international marketing operations
- Understand and be able to assess the risk involved in international operations
- Consider how profits are repatriated to the home organization. Having completed this unit you will be able to:

1 Understand the financial implications of different international marketing strategies

2 Evaluate suitable marketing strategies from any financial viewpoint.

See syllabus sections 2.3.4 and 2.3.5.

On completing the unit you will be able to:

- Explain the basis of a distribution strategy
- Identify the step-by-step approach and the impact each step might have on the overall delivery
- Review the impact of cost versus service and the management implication emanating from service-level decisions

should be able to bring an understanding of financial implications to bear on the eventual recommendations.

Financial implications of marketing to foreign markets comes under three separate headings:

- Capital requirement
- International financial risks
- The repatriation of profits.

Remember, business upon which we make no profit or for which we cannot repatriate the funds to the home office is business we can easily find in the domestic market!

Unit	Objectives	Syllabus	Summary
	• Evaluate the changing patterns in distribution and predict trends in what is happening (or likely to happen) in the future.		
Unit 11 Evaluation and control methods	Evaluation and control methods are key issues in international marketing strategy. Nothing the international marketing manager can do can remove risk completely from business decisions that are made, but careful and proper evaluation of strategy before implementation, coupled with rigorous control methods during implementation itself, can reduce these risks to levels more acceptable in highly competitive situations. In this unit you will learn how to evaluate international marketing strategy and control strategic implementation. More specifically, you will: • Review the objectives set for international marketing strategy • Evaluate strategy against the set objectives • Review the planning processes appropriate with the international business strategy • Understand the control systems necessary to ensure proper implement-ations of international marketing plans. See syllabus section 2.3.10. Having completed this unit you will be able to: • Evaluate the suitability of specific international marketing strategies • Develop control systems for the implementation of international marketing strategy.	2.3.10	In this unit we have looked at the important stages of strategic evaluation and the control of implementation. First, we considered the problem of evaluating alternative strategies for international operations and deciding which strategic option offered the best chance of achieving the organization's objectives. Evaluation will be driven largely by the organization's objectives but can be measured both internally (financial measures), externally (non-financial measures) or, ideally, a combination of the two. Second, we considered the control mechanisms that are necessary to ensure that the strategic plan is implemented in the foreign markets and the organization's objectives are achieved. We considered the range of analysis and control mechanisms which are used in different organizations including auditing, budgeting and variance analysis. Finally, we considered the nature of the corrective action that can be taken by the marketer and the variables which affect the control mechanisms and the results that these give.

About MarketingOnline

With this year's coursebooks Butterworth-Heinemann is offering readers free access to MarketingOnline (www.marketingonline.co.uk), our premier online support engine for the CIM marketing courses. On this site you can benefit from:

- Tutorials on key topics every two weeks during the term, comprehensive revision support material and access to revision days from Tactics – the highly acclaimed independent trainer for CIM courses.
- Fully customizable electronic versions of the coursebooks – annotate, cut and paste sections of text to create your own tailored learning notes.
- Access to the e-Library – electronic versions of eight classic BH marketing texts to enrich and extend your knowledge.
- Instant access to specimen papers and answers, as well as other extra material and weblinks related to the coursebooks.
- Capacity to search the coursebook online for instant access to definitions and key concepts.

Logging on

Before you can access MarketingOnline you will first need to get a password. Please go to www.marketingonline.co.uk where you will find registration instructions for course-book purchasers. Once you have got your password, you will need to log on using the onscreen instructions. This will give you access to the various functions outlined below.

Using MarketingOnline

MarketingOnline is broadly divided into six sections which can each be accessed from the front page after you have logged on to the system:

1. **The coursebooks**: buttons corresponding to the three levels of CIM marketing qualification are situated on the home page. Select your level and you will be presented with the four coursebook titles for each module of that level. Click on the desired coursebook to access the full online text (divided up by chapter). On each page of text you have the option to add an electronic bookmark or annotation by following the onscreen instructions. You can also freely cut and paste text into a blank word document to create your own learning notes.

2. **The e-Library**: click on the 'BH Library' button on the front page to access the eight titles in the e-Library. Again you can annotate, bookmark and copy text as you see fit.

3. **Revision material**: click on the 'Revision material' link and select the appropriate CIM level and coursebook to access revision material.

4. **Useful links**: click on 'Useful links' to access a list of links to other sites of interest for further reading and research.

5. **Glossary**: click on the 'Glossary' button to access our online dictionary of marketing terms.

6. **Discussion**: click on the 'Discussion' button to access our various online noticeboards. All users can access and put up entries on our public noticeboard using onscreen instructions. If your college has registered as a MarketingOnline user you may also have access to your own 'Tutor Group Discussion' where you can interact with your fellow students and tutors.

If you have specific queries about using MarketingOnline then you should consult our fully searchable FAQ section – again, this is accessible through the appropriate link on the front page of the site. Please also note that a **full user guide** can be downloaded by clicking on the link on the opening page of the website.

Objectives

International marketing strategy has always been a major factor in the success of important trading nations such as Britain. Now that membership of the EU has been secured, international marketing skills are becoming even more important to marketers. In this unit you will:

- Understand the range of tasks involved in international marketing strategy
- Review the strategic process

    See syllabus sections 2.1.1, 2.1.2, 2.2.1, 2.2.2, 2.2.3, 2.2.8 and 2.2.10.

- Understand the Diploma International Marketing syllabus
- Understand what is meant by international marketing

    See syllabus section 2.1.2.

- Understand the reasons why organizations 'go international'

    See syllabus sections 2.1.1 and 2.1.2.

- Review the principal forms of financial risk for the international organization

    See syllabus sections 2.1.4 and 2.1.5.

- Consider the role of the marketing information system in reducing the risk of international expansion

    See syllabus sections 2.1.6 and 2.1.7.

- Review the range of models that may be of use in assessing foreign market opportunities

    See syllabus sections 2.1.4, 2.1.5 to 2.1.8.

Having completed this unit you will be able to:

- Explain how to avoid problems in international marketing
- Appreciate the key questions involved in 'going international'
- Advise an organization on whether to go international and the key questions involved in this strategic decision
- Explain the role of international marketing in the overall international business process
- Identify the key drivers behind an organization's international strategy
- Evaluate the main areas of risk in international operations
- Establish ways of reducing risk in planning an organization's international marketing strategy.

Study guide

This coursebook is critical to an overall understanding of the International Marketing Strategy process. The key:

- Development of international marketing strategy
- Implementation of strategy
- Evaluation and control of strategy

come from an understanding of the organization's objectives and ambitions for its international operations.

The organization may treat its international business as an 'add-on' to its domestic operations or as an integral part of its mission. This will influence the importance that international marketing has in the organization, the resources allocated to it and the control systems applied to support implementation.

As you work through this unit, remember that:

- Domestic and international marketing work on the same principles – customers must be satisfied
- Customers in foreign markets may have different needs and may become drivers for different marketing policies
- The biggest problem in international marketing is often not the foreign customer but the international marketer.

Once you have completed this unit, read through a few of the mini-cases in the book and try to identify the key international opportunities/threats facing the organizations described.

Introduction

The International Marketing Strategy component of the Diploma in Marketing has two concise objectives:

1. To enable students to acquire expertise in developing marketing strategies for countries other than their own and thereby to extend their range of marketing understanding. To deal with international marketing situations in non-domestic markets and the impact of international competitors on the domestic market
2. To promote an understanding of the factors determining the extent to which standardization or adaptation in strategy and implementation is appropriate for success in international markets.

This is achieved by focusing on a number of key issues that logically follow each other in the strategic marketing process:

Stage 1: Where are we now and where do we want to be? (strategic financial and marketing analysis followed by strategic direction and strategy formulation)

Stage 2: How might we get there? (strategic choice)

Stage 3: How do we ensure arrival? (strategic implementation and control)

At the same time, the content of the module has been designed to complement the syllabuses for the other three Diploma papers, Marketing Communications Strategy, Strategic Marketing Management – Planning and Control and Strategic Marketing Management – Analysis and Decision (see Figure 1.1) and to build upon material at the Certificate and Advanced Certificate levels.

Given its structure, and in particular the nature of the interrelationship between international marketing strategy and the other aspects of marketing strategy, this Coursebook has been designed to provide you with a clear insight into the analysis, planning and control processes in international marketing and the ways in which these can be best applied within the international business and commercial world as well as, of course, to the CIM's Diploma examination paper.

In doing this we give considerable emphasis to the three elements that underpin all the CIM's syllabuses: knowing, understanding and doing. Thus, in each of the units we outline and discuss the relevant concepts so that your knowledge and understanding is increased. We then address the issue of 'doing' by means of a series of exercises and questions and, of course, through the mini-case study that forms Section 1 of the International Marketing Strategy exam paper. It needs to be recognized from the outset however, that a Coursebook cannot explore the complexity of concepts in the same way that a textbook can. For this reason, we make reference at various stages to three books that you may well find useful. These are:

International Marketing Strategy, I. Doole and R. Lowe, 3rd Edition, Thomson, 2001.

International Marketing, S. Paliwoda and M. Thomas, 3rd Edition, Butterworth-Heinemann, 1999.

Global Marketing Strategies, J-P. Jeannet and H.D. Hennessey, 5th Edition, Houghton Mifflin, 2001.

The first two books were written specifically for the CIM's International Marketing Strategy syllabus and with the needs of the prospective students in mind.

The third book is a very good supportive text. Between the three texts, virtually all of the syllabus is covered.

Integrated Marketing Communications	International Marketing Strategy	Strategic Marketing Management	
		Planning and Control	Analysis and Decision

Figure 1.1
Diploma in Marketing

International marketing strategy

We commented earlier that the International Marketing Strategy syllabus focuses upon three key issues: these are illustrated in Figure 1.2.

In Units 2–4 we are concerned with the various ways in which managers might identify their organization's current position and assess its true level of international marketing capability. The assessment of the organization's capability and the options open to it in its marketplaces can be seen as one of the principal foundation stones for any strategic planning process – domestic or international – since it determines exactly what the organization is or should be capable of achieving. Marketing capability by itself is, of course, only one part of the planning process and needs to be looked at against the background of the organization as a whole as well as the nature and shape of the international environment in which it is or might choose to operate. Units 2 and 3 concentrate on the nature of the international trading environment and the all-important influences upon customers that may create opportunities for the organization.

Having assessed the current capability of the organization and the opportunities and threats in the international marketplace, in Units 5–8 we start to consider practical ways in which the organization can start to turn its international opportunities into profits.

Units 9–11 assess the all-important question of how we manage, evaluate and control our marketing activities in the international environment in order to achieve the pre-set strategic plans.

Approaching the International Marketing Strategy examination

The syllabus for International Marketing Strategy is very detailed in its approach and has a number of clear and distinct learning outcomes that emerge from a successful completion of the programme. This means that at the end of your course you should be able to:

- Understand the composition and changing nature of the international trading environment and the major trends, environmental, strategic and contractual, influencing global marketing decisions
- Differentiate between marketing strategies appropriate to industrialized, developing and less-developed countries
- Describe and understand the information needs, methods of data collection and analysis in support of the international decision and international marketing generally
- Compare, contrast and evaluate strategies for exporting, international, multinational and global marketing and understand the organizational changes as an organization moves through the globalization spectrum
- Evaluate the factors which influence the planning, organizing and controlling of the marketing mix – product, price, distribution, marketing communications, people, physical evidence, and process in a non-domestic context
- Understand the financial, human resource, operational, logistical and internal marketing implications of different international marketing strategies.

Study tip

After each examination the senior examiners write a report for the Chartered Institute in which they discuss how the students coped with the examination and highlight any particular problems that have been experienced. In looking back at the reports which have been written over the past few years, there are several issues which have been referred to on almost every occasion. Obtain a set of examiner's reports for yourself and make sure that you don't forfeit marks needlessly.

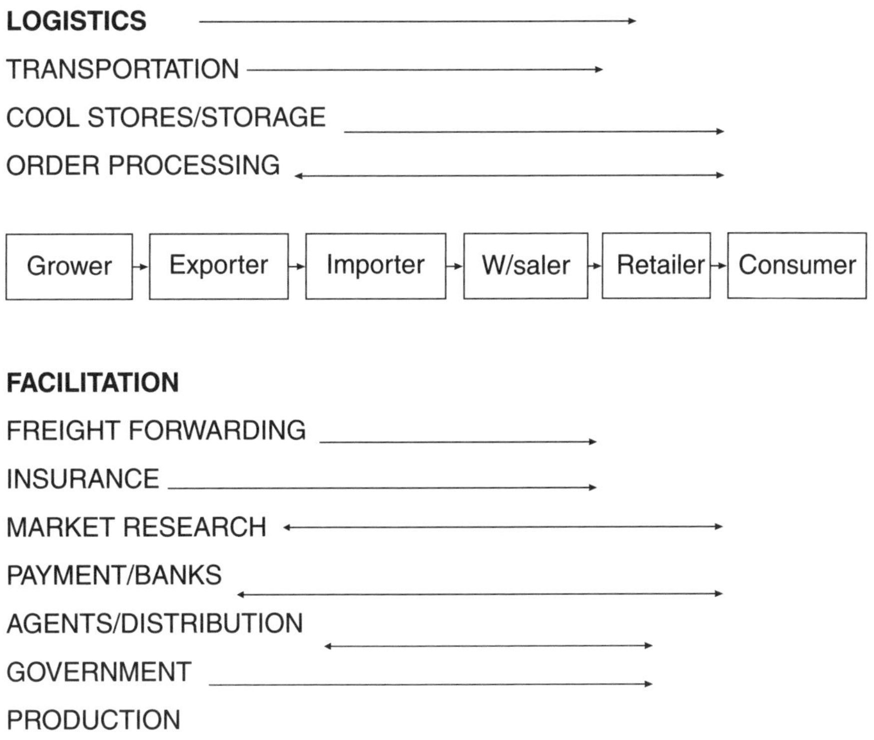

```
LOGISTICS          ─────────────────────────────►

TRANSPORTATION ──────────────────────────►

COOL STORES/STORAGE ───────────────────────►

ORDER PROCESSING ◄───────────────────────────

┌────────┐  ┌──────────┐  ┌──────────┐  ┌──────────┐  ┌──────────┐  ┌──────────┐
│ Grower │►►│ Exporter │►►│ Importer │►►│ W/saler  │►►│ Retailer │►►│ Consumer │
└────────┘  └──────────┘  └──────────┘  └──────────┘  └──────────┘  └──────────┘

FACILITATION

FREIGHT FORWARDING ──────────────►

INSURANCE ─────────────────────────►

MARKET RESEARCH ◄──────────────────────────

PAYMENT/BANKS ◄────────────────────────────►

AGENTS/DISTRIBUTION ◄────────────────►

GOVERNMENT ─────────────────────────►

PRODUCTION
```

Figure 1.3
The International Supply Chain. High value horticultural produce

---

Exam Question 1.1

As a Marketing Consultant, advising a lesser developed country (LDC) provider of horticultural produce wishing to export to a developed country (DC), write a report showing the role of the international supply chain in creating value. Use 'petrol' as an example for comparison. (December 2001, Question 2).

Go to www. marketingonline.co.uk or www.bh.com/marketing to access Specimen Answers and Senior Examiner's advice for this exam question.

One of the most important factors in international marketing, and in international business generally, is not the new and different techniques which have to be learned to deal with overseas markets but in the mindset of the managers attempting to satisfy overseas or international market needs. Every manager or marketer is the product of his or her own culture. The end result of centuries of conditioning in what our domestic culture considers to be acceptable and non-acceptable modes of behaviour colours all our perceptions of foreign market and customer behaviour. The single most important problem any organization faces within its international setting often comes not from the environment but from its own reactions to that environment.

James Lee refers to the self-reference criterion (SRC) and compares this 'cultural conditioning' to an iceberg: we are not aware of nine-tenths of it. The sequence of comments uttered by many domestic marketers considering international markets for the first time is often as follows:

'That's interesting!'

'That's different (from what we do at home).'

'That's wrong! (it's not what we do at home).'

The third comment is driven directly by the manager's SRC and often results in the application (normally unsuccessful) of domestic marketing policies in overseas market situations. In order to avoid errors in business decisions, the SRC must be recognized and isolated so that its biasing effect is minimized, if not eliminated completely, from international marketing strategy decisions.

The key questions in international marketing

There are six broad questions which are relevant to the international marketer and the company considering international operations for the first time. These questions can be addressed in a sequential order.

Whether to go international?

There are between 190 and 200 countries in the world with governments which can lay claim to being independent – the number tends to change on a weekly basis! Although they are often classified as being either 'industrialized', 'less developed' or 'advanced' such simplicity is misleading to the international marketer. Organizations operating internationally must analyse the environment in which they will be working; how people think and act – be they customers, agents, employees or governments. It is the organization's international environment which will largely determine the actions that can be taken and the kinds of adaptation that must be made in international operations. In Units 2 and 3, we will look in detail at the ways in which the international environment can be analysed and in Unit 3, we will spend some time considering the mechanical approaches of market research that may be required to uncover the important parameters of the international environment.

Where to operate?

Of all the various markets and the different opportunities that appear to be open to the organization, where should the marketer concentrate his or her efforts? Despite the talk of collapsing national boundaries and the global information infrastructure, the world still remains a very big place. Rather than spread the resources of the organization too thinly (the Marmite approach!) it is important that the international marketer is able to focus the resources of the organization on the market or markets where it is felt the returns may be the most promising. How can these markets be selected? In Unit 3, specifically we will address the question of target markets selection and the basis upon which an informed choice might be made.

What are the rules of engagement?

Allied to the previous point, it is not just a question of identifying a market which may promise the best returns, but identifying the 'rules of engagement' as these differ substantially from country to country. These 'rules' include factors like tariff and non-tariff barriers, attitudes to multinational involvement such as involvement of local resources and shareholders. Operating in the United States of America for example may be very different from operating in Zambia or Malaysia. It is essential to assess these factors in advance and take them into account in international decision making.

What to market in the overseas environment?

Although most organizations would prefer to market a single product or service to all international markets, the market pressures are such that some adaptation will often have to be made. These adaptations may be caused by differing use conditions, tastes or habit or government regulation. Other areas of product mix may need modification, for example packaging (language or literacy requirements and different transport and distribution systems) or brand and trade marks (may not travel well due to differences in language, idiom or aesthetics). In Unit 7, we will discuss the implications of product policy for overseas markets in more detail.

How should we operate internationally?

Once the organization has decided where it will operate and concentrate its effort, and what the market requires from it, the final decision is how to operate in those overseas markets. Decisions such as method of market entry and whether to use local agents, distributors or develop a wholly-owned subsidiary will be considered in greater depth in Units 8 and 9.

For organizations already active internationally, there are similar questions. Too often, international marketers simply 'live with' the reality of being international and do not question the reasons why the business operates this way. For the international organization, the above questions are still valid and should be asked on a regular basis. Markets and environments change and should the attractiveness of international operations decline, withdrawal needs to be considered.

What are the likely currency fluctuations?

Whilst an evaluation of likely currency movements is usually confined to an international 'environmental' analysis, it should be at the forefront when considering in which countries to operate. Large sums of money can be lost almost overnight by devaluations and the effects on investment and returns on investment can be dramatic. Huge devaluations can affect the costs of operations and make inputs of necessary materials for example, very expensive, making domestic prices prohibitive. Of course revaluations of currency can have the opposite effect and devaluation should aid exports. But not for all countries, especially those that are exporting commodities and goods which are subject to world fixed prices, for example, tin and horticultural products. Good examples of recent devaluations are Zimbabwe and the 'Asian Tigers' in 1997/8, resulting in a reduction in the demand for internationally traded products within these countries.

Question 1.2

As an organization evolves from a domestic to a global operator what are the principal factors that it must consider?

Understanding the international marketing strategy process

In order to understand the international process it needs to be viewed schematically from the first decision-making processes through to implementation and control. This entire process is outlined in Figure 1.4 which can be explained in more detail as follows.

Information: foreign market potential

Any decision to go international must be based on solid and reliable market information on the potential to the organization from the foreign market.

Organization's objectives

A clear understanding of the organization's corporate and marketing objectives will help the marketer to understand whether international marketing and/or the selection of particular key markets is in line with the organization's objectives and ambitions for the future.

Decision to go international

An organization deciding strategically to take an international role in its business rather than opportunistically following up the odd foreign sales lead has a very different effect on it and the way it approaches its international markets. With a corporate decision to take international business as a serious activity, the organization is likely to put the resources required behind the effort and to treat it as a key activity in the future.

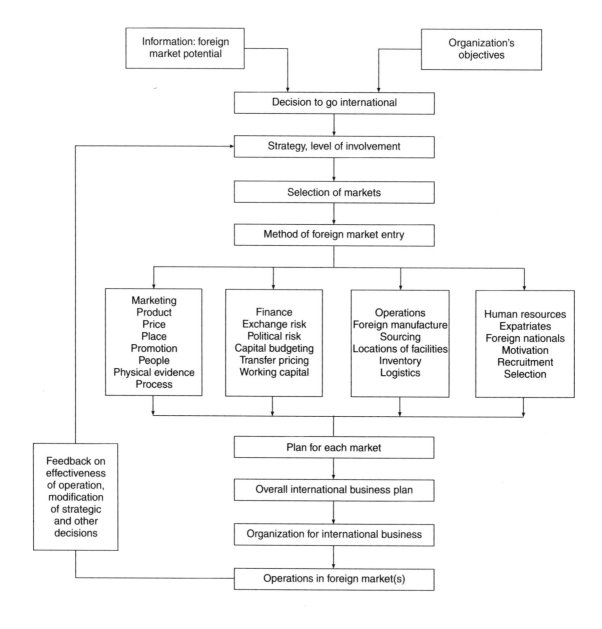

Figure 1.4
The international business process (Source: Fifield and Lewis)

Strategy 'level of involvement'

The first strategic decision the organization makes on its route to internationalization, is to decide how deeply involved it wishes to become in the international marketplace. The organization's chosen level of involvement in international business will determine (at least in the short term) the marketing, financial, operation and human resource strategies that can be employed. The different levels of international involvement range from active exporting through joint ventures to marketing subsidiaries overseas as far as foreign production and foreign marketing. These options will be analysed and described in more detail in Units 6 and 8.

Selecting the markets

The organization should resist the temptation to attack too many markets thereby spreading effort and resources too thinly to be successful. The most successful international operations often come from making an initial effort into a single market and then extending this to other possibly neighbouring markets as learning in international business increases. Market selection can be based on three criteria: market potential, similarity to home or other foreign markets and market accessibility. These methods of market selection will be considered in more depth in Unit 4.

Method of foreign market entry

Unlike domestic marketing, the organization often has a clear choice of how it proposes to enter overseas markets. How the method of market entry is selected will determine the freedom of action the organization has over the various elements of the marketing mix. As with level of involvement, method of entry may dictate marketing activities in the short term. Alternative methods of market entry will be considered in more detail in Unit 6.

Foreign market planning

Although the international marketing strategy syllabus is primarily concerned with marketing activities in overseas markets, the modern marketer can ill afford to ignore the international aspects and pressures upon other functional areas of the business. Not only must decisions be made on the marketing mix most appropriate to international markets, but also the other functional requirements of the organization must be considered if any strategic marketing activity is to be successful. Financial considerations of international operations are considerable and will cover issues such as exchange risk, political risk, capital budgeting, transfer pricing and working capital requirements. International operations may also represent a major cost centre and questions such as foreign manufacture, working stock and location of facilities are key issues. Human resources are an equally important area. All these issues are considered in more depth in Unit 9.

Question 1.3

Citing an organization of your choice, identify the internal factors which should be considered when it evolves from a solely domestic to a global operator.

Plan for each market

In order to control the marketing and business operations in overseas markets it is important that a plan is developed for each individual market based upon the differing marketing characteristics and customer expectations from that marketplace (see Unit 4).

Overall international business plan

International business planning requires that the individual market plans be coordinated and controlled for international operations. Unlike the domestic situation where there is a single market and easily understood planning parameters, the international environment tends to be much more fragmented and may require differing resources at different stages and levels of allocation. It is important that the organization attempts to remain in control of the situation and the coordination of (often diverse) national or market plans becomes a major strategic activity.

Organization for international business

Structure can be a severe brake on any organization's international ambitions and new organization structures may be required in order to facilitate and promote international business. This will be discussed in more detail in Unit 3.

Operations in foreign markets

As operations and activity 'on the ground' begin to unfold, it is important that evaluation and control methods be in place for the organization continually to improve its activity in international markets. Evaluation and control methodology will be considered in more detail in Unit 10.

Some reasons for 'going international'

There are many reasons why an organization might consider going international and the following are some of the most common:

1. *Saturated home market* If the home market for an organization's products or service is saturated or competition is so intense that it can no longer gain any significant market share improvement it might consider extending its market activity to overseas markets. This move might be considered under market extension or even diversification strategies in the Ansoff matrix. Remember that success in international markets will depend on whether the products and/or services offered by the organization are attractive to the international customer. Success in the home market does not, of itself, guarantee this!

2. *Competition* There are two separate but interrelated reasons why an organization may decide to go international in this instance. The first case is that competition may be less intense in overseas markets than in the domestic market. Competition, as we all know, may have benefits for customers but it is always extremely expensive for the organization. Despite the often increased risk of operating overseas it may be that the organization faces a better potential return by operating in markets where there is less intense competition for its products and services. A second competition-related factor in moving internationally may be that an organization is faced by particularly virulent international competition in its domestic marketplace. In some instances it is difficult to compete from a domestic base against international competitors. In such cases the organization may consider moving internationally in order to be able to compete on a more equal footing with the opponent organization.

3. *Excess capacity* Where an organization is operating successfully in its domestic marketplace but is operating at below optimal capacity levels there is excess capacity available for production. In these instances it may be wise to consider international operations where the product or service can be costed at marginal cost, thereby giving a potential price advantage for overseas marketing operations. Because the organization can produce at marginal cost does not, of course, mean that it ought to enter foreign markets at a lower price. It could decide to use the extra margin for marketing support. Big price differences may, too, produce the risk of parallel imports back to the home market and could disturb prices there.

4. *Comparative advantage in product, skill or technology* The organization may discover, when analysing overseas market opportunities, that it has a comparative advantage against local competition in the foreign market. This advantage might be in product, skill or technology but, always subject to local market demand and tastes, it could be the makings of a profitable venture. Comparative advantage is often the case when organizations are based in advanced countries and consider marketing internationally to lesser developed countries.

5. *Product life cycle differences* As you will know from studies in domestic marketing, as a product or service progresses through the life cycle it often changes in style, performance or efficiency. When considering international markets the marketer may discover that foreign markets are at a different point of development in the product or industry life cycle. The marketer may decide to exploit these differences, either by exporting product which is no longer suitable for the domestic market place (the life cycle requirements have moved on) or by entering the foreign market with a more advanced product than the local competition has yet developed.

6. *Geographic diversification* Linked to items above, an organization may discover in its domestic marketing strategy that either its market is saturated or competition is becoming more intense in established markets. To continue to grow and develop it must extend its operations in terms of either products or markets. The classical development of the Ansoff matrix (see Strategic Marketing Management coursebook) normally considers just domestic operations but international options can be considered too. When considering 'market extension' strategies the organization can include international markets as well as other domestic markets for further growth. A number of companies have preferred to focus their attention on a single product or very limited range of products in a number of markets for growth rather than take on the risk of developing new products or extending their activities into markets that they do not understand.

7. *Organizational reasons* Often an organization may find itself haphazardly involved in international business and marketing operations through the acquisition of random activities during acquisition and merger operations or through the organically-grown exporting activities of its own subsidiaries. Soon a point in the organization's development arrives when it is time to put order into the previously piecemeal approach to international operations. This often results in the creation of an international marketing division where the various activities are brought together, rationalized and coordinated. This 'house keeping' often provides areas of significant international potential.

8. *Financial reasons* There are a range of financial reasons why an organization may decide to take the international route to its business and these might include investment incentives in overseas markets and the availability of venture capital as well as the option to maximize profits or minimize losses through international rather than simple domestic operations.

Whatever the original reason for considering international operations, no organization should forget the golden rule: international marketing will prove to be a more successful venture for the organization that is exporting a positive advantage than for one exporting to cover a domestic weakness.

Financial risk in international operations

One major difference in operations carried out internationally rather than domestically is that the fund flow occurs in a variety of currencies and in a variety of nations. These currency and national differences, in turn, create risks unique to international business which are explored in greater detail in Unit 9.

There are two types of financial risk unique to international marketing operations:

1. *Foreign exchange risk* This arises from the need to operate in more than one currency. Since January 2002, most of the countries which make up the EU have adopted the euro as a common currency. Hopefully, this will make the risk of foreign exchange fluctuations, in Europe, a thing of the past. The UK has decided to remain outside of 'Euroland' for the time being.

2. *Political risk* This is a term used to cover those risks arising from an array of legal, political, social and cultural differences. Political risk normally produces losses when there is a conflict between the goals of the organization and those of the host government.

Home country (domestic) law is also important in that it defines acceptable behaviour for the organization in all its activities – whether at home or abroad. Figure 1.5 below demonstrates the nature of this relationship between the organization, the host government and home government.

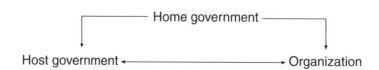

Figure 1.5
The organization and 'political risk'

The international management information system (MIS)

It will be seen from the above that the establishment and maintenance of a high-quality management information system is essential for two primary reasons:

1. Helping the organization to decide whether to follow an international route by quantifying opportunities

2. Helping management to develop and implement suitable marketing strategies and programmes that will allow the organization to exploit the foreign opportunities to the full.

These two key drivers create the need for two different types of data:

1. *Feasibility data* The decisions which the organization needs to make in terms of whether it should go international and if so which markets it should enter are all to be captured under the title of feasibility data collection. Data in this area will facilitate decisions such as whether to go international or not, where to go, what to offer.

2. *Operational data* The second form of data required by the organization is that which will allow it constantly to offer the products and services that the markets require, and according to terms and conditions which the local customers and governments find acceptable. As we will see, market conditions and governmentally imposed regulations are subject to regular change. Long-term profitability depends upon the organization's ability to anticipate and, if possible, avoid such restrictions. The operational data collection process should highlight the likely imposition of such restrictive measures in time for the organization to take action.

The market information and analysis process will be discussed in more depth in Unit 3.

Activity 1.1

What information does your company collect for its international markets? What gaps, if any, can you identify?

Models to assist in the assessment of risk and opportunity

There are a number of models that have been devised over recent years in order to help organizations assess the opportunity/risk in international markets. This Coursebook is not designed to be a complete international marketing textbook so we have not analysed or explained the most popular models here. As part of your preparation for the Diploma exams you will need to be reading widely and from the recommended texts you will be able to identify the various approaches and advantages/disadvantages of each of these models. The theoretical models you may come across might include:

- Harrell and Keifer model
- Gilligan and Hird model
- Harrell and Kiefer model

  (for these see the Doole and Lowe text)

- Business Environment Risk Index (BERI)
- The Uppsala school.

  (For these see Hollensen, S., (1998) Global Marketing: A Market-Responsive Approach, Prentice-Hall, Europe)

In your studies you are likely to encounter a number of different models which apply to various areas of international marketing. You should bear in mind when assessing these models that many have been developed not with a larger view of international or global strategy in mind but to meet the specific needs of a particular market or industry or product sector. Greatest success is likely to come if you are able to tap into the models at a conceptual level, understanding what they mean in broad strategic terms rather than treating them as a blueprint for guaranteed success under any circumstances. Often you will find that blending one or two models will give you a greater insight into the existence (or not) of international marketing opportunities for your organization or the case study.

The world of international marketing is growing and developing all the time. You should remember that many models are simply the codification of observed success in the (international) marketplace. You should pay close attention to what is going on in the real world and assess business activity on your own. Remember that what you spot happening today is probably the business model of tomorrow!

International marketing and the internet

Much has been written recently about the internet, some hype and some important – how to tell the difference?

An e-revolution?

Well is it? Great minds are divided at the moment, no doubt depending on whether or not they own any internet shares. The great debate seems set to rattle on for a while yet but the arguments are simple, is it:

- Anarchy
- Youth
- New paradigms
- A global business revolution.

Or is it:

- Just another international channel
- Hope
- Desperation
- The emperor's new clothes.

The pages of the business magazines are full of the debate and we have no intention of spending much time on it here. But questions are sure to be raised in the examination, do you have a view? Have you looked at the situation dispassionately? How will you respond?

Whichever way we look at it the internet has rapidly grown in recent years, see Table 1.1

Table 1.1 Internet Consumer Trends 31 October 2000					
Users (%)	UK	USA	France	Germany	Sweden
Internet users	33.3	54.3	15.6	20.8	56.8
Online shoppers	37	19	13	31	31
E-banking customers	5	18	2	6	27
Source: Metro 2 February 2001					

As at February 2000, Tesco, the UK supermarket, was the world's biggest online grocer with sales at £200 million. The UK's total online sales of £390 million represent 0.4 per cent of the global market, ahead of the USA. It is estimated that the number of households doing their food shopping online in the next few years will rise dramatically so that by 2005 online sales will account for more than 5 per cent of the British market, a turnover in excess of £6 billion.

Questions

As a check on your understanding of what has been covered in this unit, consider the following questions:

Question 1.4

1. How is the organization affected by international business trends?
2. How can the international marketer's own cultural background affect the organization's international market strategy?
3. What are the four key questions in international marketing?
4. What are the two key drivers which may start off an organization's entry into foreign markets?
5. What is meant by 'level of involvement'?
6. What tactical effects will the strategic decision on 'how to enter a foreign market' have?
7. What are the three criteria for foreign market selection?
8. What are the special factors to be taken into account when planning for international marketing strategy?
9. What are the main reasons that an organization might consider going international?
10. How might intense domestic competition encourage an organization to develop markets abroad?
11. How can we apply the concept of the product life cycle (PLC) in international business?
12. What are the two main forms of financial risk in international business?
13. What are the two particular management decisions that research can help support?
14. What are the two types of international data that might be collected by an organization?

Extending knowledge

For a more detailed treatment of what international marketing strategy means, read:

International Marketing Strategy, I. Doole and R. Lowe, 3rd Edition, Thomson, 2001, Chapter 1, pp.5–31

International Marketing, S. Paliwoda and M. Thomas, Butterworth-Heinemann, 1999, Chapter 1, pp.1–41

Summary

In this introductory unit we have considered the format and approach that this book will take in addressing the international marketing strategy syllabus and the importance of using this book in conjunction with other international marketing texts recommended for the examination. We have also considered the detailed analysis of the syllabus as well as the all-important learning objectives and outcomes required for a successful attempt at the examination itself. Finally, we considered the overall nature of the international marketing strategy tasks and we concluded that:

- There is little conceptual difference between international marketing and domestic marketing.
- The focus of the international marketer's activity is the customer (as in the domestic situation), but the customer happens to be in a foreign market with all that that entails.
- A primary problem in successful international business is the social/cultural conditioning of the international marketer (remember the SRC).
- International marketing consists of four interrelated questions: Whether to? Where to? What to? How to?
- The international marketing strategic process can be seen as a logical series of steps which will take the business from a domestic organization to an international organization and possibly to a global organization.

In this unit we have seen that there are a number of very good reasons why organizations may decide to 'go international'. The opportunities and potential profits for an organization can often be quite sizeable. At the same time, there are some significant risks in such operations, particularly foreign exchange risk and political risk. In any event, some detailed market research and analysis is required in order to uncover likely marketplace opportunities for the organization and a range of models exist to help you in this evaluation process.

One final word of warning is that you should bring some common sense to bear on the market research data when available. The data analysis and scanning may identify gaps in the marketplace – the international marketer has to decide whether there is a market in the g!

Objectives

In this unit we highlight the growing importance of international marketing and the changes that are accelerating its importance. Understanding the changes that are underpinning the development of world trade – events that are shaping everyone's life wherever they might live and work. In this unit you will:

- Appreciate the growth and scale of world trade
- Consider just how 'international' our everyday lives are

    See syllabus sections 2.1.1 and 2.1.3.

- Understand the macro forces at work shaping the business world of today and the future

    See syllabus section 2.1.3.

- Study the factors that are increasingly important in defining success

    See syllabus sections 2.2.2 and 2.1.3.

Having completed the unit you will be able to:

- Identify the key drivers in world trade
- Appreciate what is creating convergence in consumer behaviour
- Understand the changes in international business
- Recognize that domestic horizons are increasingly meaningless in the fast-changing 'global village'
- Explain the essential balance of trade between the key trading nations
- Discuss potential future developments and the impact of the emergence of new giant economies
- Debate whether regionalism will be a force for good or bad
- Understand barriers to trade and their impact
- Initiate discussion on the role of the key facilitating agencies (e.g. GATT/WTO) and relate their relevance to the nation state and the individual firm.

Introduction

This is a live topic and much of what will be discussed is not contained in the textbooks. International business is on-going and incredibly dynamic. It is vital students are fully aware of what is going on in today's business world. The quality press contains news virtually on a daily basis of new developments in mergers and acquisitions, to say nothing of technological innovations which are revolutionizing our lives as global consumers – for this is what we are (or are rapidly becoming). Students are strongly advised to read and digest world and business events, e.g. upheaval in South-East Asia and South America; harmonization and unification in Europe and see how today's companies are reconfiguring to meet these massive changes in the international business environment.

Why all businesses need to think international:

1. If all you are preoccupied with is your local market and local customers the chances are you could be out of business sooner than you think. The world is shrinking and the 'competitor from hell' could be around the corner eyeing your customers as juicy prospects for profit from a faraway country, e.g. China, India, Korea, Malaysia; or

even closer to home within the European Union, now that this region is experiencing increasing harmonization in a levelling out playing field.

2. But what's going on is much more important and significant than the perception of the individual firm. It is customers that matter and customers are discovering for themselves the benefits of seeking products and services from an international shopping mall – some of which is a virtual activity. Your customers are international shoppers and frankly don't care where or who they buy from as long as it is what they want, available, and at a price they are content with. This is one of the reasons why UK car buyers are scouring Europe on the Internet or other ways, to secure their desired brand of car at the most favourable price.

Macro forces underlying international business

That international trade is expanding is not challengeable – despite the setback in South-East Asia in 1997/98. The decade of the 1990s saw world trade in everything accelerate. There is a global market for most things. It's a cliché but think in terms of your daily routine which (if you're a male executive) might go along the following lines.

Woken by a Sony alarm radio, listen briefly to the summary of the world's financial markets; news from the Hang Seng to Wall Street. Hurrying through the toiletry routine using a Gillette razor, Imperial Leather soap, Colgate toothpaste. Breakfasting on Kellogg's and Nescafé you place a call with your Nokia mobile phone, get off to work, log on your Compaq PC sending e-mails worldwide. Then get ready for a pan-European video conference. Have you noticed how many consumer products are made in China these days?

Well the point is made. It's a global world with global consumers, global meetings and a twenty-four hour virtual reality situation which five years ago – even one year – would have been far fetched to most executives. Incidentally, leaving aside the shaving aspect the rest of the description is unisex. So, welcome to the global village. You're part of it!

Activity 2.1

To reinforce the points made so far, wander around your home and list four international products or services which are part of your everyday life. Give thought as to where they come from, i.e. country of origin. Ask yourself the following questions:

- Could I get by without international products/services?
- Where were they made, i.e. country of origin?
- Why were they made there?
- Why were they not made in your own country?
- How did they arrive in your country? i.e. consider the international supply chain
- What is their competition? Could I have got them anywhere else?
- Why didn't I buy them from somewhere else?
- Could I get by without them?

The global village

A phrase coined in the 1970s is here and globalization is an everyday topic in business. Yet Ted Levitt only conceived his seminal text in the *Harvard Business Review* in 1983 and it has been one of the hottest topics in business ever since. The 1960s saw the development and expansion of multinational corporations who at that time were more concerned with geographic spreading than international marketing. Yet today large regions of the globe are addressed in similar ways from a production and a marketing perspective, based on the discovery, creation and development of similar customer behaviour patterns – maybe not identical but with sufficient similarity to effect a satisfactory product/market match.

Let's spend some time in examining the macro forces that are creating a world of similarities. However, it is essential to keep a sense of perspective about these forces. No one is suggesting a world of identical clones. Customers, countries, nations will remain deeply participative of their native cultures yet will adapt to products or adapt the products to the culture they enjoy.

Wealth

People, i.e. customers, are getting richer. The rich are getting rich fastest but the poor are also increasing their personal wealth measured in terms of disposable incomes. While there exist pockets where the situations to the contrary applies, most of the citizens of the world are enjoying the benefits of increased wealth. Villagers in rural India congregate around the communal television. Mobile phone ownership is rising dramatically. Electricity is reaching deep into traditional wildernesses. The Indian middle class exceeds the total population of the European Union – of course they don't have the equivalent spending power but all these things are relative.

Technology and communication

As you actually read and learn vast changes are taking place. The ones that really shape the future are concerned with communication. Computers are changing the way we communicate yet they are only in their infancy and remain over-priced. In five years from now your average desk-top will probably cost 20 per cent of what you pay today and, in fact, the desk-top computer may well be on its way to being history. Just think about and get ready for the £100 alternative. What'll it be? I don't know. But I do know that the pace of change dictates incredible surprises, shrinking distances and consigning some of the major corporations of today to the dustbin, leaving them to be taken over or sunk. It would be a useful exercise for you to think through very carefully the implication of technological change in your marketplace. Forget industry – think customers. British Airway's future competition for business-class customers may not be other airlines but video conferencing. Time is money. Companies are increasingly global in their supply and distribution networks. Everyone is seeking to cut costs. Business travel may well decline, we are not saying it will – but if you can't see the leverage from the alternative described then you are in trouble. There's a lot more that could be discussed on this subject area but I leave it to you to explore. Make sure you do it – your future career could and probably will hinge on it.

Activity 2.2

Select an area where technology is leading product development. Try to identify a company/product that made a breakthrough in the way Sony did 15 years ago with its Walkman. Work out how long it took for competitors to imitate.

Multinational and trans-national corporations

The big are getting bigger. We're in a curious state of business development. On the one hand Godzilla lives, i.e. mega corporations are buying others or merging with them. Yet at the other end of the scale we have the creation of new species – small entrepreneurial, innovative companies setting out on the path to humble giant corporations – and sometimes succeeding. Yet the two seemingly contradictory pathways converge. The small guys need the large guys to grow and the large guys need the little guys to both challenge them and to supply new ideas and ways of doing things. Today the gulf between 'little and large' is shrinking. Can you recall Yahoo!, Excite, and AOL/Netscape as being giant corporations two or three years ago? Well today they rank as leaders of the pathways to the future. Laggards describe Yahoo! and Excite, etc., as search engines. They are wrong, as they are portals to information, knowledge and power. They are the brands of today and tomorrow. Davies and Meyer in their book *Blur* published by Capstone (1998) describe the future as being about speed, connectivity and intangibility. Yahoo and its like have this in abundance. Back to multinationals. The world's biggest 500 companies account directly/indirectly for:

- 30 per cent of gross global product
- 70 per cent of global trade
- 80 per cent of international investment.

They are setting the agenda for the future and in doing so shaping how we, as customers, live our lives. There is only one major computer software company – Microsoft – and two major aeroplane producers – Boeing and Airbus. Today there are six major computer manufacturers, tomorrow this will shrink to four and there is huge over-capacity in the motor car industry. Watch out for the 'car boot' sale of the century as the industry seeks to consolidate. Tom Peters says, 'there is a surplus of just about everything in today's world' (BBC2 video, *The Money Programme*). Somebody is going to take the costs out of the market.

Finally, money incidentally is a global product that currently flows freely around the world. Well over $1 trillion dollars cross national boundaries daily seeking the minute profit percentage in playing the global casino. Current thinking is that international monetary forces and facilitation need to rethink the global casino analogy as it has been proven to wreak havoc on specific economies in 1997–98 especially South-East Asia and more recently Russia and Brazil. It would seem even financial speculators such as George Soros seek some stability.

Activity 2.3

Write a list of multinational/global corporations. What products/services are they famous for and why?

Global consumers

Everything discussed so far has accelerated the convergence of behaviour. Today in the developed world, which accounts for around 80 per cent world GDP, customers are behaving with increased similarities. Nike, Levi, Coca-Cola, Marlboro, Sony, McDonalds, Honda, Microsoft, Ford, Benetton are all marketing global offerings to all intents and purpose. The physical product may differ marginally country by country but the proposition and the market positioning remain constant. The list is far more extensive and I have already indicated that it isn't feasible to lead a 'normal' life without being a global consumer. This is far more the case for younger members of society and as they mature they will consolidate patterns of behaviour albeit within their cultural surroundings. Kenichi Ohmae, the Japanese guru on globalization, has claimed that no matter who you are or where you live once people earn a wage of around $15,000 or local equivalent in purchasing parity they behave similarly. First they buy a fridge, then stock it with pre-prepared packaged goods, then they buy a television, and then they plan a holiday. Accepting there are local variations, the pattern is not dramatically different, e.g. for holiday substitute personal motorized transportation – scooter, motorbike or car.

Urbanization

Consolidating the theme of global consumers is the trend towards living in cities and fleeing the countryside (with the exception of post-industrialized societies). Mega cities are springing up fast. Tokyo tops 30 million, Mexico City 15 million, Lagos 13 million, etc. In 1997 around 26 per cent of the Chinese population lived in cities. By 2025, it is anticipated that it will exceed 50 per cent. The implication of this are mind boggling, for city dwellers live very patterned lifestyles that require information, communication, energy systems, specific point of purchases, with most consumables packaged for them. This means huge opportunities for international business development. Your customers will be all in one place, easily and cheaply accessible.

World brands

Continuing the theme, global customers, city dwelling, richer than yesterday will seek products and services that will conform/meet their needs. They won't want to search. They will seek familiar patterns in their choice of what to buy. This means that branding (world branding) will become even more important. The development of world brands has arrived with bewildering speed. Disney, Ford, IBM, Microsoft, Sega, AOL, Nike now straddle the world yet were relatively modest corporations a decade or so ago. It is safe to say that ten years from now 25 per cent of the world's brands will be for companies you might never have heard of. The giants of the future look like being communication interfacers, i.e. corporations whose portals carry and process information turning it into knowledge and from there to power.

Exam Hint

Very frequently examiners ask questions demanding that you demonstrate your knowledge via examples. So, at the end of this unit or major activity, write down examples and commit them to memory. This will save you desperately trying to 'think on the spot' in the examination. International Marketing Strategy, on average, requires more examples than, say, Planning and Control.

Activity 2.4

Write down a list of world brands. What 'values' do they stand for internationally? There is frequently a question on globalization in the examination, so be prepared with your examples.

The shape of things to come

International business is expanding. Customers are increasingly seeking and experimenting with international firms and developing international 'relationships'. International corporations are no longer within the influence of national boundaries. National governments are now subject to the new world order of globalization, but in terms of supply and consumption. The outcomes for everyone concerned with this on-going process include:

- Better opportunities to succeed, yet the global market is also the global snake pit
- Information technology and communication will be the main driving force and will continue to shape and configure patterns of business supply and delivery mechanisms
- Businesses will increasingly need to think deeply about internationalizing their 'offers' be they small or large enterprises
- Customers' needs are converging, driven by increasing affluence which translates into greater profit opportunities
- Relationship marketing and information processing will need to be woven or crafted into the marketing mix faster and more effectively

- To meet this massive change in the 'environment', companies will need to reconfigure their entire approach to dealing with customers
- One way will be to both compete and collaborate simultaneously to deliver satisfaction to customers as competition intensifies. This is a paradox yet opposites will be attracted to one another.

To meet the challenge, companies will need to:

- Think outside the box, e.g. Sony is entering the banking business and Microsoft is entering the video games console market
- Step outside the industry rules, e.g. Sony's biggest product is its PlayStation
- Think customer, first and last, e.g. EasyJet (a European low-cost airline) is now offering car rental
- Internationalize the operation
- Be entrepreneurial. Take risks
- Collaborate and compete, e.g. the creation of 'One World', an alliance between five international airlines, including British Airways
- Create a thinking and learning organization.

All of this should excite you. If it doesn't, you're on the wrong course.

Patterns of world trade

Growth in world trade

World trade has grown enormously over the past twenty years expanding from around $4 trillion in 1980 to in excess of $10 trillion by the year 2000. This growth has been fuelled by many of the factors identified but also by the liberalization and deregulation of markets (countries). Barriers have been reduced, openness has been the order of the day and we now live and trade in what might be described as the 'borderless world' to quote Kenichi Ohmae.

Billions of dollars, pounds, marks, yen and other front-line currencies are traded daily. Businesses establish operations and borrow capital in an open marketplace. Furthermore, each country's economy is interwoven with the economy of many other countries. There is transparency and massive interdependence to the extent that countries cannot 'go it alone' anymore. The fact that in the UK government policies (Labour or Conservative) are virtually indistinguishable from each other in the macro sense is no accident. The options and alternatives facing them are the same. The key agendas are run by global corporations and regional decision makers, e.g. the European Bank.

The one world marketplace

We will return to the growth of world trade in a minute but it is worth recording the events of the past decade:

The fall of communism in Russia and Eastern Europe opened up new horizons for Western (and Eastern) capitalism, doubling the size of the greater-European market.

The opening of China, with its march away from command economy mentality has liberated over 1 billion consumers and equally importantly businesses. The Chinese have the longest tradition of mercantile trading and despite a half century of isolation have not lost these business skills which are to a certain extent based on guanxi (Chinese for 'connection'). The Chinese are described by Naisbitt in his *Mega Trends Asia* text (Avon Books, 1995) as the biggest tribe in the world, i.e. their relationships and connections are extensive. For example, 90 per cent of Indonesian businesses are Chinese owned and there are 200 million Indonesians, making the country the world's fourth most populous.

The decline of socialist policies virtually everywhere (Western European socialism is mercantilist/capitalist nowadays). This decline in socialism has seen the opening up of the Indian subcontinent with its 900 million – soon to be 1 billion plus customers.

What these factors imply is that up to 40 per cent of the world's consumers have been excluded from the world economy until a decade or so ago. Can you think for a minute of the incredible opportunities – balanced by compensatory threats – which are available to entrepreneurs and businesses? There has never been a better opportunity to 'get rich' in the history of mankind. But getting rich means marketing and selling to international customers.

Nations trade with nations

We have identified the interdependence of nations. Perhaps now is the time to add some substance to illustrate the importance to selling to overseas customers – generally expressed as exporting. Although a little dated the figures in Table 2.1 illustrate the position convincingly.

Table 2.1 Imports and exports as a percentage of gross domestic product (GDP)			
	GDP ($ billion)	Imports (% GDP)	Exports (% GDP)
Industrialized countries			
USA	7081	11	8
Japan	5052	6	8
Germany	2145	18	22
UK	1129	22	21
Holland	392	34	38
Switzerland	310	23	23
Developing countries			
Korea	459	28	27
Mexico	319	23	25
China	740	21	21
Source: Adapted from World Outlook 1996, Economics Intelligence Unit 1996.			

Table 2.1 poses an interesting point. Japan far from being the export tiger of the world decimating 'local' economies with its aggressive export policies is actually in real terms a modest exporter when seen as a percentage of GDP. The major thrust of Japanese growth is the internal domestic market. Of course this is now rather evident as Japan plc is struggling in economic terms as it domestic consumers have stopped spending – putting their disposable incomes into savings. The USA likewise, although the dominant player in the world marketplace shaping and leading the transformation of customers' lives and culture in many instances, is in reality a rather parochial economy inward looking in terms of its macro-economic thinking. Exporting is not the foremost activity. Consider Germany next. It is the export champion and so is the UK. The Germans are an interesting case study. The 1990s saw the country embark on a massive transformation of the internal economy and creation of a new social order with the reunification of the East with the West. Coincidental with this immense project, German industry found itself becoming uncompetitive in world markets, forcing a rapid rethink among the major industrial corporations. The result has been twofold. First, a huge transformation of German industry – business reengineering processes, etc., and second, a massive overseas investment expansion via mergers and acquisitions the most recent being the creation of Daimler-Chrysler. At the end of the decade Germany has regained its position of prominence in world trade. As a student of international business you should compare this with the performance of Japan plc.

The interdependence factor – regionalism

The global village concept was explored earlier together with the factors underpinning it. In this unit we have discussed the interconnections with import and export performance. But it's not that simple. Today's nations are seeking synergy for the alternative – to compete in a 'dog eat dog' scenario with approximately 200 nations all scrapping for the same bone suggests a savage reality of outright winners and losers. To prevent this, nations are creating consolidations of self-interest and aggregating themselves into distinct economic (and social) regions. There are three key trading regions and the interdependence between them is expressed very clearly in Figure 2.1.

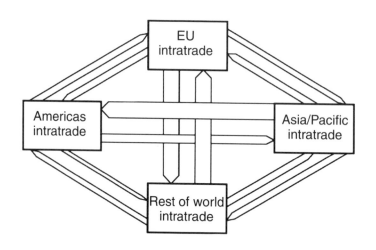

Figure 2.1
Relative world trade flows

The three key regions are the European Union, North America Free Trade Area (NAFTA) and Asia and Pacific (Asia Pac) – the Triad. Between them they account for about 85 per cent of world trade. They dominate the world economically. Not just that, they set the agenda of the future direction and development of the planet and everyone who lives on it (with very few exceptions).

The European Union (EU) is probably the foremost and most developed in the move towards regionalism. In less than forty years, Europe has moved from a 1000-year tradition of warring nation states to one nation economically and very likely socially and politically in the near future. This could well be the most significant global development of the twentieth century – or not. We simply don't know. The process is dynamic and for many independent observers the 'jury is out'. What we do know is that macro-economic policies are converging and with it is the development of a single currency effective from a business perspective from 1 January 1999 and from a customer perspective (notes and coins) from 1 January 2002. In this scenario, nations will not be trading with nations but companies will be trading with customers – all 370 million of them in a broadly similar strategic paradigm. Again momentous opportunities or catastrophes may occur dependent on the readiness of companies to keep up with customers' behaviour. Please don't forget it is customer who will benefit and seek to make relationships not companies. Companies will have to run to keep up – customers will not wait or forgive! Companies will increasingly merge, consolidate, acquire, and create joint ventures and alliances to compete in the vastly enlarged market.

NAFTA, the North American Free Trade Area, comprising USA, Mexico and Canada, is a broadly similar but looser arrangement. It has set the agenda to expand and consolidate and in doing so expand the interdependence of nations in Central and South America.

ASEAN – although a late starter in the development of regional interdependence – is a regional entity. Nothing like as powerful or coordinated as the European Union the countries of Singapore, Malaysia, Indonesia, Thailand, Philippines, Brunei, Vietnam, Laos, Cambodia and Myanmar are forging corporate agreements and are undertaking (some) joint planning agreements.

Please note that there are other economic groups involving countries, e.g. Ecowas (West African states), ANCOM (Western South America) and AMU (North Africa).

The threat of interdependence

The term 'Fortress Europe' has been mentioned in connection with the European Union, which could, if it chose to, deny access and privileges to non-member states. The clarion cry of the moment is 'unemployment' and xenophobic nationalists could seek leverage from excluding 'foreign' goods particularly from low- (labour) cost nations. To do so would be a disaster of global proportions for it would invite retaliation and a return to the 'beggar my neighbour' economic and political policies of the 1920s and 1930s which resulted in the biggest depression in world history.

What is more likely is that the major trading blocks will engage in a series of bi-lateral and tri-lateral agreements although the path ahead will undoubtedly be a bumpy one. A current example of the stresses between the trading blocks is the banana issue between the USA and the European Union concerning preferential treatment on the part of the EU to Caribbean producers. This is an appropriate point to end this section on patterns of world trade and move to a discussion of the global institutions facilitating the development of world trade – starting with the WTO.

Facilitators of world trade

International organizations

We have considered the rapid expansion of the volume of world trade together with the underlying forces. However, this growth has been far from accidental and although little of the growth can be attributed directly to any one event or set of circumstances, there is no doubt that it could not have come about without the help and assistance of a number of worldwide organizations that together have created a climate for growth through liberalizing trade, reducing regulation and coming to the rescue of nations encountering difficulties in adjusting to the emerging new world order – usually through economic mismanagement of the country's development. There is an extensive list of worldwide organizations and in this section we will limit discussions to a few key facilitators.

World Trade Organization

The World Trade Organization was referred to as GATT (General Agreement on Tariffs and Trade) until 1995. GATT was founded in 1947 in line with many of the other international organizations following the Second World War. The political thinking of the age was far reaching and enlightening as the alternative was descent into national rivalries and enormous economic depression. The purpose of GATT was to reduce tariffs and other obstacles to trade via a series of regular meetings between member countries (actually called 'rounds'). For example, the average tariff rate on manufactured products percentage of value, on trade between industrial nations like theUSA, Britain, Japan and Germany, has fallen from between 10 and 25 per cent to 4 per cent from 1950 and 2000. Furthermore 90 per cent of disputes between trading nations were settled. During this same period the volume of trade increased twenty-fold China has recently joined WTO and the effects of this are eagerly awaited. With a market of 1 billion plus, (not all, it has to be said, have the income to participate in the market economy), the potential is enormous. Even now, many consumer goods, manufactured in China, are entering the markets of the West. Conversely many Western countries are investing in China, taking advantage of the relatively low costs of production.

The eighth round began in 1986 in Uruguay and was concluded in 1995. Despite considerable animosity and hard bargaining the outcome was dramatic. Tariffs were reduced by a further third and new ground rules were established for trading among industrialized nations. For example, there is more money made from trading financial services than trading in physical goods. Furthermore the WTO is an authority with power – GATT with teeth! It can compel nations to conform whereas the previous arrangement was that GATT acted as a pure facilitator. The role and contribution of GATT/WTO has been extremely important to world trade and although the organization has from time to time been derided, it will very likely gain in power and influence to the benefit of nations, companies and customers. It is expanding in membership – currently 120 or so with further associate members.

The World Bank

The role of the World Bank, or the International Bank for Reconstruction and Development to give it its official title, is multifunctional but it is best known as the provider of 'soft' loans to governments to assist economic development frequently through the creation of infrastructure systems, e.g. airports, hydroelectric schemes and railroads. The billions of dollars and other currencies provide the springboard for thousands of businesses, both international and local, to develop. International competitive bidding is a requirement and such is the prudence and reputation of the World Bank there has never been default. This brings confidence to the marketplace and the international business community.

However, it is very important to recognize that the methods employed by the World Bank are sometimes at odds with the social values prevalent in certain countries. Many African nations, trying to develop economic models different to those of the Western oriented capitalist ones have either resisted the methods of the World Bank or even rejected them. The same is true for the IMF.

International Monetary Fund (IMF)

Yet another post-1945 institution, the IMF is the hard man of world governance and is frequently referred to as the 'bank nations love to hate'. Its remit is simple:

- To foster orderly foreign exchange arrangements
- To foster convertible currencies
- To stabilize and reduce balance of payment disequilibrium.

In this respect, its duty is to oversee the interests of nations in a workable international monetary system that benefits all. Its most frequent contribution is to offer financial support and advice to nations whose economies and currencies are in turmoil and crisis. In doing this it operates like a bank helping a business overcome a temporary crisis. But like any prudent banker the IMF can impose draconian conditions on borrowers leading to temporary unpleasant experiences to the politicians and the citizens of a country. Thus the title the bank nations love to hate.

The United Nations (UN)

Unquestionably the best-known worldwide organization. Its high profile role is that of international peacekeeping between warring groups or nations but it does have a role and responsibilities in fostering and developing projects in less developed countries (LDC). It undertakes and underpins technology transfer in the fields of irrigation, education, health, agriculture and commodity extraction from developed countries to underdeveloped ones. The specialized agency (one of about fifteen including the World Health Organization) that is responsible for the transfer _____ UNCTAD (The United Nations Conference on Trade and D_____

European Bank for Reconstruction and Development (EBRD)

Created in 1990, its initial remit was to assist the former communist economies of Eastern Europe to adjust to the market-force economic trading environment.

Exam Question 2.1

In terms of potential market and channel development, what are the implications for organizations which are intending to market their products or services in countries which are experiencing World Bank inspired change from a 'command' to a 'market' economy. (June 2000, Question 4)

Go to www.marketingonline.co.uk or www.bh.com/marketing to access Specimen Answers and Senior Examiner's advice for this exam question.

Exam Question 2.2

Explain how the development of regional economic blocs e.g. the EU, ASEAN, is making it increasingly difficult for global marketers to implement classic 'market entry strategies'. (December 2000, Question 6)

Go to www.marketingonline.co.uk or www.bh.com/marketing to access Specimen Answers and Senior Examiner's advice for these exam questions.

1. Opportunities
   - Reduction of tariff barriers and quotas
   - Opening up of trade borders
   - Reduction of restrictions on goods movements, imports and exports
   - Greater availability of foreign exchange
   - Devaluation of domestic currency
   - Reduction in public sector (abolition of state enterprises)
   - Inward investment programmes/EPZs creation
   - Reductions in restrictions on currency movements.

2. Problems
   - Price rises for domestic product/sources
   - Lack of market demand through currency devaluation/unemployment
   - Rise in import prices
   - Unemployment caused by inflow of foreign goods, reduction in public sector employment requirements
   - Infrastructural problems due to lack of government investment
   - Poor quality of domestic production due to 'closed' economy
   - Lack of channel of distribution
   - Lack of variety of media
   - Lack of money
   - Lack of 'transactional' institutions, i.e. credit.

Barriers to world trade

Having discussed the key facilitators we should end with a very brief review of the barriers the world organizations were established to overcome.

Export and import flows are eased by the removal of barriers. The recommended text contains detailed descriptions of the subject. The intention here is simply to list the key barriers leaving the reader to discover the fuller ramifications of each. Basically there are two recognized forms of barriers and one which, although not overt, can cause 'outsiders' some form of difficulty.

1. **Visible barriers – tariffs and quotas.** Quotas are self-evident restrictions. A tariff can take one of two forms:

    1. A tax on volume, e.g. £1 tax on a 70 cl bottle of wine entering the UK
    2. A tax on value, e.g. the 10 per cent tax levied on importing a car into the UK from anywhere outside the EU. In this instance there is a further addition of 17.5 per cent VAT.

2. **Invisible barriers** – These can take several forms and include:

    3. Government regulations
    4. Technical specifications
    5. Complex administration
    6. Embargo and other quantitative regulations.

3. **Trading blocs** – The EU, ASEAN, etc.

    While one of the objectives of economic integration is to foster trade for the member states, changes to the way business is done in economic blocs can cause some major changes in, and possible barriers to, trade. A classic example of this is the ongoing debate in the European car industry regarding the selling of cars through exclusive retailers. Currently the EU is considering legislation, to be introduced circa 2002, to enable car retailers to sell other makes of car rather than have to exclusively enter an agreement with one manufacturer only. This is causing some European car manufacturers to rethink their retail strategy. Moreover, the effect of this move on non-EU car manufacturers could be far-reaching. They may find themselves competing for retail space with other marques in the same retailer.

    Changes in legislation, quota impositions, rules on ownership, import duties etc., imposed by economic blocs, can have far reaching effects on 'outsider' nations and organisations wishing to do trade with them. These changes can effect the 'rules of engagement' and modes of market entry. For example, changes in packaging and phytosanitary regulations by the EU can dramatically affect the exports of horticultural produce to the EU by Zimbabwean and Zambian producers, causing their costs of production and marketing to rise with the resultant reduction in producer margins. Similarly changes in Education legislation by the Government of Malaysia has caused the 'distribution' of education by UK providers to change from a UK-based focus to a Malaysian-based focus.

    Economic blocs are growing and increasing their 'integrative' processes, for example the single European currency – the euro. These developments can cause great changes to the way business is conducted within and without these blocs, and it behoves global organizations to monitor these changes carefully. Who would have thought that the UK would be facing a total car industry crisis at the end of the year 2000 having, seemingly, established a world-class industry? Partly blame the decision of the UK to stay out of the single European currency, partly blame the effect of overcapacity and falling European demand, but mainly consider the effect of a 'globalization' decision made in Detroit, USA by the car manufacturer's headquarters.

Questions

To check on your understanding of what has been covered consider the following questions:

Question 2.3

- Why is international marketing so important to UK firms?
- Identify five prominent UK companies seriously involved in worldwide marketing. Choose one, preferably one close to your town/city. Study the comments made by the chairman about international marketing – examine its importance to the firm.
- In what way is your life, particularly your business career, related to development on international marketing? Think personally on how events might shape your future career. What will your firm/industry look like 5 or even 10 years from now?
- The big are getting bigger – the paradox is that this leaves more opportunities for small, nimble organizations to prosper. Identify a industry (market). Plot the shapers in terms of macro factors, then see if you can come up with ideas for niche operators.
- From an international perspective, what can be learned from an examination of the make-up and patterns of world trade?
- What is GATT (now renamed the World Trade Organization)? What is its role in international marketing – and what factors threaten its future?
- South-east Asia seems the growth market for the twenty-first century. What advice might you give to the UK firm in:
  1. Entering the region?
  2. Facing competition at home from it?
- Why might a UK company deeply involved in international marketing feel threatened by the formation of the Triad trading blocs? How might it react?
- Who/what are the major institutions facilitating world trade? What are they there for? Do we need them?
- Why is trade in services so difficult to manage? What do you think will be the future reaction of nation states to the accelerating growth of international services? What in your opinion should happen?
- In terms of their impact on your nation's economic well-being explain the similarities and differences between tariff and non-tariff barriers.

Extending knowledge

There are probably many gaps to fill in your knowledge base in the unit. It is important you read widely as the syllabus is now more strategic.

International Marketing Strategy, I. Doole and R. Lowe, 3rd Edition, Thomson, 2001, Chapters 1 and 2. pp. 5–52.

International Marketing, S. Paliwoda and M. Thomas, 3rd Edition, Butterworth-Heinemann, 1999, Chapters 10 and 11, pp. 392–495.

Global Marketing Strategies, J.-P. Jeannet and H.D. Hennessey, 5th Edition, Houghton Mifflin, 2001, Chapters 1 and 2, pp. 2–76.

Summary

Having read this unit you should be in no doubt that international marketing is a driving force in developing world trade. Fewer firms can restrict their thinking to the narrow confines of domestic marketing. International influences are affecting everyone's behaviour. Reliance on the 'home' market can only be sustainable where government protection prevails – and that is in decline. Facing up to international trends in planning for inward competition is an essential prerequisite of every organization.

Trade between nations is the engine that drives the world economy. It needs supporting otherwise the alternative (i.e. a breakdown in international trade) will result in misery for everyone. Yet unfettered trading can also create a perilous scenario. Of crucial importance is balance – equilibrium with openness and liberalization held in perspective by world forces. But this balance is constantly under threat as individual nations protect and encourage home industries. Tensions are forever arising as nations expand or decline on the world scene. World trade is not static, it is forever changing.

Objectives

Customers and an understanding of customer needs and motivations are key to any successful marketing strategy – domestic or international. In international marketing strategy the problem is made more complex for two reasons. First, customers tend to be in different countries and different markets with different environmental effects acting upon them. Second, the self-reference criterion makes it difficult for marketers of a different culture to understand fully how and why a given customer in an overseas market may act differently to the same marketing stimulus. In this unit we will look at the key factors which impinge upon customer behaviour in overseas markets and we will attempt to build a picture of how the international marketer might go about trying to understand the nature and complexities of the foreign market selected.

The best way to understand customers (or to attempt to!) is to analyse and identify those factors of the environment that affect the way that they think and behave. In this unit you will:

- Review the factors that affect buyer behaviour
- Evaluate the key elements of culture
- Consider the main aspects of the international legal environment
- Consider the main aspects of the international political environment
- Consider the main aspects of the international economic environment

  See syllabus sections 2.1.4, 2.1.5 and 2.1.6.

- Review the process of international market selection

  See syllabus sections 2.1.4, 2.1.5 and 2.1.8.

Having completed this unit you will be able to:

- Understand the differences in business and social/cultural conventions which affect buying behaviours in international markets
- Understand how different stages of economic growth affect buying behaviours
- Appreciate how marketing approaches for different foreign markets are driven by local needs and environmental conditions
- Prioritize and select foreign markets.

Study guide

This unit might be considered to be the most important in the whole question of forming international marketing strategy. Good marketing (international as well as domestic) must begin with the customer – not the product.

Success in international operations comes not from skilful manipulation of product or promotional strategies but from a good depth of understanding of what our customers want, what drives them and how to read the local environment to understand customers.

The candidate should read this unit more than once. It should be worked in conjunction with all the other units in this book.

> Once you have completed this unit, try to apply the data as a key to understanding a foreign market that you know, perhaps one that you have visited on holiday. What can you see from an analysis of the market? Can you place some of the 'different' behaviours in context? What special aspects of the local environment are driving the different behaviours?

Environmental factors

The comparative analysis of world markets is concerned with the environment in which international marketing takes place. The kind of steps that the international marketer can take and the adaptations that organizations must make will be determined largely by this environment. In this unit we will be concerned primarily with the international marketer's sphere of operation, dwelling particularly on the uncontrollable variables and how they affect the international marketing task.

There are a number of ways of categorizing the environment and in international marketing strategy the SLEPT method is preferred (i.e. social, legal, economic, political and technology factors).

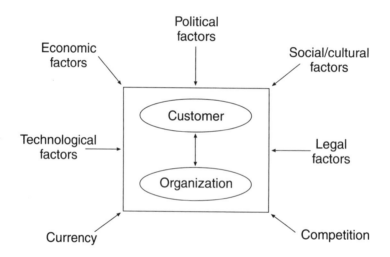

Figure 3.1
Environmental factors in international marketing

Figure 3.1 identifies these various factors which are the most important variables that affect the relationship between the organization and its customer in the foreign market operation. The rest of this unit will consider these factors separately and intends to identify how they impinge upon the international marketer's task.

Note that a further discussion on environmental factors appears in the module 'Marketing Operations' in the Advanced Certificate in Marketing.

The social/cultural environment

It is only in relatively recent years that socio-cultural influences have been identified as critical determinants of marketing behaviour. In other words, marketing is a cultural as well as an economic phenomenon. Culture is so pervasive yet so complex that it is difficult to define in short, simple terms. The easiest way to grasp the complexity of culture is to examine these varied aspects. Up to 73 'cultural universals' (human behaviours that are to be found in all cultures in the world) have been identified, but we have reduced these to eight 'cultural components' for our purposes (see Figure 3.2). While this brief survey is not sufficient to convey any expertise in the area, its main purpose is to alert the prospective marketer to the kind of cultural parameters that can affect international marketing programmes.

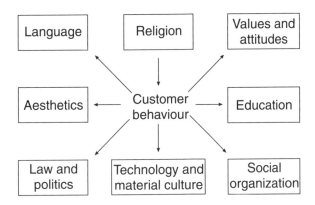

Figure 3.2
The components of cultures (adapted from Terpstra)

The key components of culture in the international marketing environment are as follows.

Language

Foreign markets differ from the domestic in terms of the language which the people speak and the language which is written. In some markets the official language differs from the actual one used, in other markets there is more than one language to deal with in the same population. Countries with more than one official language are relatively easy to spot (Switzerland has four), other countries with widely differing dialects are sometimes more difficult (India = 500, Papua New Guinea = around 750). In other markets there are differences in the language spoken by the males and the females of the population (Japan).

35

Language differences will affect not only the organization's promotional strategy in international markets, but will add complexity in interpersonal relationships and internal written/spoken communications.

Religion

Religion is a major cultural variant and has significant if not always apparent effects on marketing strategy. For example, the identification of sacred objects and philosophical systems, beliefs and norms as well as taboos, holidays and rituals are critical for an understanding of marketing interest in a given product or service. Religion will affect the food which people eat and when they eat it as well as people's attitudes to a whole range of products from deodorants to alcoholic drink.

Values and attitudes

The values that a market has towards things such as time, achievement, work, wealth, change and risk taking will seriously affect not only the products offered but also the packaging and communication activities. 'Old' and 'New' have quite different meanings in the East and in the West and even within Europe. Motivation of the organization's personnel is also strongly influenced by the local culture and practice. Encouraging local sales forces to sell more by offering cars and more money, for example, may not work in all cultures. The SRC is a major obstacle in this area.

Education

The level of formal primary and secondary education in a foreign market will have direct impact upon the 'sophistication' of the target customers. A simple example will be the degree of literacy. The labelling of products, especially those with possibly hazardous side-effects, needs to be taken seriously for a market that has a very low literacy rate.

Social organization

This relates to the way in which a society organizes itself. It should consider kinship, social institutions, interest groups and status systems. The role of women and caste systems are easily identifiable examples. If your organization has a history of successfully marketing to 'the housewife/homemaker', life becomes more difficult where women have no social status at all. An example close to home would include Switzerland, where the majority of people rent rather than own their houses and expect to rent property with domestic appliances installed – in this case the banks are the largest single purchasers of washing machines!

Exam Hint

In case you are asked to quote an example, it can be useful to try to understand, in reasonable depth, one or two international markets (culture/ technology, etc.) and how things really work. One advanced and one less advanced market is usually enough. Depth knowledge used in one question could make all the difference.

Technology and material culture

This aspect relates not to 'materialism' but to the local market's ability to handle and deal with modern technology. Some cultures find leaving freezers plugged in overnight and servicing cars and trucks that have not yet broken down difficult concepts to manage. In instances such as these the organization is often faced with the choice of either educating the population (expensive) or de-engineering the product or service (often unpalatable to domestic engineers).

Law and politics

The legal and political environments in a foreign market are often and rightly seen as consequences of the culture of that market. For example some forms of punishment for crimes committed in Islamic cultures may be difficult to accept by 'Western' cultures. Legal and political systems are often a simple codification of the norms of behaviour deemed acceptable by the local culture. These two aspects will be dealt with in more depth below.

Aesthetics

This area covers the local culture's perception of things such as beauty, good taste and design and dictates what is acceptable or 'appealing' to the local eye. An organization's decision as to aspects of the product or service involving colour, music, architecture or brand names needs to be sympathetic and acceptable to the local culture if purchase is to take place. For the unwary there are many, many traps in this area. Colour means completely different things in different cultures and brand names often do not travel well!

International marketing and the internet

Leaving the 'e-' to one side for a moment, what is it all about? Any business, 'e-' or 'non-e-' has got to be about three things:

- Buying and selling something
- Customers (who make the money to make the world go round)
- Profits (that allow the companies to survive).

E-customers?

So what do we know about e-customers. Not too much at the moment, but we can gather a great deal of intelligence from analysing how the current internet businesses seem to be treating their customers. E-customers appear to be patient, time-rich and homebound individuals who are wired to the internet twenty-four hours a day. They also appear to be 'shop-o-phobic' to an unnatural degree and solely driven by price.

Even better, to judge solely by current activity, all e-customers are the same – there is no allowance being made for differences in needs, lifestyle or demographics. Go on the internet and immediately you are a global company – whatever happened to all the pitfalls of international business with different needs and different cultures? The myth of the homogeneous customer has always been attractive but it remains a myth nevertheless. As much as a myth as the standardized 'global product'.

Where is internet usage currently? Is North America your chosen international market? Just how established is the internet in the developing and underdeveloped world? Is it all in American English? How many languages is Yahoo! presented in? Can everybody understand it?

Now, how important is the internet going to be for the international business – and how fast?

The answer to some of these questions can be found in Table 3.1.

Table 3.1 Numbers on line Nov. 2000		
	Millions	%
Africa	3.11	0.8
Asia Pacific	104.88	25.6
Europe	113.14	27.8
Middle East	2.40	0.6
Canada and USA	167.12	41.05
Latin America	16.45	4.15
World total	407.1	100
Source: Nua Internet services at www.nua.ie *Jan 2001*		

There is evidence to suggest that the biggest user of on line purchasing is the business to business sector, followed by the consumer retail sector, especially financial services. At the end of 2000, many dot com companies in the USA and the UK ceased trading and there was evidence that consumers in the USA and Europe were foresaking the medium, some 25 million coming off line in the USA alone. However, internet use continues to soar in Canada and Southern Africa, even in Swaziland. It is estimated by various sources that by 2005, despite all the hype, internet trading will only account for 5% of world trade.

The political environment

The political environment of international marketing includes any national or international political factor that can affect the organization's operations or its decision making. Politics has come to be recognized as the major factor in many international business decisions. It is a major factor in deciding whether to invest and how to continue marketing. The best way to deal with this problem is for management to become fully informed of the situation and the firm must go beyond traditional market research to include the political environment.

There are a number of aspects to the political environment that should serve to guide you through this area and they are as follows.

The role of the government in the economy

What is the role of the government in the targeted local marketplace? Is it primarily undertaking a 'participation' role (strongly involved in the day-to-day activities of the economy) or is it primarily a 'regulator' (fixes the rules and regulations but tries to leave the market open to local competition and market forces)? For example, over the last 20 years or so, many countries in Sub-Saharan Africa have been undertaking World Bank supported structural adjustment programmes i.e. a change from a 'command' to a 'market' economy. This has meant that governments, for example Malawi, have changed their stance from 'participation' to 'facilitator/regulator'. Basically the Government has been denationalizing and withdrawing from hitherto state-owned industries.

Ideologies and marketing

The ideological background of the government can give good insights into how it is likely to act/react with a foreign company operating in its marketplace. Ideologies such as capitalism, socialism and nationalism will clearly affect the way the government deals with overseas organizations and its likely approach to your marketing programmes when they are implemented. Beware new 'labels'. The recent (so-called) collapse of communism may have produced apparently new capitalist markets to explore – it normally takes more than a declaration for managers and customers to behave differently. Change certainly doesn't happen overnight. For example, while in theory, many of the 'Asian Tigers' have now adopted a 'Western' approach to market development since the 1997/8 financial contagion, in reality the 'Asian' development model still persists, e.g. South Korea.

Political stability

How stable is the government? Here much depends upon the organization's level of involvement and the amount of risk that the organization is prepared to take. Pure exporting is a very low-risk scenario and the political stability is of minor concern. If the organization is planning longer-term involvement and higher investment in the market, longer planning horizons may require a more rigorous analysis of government stability and governmental policy. For example, potential investors are more likely to favour investment destinations like the EU and the USA at present to the politically uncertain destinations like Zimbabwe, the Democratic Republic of Congo and Liberia.

International relations

Two forms of international relations are important here: first, the relationship between the home government and the various host government or governments and second, the ongoing relationship between different host governments in those markets in which the organization wishes to operate. In the 1980s, owning a subsidiary which operated in apartheid South Africa was a major liability for many international organizations. In the 1990s, organizations thought to be supporting the apartheid regime might have similar problems dealing with the new government, although this is now a rapidly fading phenomenon in the current South African climate of reconciliation.

We are also witnessing a resurgence of 'nationalism' and 'back to roots' in some parts of the world as frontiers and political orientations change. East Timor and Aborigine situations in Australia are cases in point.

Activity 3.1

If you work in an organization, find out how well your managers know the cultural aspects of their target markets. How well is this knowledge used in international marketing planning? Alternatively, analyse a well-known company and assess how well they do it.

The political threats

The primary consequences of wrongly assessing the political environment can prove extremely costly for the international organization. In the event of a serious 'falling out' between the organization and host government, local officials may have the power to confiscate company assets, expropriate them or simply increase governmental controls over the company assets located in their country. There are a number of instances where these actions have been taken and, despite loud voices and sabre-rattling on the part of the home government, the costs to the international organization have been significant. White farmers in Zimbabwe are still facing the real threat of nationalization/expropriation of their lands to be 'redistributed' or 'resettled', despite previous assurances from the government. Recently, Bosnia, Serbia and Indonesia have also experienced political intervention and suffered the consequences in terms of loss of investment and trade.

The legal environment

The legal environment is generated from the political climate and the prevalent cultural attitudes towards business enterprise, that is, the nation's laws and regulations pertaining to business. It is important for the firm to know the legal environment in each of its markets because these laws constitute the 'rules of the game' for business activity. The legal environment in international marketing is more complicated than domestic since it has three dimensions: (1) local domestic law, (2) international law and (3) domestic laws in the firm's home base.

There are a number of key aspects to the international legal environment:

- *Local domestic laws* These are all different! The only way to find a route through the legal maze in overseas markets is to use experts on the separate legal systems and laws pertaining in each market targeted.
- *International law* There are a number of 'international laws' that can affect the organization's activity. Some deal with piracy and hijacking, others are more international conventions and agreements and cover items such as the IMF and World Trade Organization (WTO formerly GATT) treaties. They also deal with patents and trademark legislation (some of which differ by markets) and harmonization of legal systems within regional economic groupings such as the growth of EU laws which bind member states.
- *Domestic laws* The organization's domestic (home market) legal system is important for two reasons. First, there are often export controls which limit the free export of certain goods and services to particular marketplaces and second, there is the duty of the organization to act and abide by its national laws in all its activities whether domestic or international.
- *Laws and the international marketing activity* It will be readily understandable how domestic, international and local legal systems can have a major impact upon the organization's ability to market into particular overseas countries. Laws will affect the marketing mix in terms of products, price, distribution and promotional activities quite dramatically. 'Ignorance is no defence' tends to be universal in all markets.

The economic environment

The economic environment has long been recognized as an uncontrollable factor in the task of marketing management generally. The economic environment of international marketing is peculiar in two ways. First, it contains an international economic structure that affects marketing between nations, and second, it includes the domestic economy of every nation in which the firm is attempting to market. Thus the international marketer faces the traditional task of economic analysis but in a context that may include a hundred countries or more. This investigation will be directed towards two broad questions: (1) how big is the market and (2) what is the market like?

The first issue confronting the international marketer is to identify the likely size of the target market or markets. We can assess this in a number of ways:

- *Population size and growth* How big is the population and how fast is it growing? This will give an indication of likely current and future demand.
- *Population density and concentration* Where is the population located? How dense is the population and is the population concentrated in specific areas? Population concentration is important for two reasons. First, there are obvious questions of distribution and logistics. Second, when population becomes concentrated it often tends to take on a separate character. 'Urbanization' (see Unit 2) produces the need for different products and services.
- *Population age and distribution* How old is the average population and what is the distribution among the various age levels? The advanced economies of the West have rapidly ageing populations that offer certain market opportunities for particular products. Some African countries, on the other hand, have 50 per cent of their populations below the age of 15. This offers a completely different market opportunity for the international organization.

able income and distribution What is the available income in the population? Can people afford the proposed products or services that the organization can e? Equally important, is the income concentrated into particular groups of people widely distributed through the population? Remember that even in the poorest markets there are often pockets of extreme wealth that can afford and demand certain high quality luxury goods.

Activity 3.2

Find out how the United Nations and/or the World Bank classifies nations according to these classifications or others.

What does the classification tell you about their understanding of world trade and politics?

What are the implications for the international marketer?

As well as the market size the international marketer should also try to understand the nature of the economy in which he or she proposes operating. There are a number of dimensions to this question:

- *Natural resources* What resources are available in the local marketplace that the organization may wish to use for its production? This may include natural resources (raw materials) as well as local management ability. Some countries require an agreed amount of local content as a basis for foreign investment in the first place.

Activity 3.3

Spend some time with an atlas. Look at the world and at the natural topography. Even today these features can affect marketing plans and implementation. Can you see how?

A few hours' study of a good atlas will almost certainly pay dividends on the day of the examination. Geography lessons at school are long forgotten and population figures change rapidly. Newer atlases will be needed to show up states in the former USSR and the exam could ask questions based on the new, emerging nations.

- *Topography* This relates to the physical nature of the marketplace, rivers, mountains, lakes and the like. Natural features such as mountain ranges and rivers can provide serious barriers to communication, both physical and electronic in even the most advanced markets.
- *Climate* The climatic situations prevalent in a marketplace may require adaptations to product or to services from the domestic standard. Climate can affect both the delivery and the operation of the product and service. Consider water-cooled engines in drier climates and the management siesta in the Mediterranean!
- *Economic activity* What is the primary economic activity of the marketplace? Is it basically agricultural or is it industrial? Such indicators will give a good key as to the likely demand, lifestyles and product/service requirements.
- *Energy and communications* Energy sources and communication infrastructures that we take for granted in the advanced Western economies tend to be less readily available or less reliable in underdeveloped or less developed markets. If the organization's business

relies strongly upon speedier reliable communications then overseas markets need to be assessed carefully before entry is made.

- *Urbanization* To what extent is the local market urbanized or rural? The level of urbanization will affect not only the types of products and services that are demanded but also the way in which these are delivered.
- *Differential inflation* What is the level of inflation relative to that of your domestic market or another market with which the target will be linked? If the organization is used to operating in areas and markets of low inflation, annual inflation rates of 500 or 1000 per cent may be beyond the realm of management expertise.

Activity 3.4

What is the current rate of inflation in the UK/your home market? What country currently has the highest rate of inflation in the world? What rate is it? How do people manage on a day-to-day basis? How would it affect a company exporting from your home country into the high-inflation market?

A number of models exist to classify various markets around the world according to different stages of economic growth and development. Examples of these classifications would be:

1.

   a. Less developed countries (LDCs)
   b. Newly industrialized countries (NICs)
   c. Advanced economies.

2.

   a. Self-sufficiency
   b. Emergence
   c. Industrialization
   d. Mass consumption
   e. Post-industrial society.

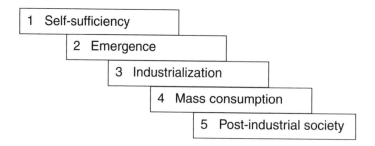

Figure 3.3
Stages of economic development

Many of these classifications are useful shorthand and give an instant view of the various economic marketplaces throughout the world. However, it is difficult to capture the special characteristics of individual markets in this way and oversimplification of this sort can be dangerous in any in-depth analysis. For example, the second model (illustrated in Figure 3.3) is based strongly on the natural evolution of economies through a regular and understood industrialization process. It has difficulty in dealing with economies which are either artificially distorted by, for instance, sudden oil revenues or even those markets that are, or have been, artificially controlled by Communist governments. For example, many oil-rich states in the Middle East seem to display characteristics of stages 1, 2, 3 and 4 at the same time! The moral here is to treat such models as useful guidance but to temper this approach with some degree of commonsense.

The technological environment

Technology is no longer subject to national boundaries although it is, to some extent, still subject to economics – not every company can afford to purchase the very latest technology. Technology can be very expensive for many organizations and countries, certainly if they wish to acquire the state-of-the-art technology which is often necessary just to keep in the race as products and services become more and more developed. On the other hand, technology is also reducing the barriers to entry to many industries by reducing the necessary scale of operations required to reach economically competitive cost levels. Therefore it is becoming more feasible for the installation of local operations in smaller markets and smaller countries.

The internet may eventually open up new markets but we should beware of the hype – at least in the short term. Remember that 40 per cent of all internet connection is still confined to North America, with Europe and Asia together accounting for 53 per cent. Third world and developing areas are well behind.

The final important aspect of technology, as it increases its worldwide reach, is for a tendency for production and services to increase on a global scale. As a result, pressures on price and margins at a global level increase apace.

The competitive environment

Competition worldwide is increasing at both a global and a local level. Local markets are increasingly subject to international and global competition and, in addition, technology is facilitating competition from previously unexpected quarters. No longer are LDCs satisfied merely by exporting raw materials, they also want the additional margin that comes from manufacturing.

Activity 3.5

For a company and a market of your choice, can you identify:

- All the different forms of competition they face?
- Exactly how competition affects the development of international marketing plans?
- Can you name the five different competitive forces?

At an international level advanced markets are seeing significant competition from both LDCs and NICs who are using modern technology and lower labour prices to compete in hitherto 'protected' marketplaces.

Exam Hint

Competition is critical to the development of any form of marketing strategy – including international. Are you confident that you can apply Porter's competitive forces model to international marketing? You need to know how.

The complexity of international competition has been heightened by the strategic use of international sourcing of components to achieve competitive advantage (reference the Japanese electronics industry).

The currency environment

The world currency environment, stimulated by worldwide trading and foreign exchange dealing, is an additional complication in the international environment. On top of all the normal vagaries of markets, customer demands, competitive actions and economic infrastructures, foreign exchange parities are likely to change on a regular if unpredictable basis. Such changes can be stimulated by a number of different factors, most of which are completely out of the control of the international marketing organization.

Difficult as it may be, foreign exchange movements need to be understood and, to some extent, predicted where possible. With increasing levels of competition and the consequent reduction in international margins, unpredicted exchange movements can, at a stroke, turn a brilliant strategy into a shambles – and profit into loss.

Rapid and abrupt movements in currency in foreign markets can be a real challenge to the international marketer. Differential inflation rates are a problem, up to 2000 per cent has been noted in some South American countries and these days could return. The emergent Russia has shown what happens when a currency effectively collapses and the market is forced to return to the black market and foreign currencies in order to survive.

The question of currency also raises the issue of the EU and the euro or common currency. Whether or not the UK eventually joins the European Monetary Union (EMU) is far from clear. Whether the Euro succeeds in its aims is still a question. Although the issues are still far from clear, the international marketer needs to be prepared for any eventuality and a new currency is no small matter, especially for multinationals or financial services organizations. The Diploma examinations could ask a question in this area, do you have a view? Is your view reasoned and supported by facts?

Question 3.1

The recent collapse of economies in South-East Asian countries has highlighted the difficulties of the 'pricing' decision in global marketing. What are the major considerations for pricing goods and services for the international market, and what contingencies should be planned to offset currency collapse? (June 1999)

Go to www.marketingonline.co.uk or www.bh.com/marketing to access Specimen Answers and Senior Examiner's advice for this exam question.

Question 3.2

Write briefing notes to the Chief Executive of a global consumer electronics manufacturer critically analysing the effect of the growth of e-commerce on global channels of distribution, Illustrate your case with relevant examples. (June 2001 Question 6)

Go to www.marketingonline.co.uk or www.bh.com/marketing to access Specimen Answers and Senior Examiner's advice for this exam question.

arge component of international business involves business-to-business activity. The many texts in the area tend to stress the key aspects of business-to-business marketing in the domestic environment and focus on issues such as:

- The composition of the DMU
- Organizational factors affecting the purchase
- The role of technology
- Personal characteristics of the business buyer
- The business/industrial buying process.

All these factors are influential in the international situation with the added aspects of the SLEPT factors discussed above. Culture especially, will be a key factor in this area and its effects on personal and interpersonal relationships should never be overlooked.

It is absolutely essential to evaluate either business-to-business or consumer behaviour in a global or international market opportunity analysis context. Without a consumer or business which has the desire and money to spend on goods or services there is no market, hence no market opportunity. Having identified possible market opportunities then business decisions are taken in order to meet them. Changes in technology and other environmental factors, can have an effect on consumer or business-to-business behaviour and international organizations must be alive to these changes. For example, the development of e-business has affected the way consumers behave and buy in many goods and services and has definitely led to the evolution of new communications and channels of distribution. Businesses need to be acutely aware of these changes when evaluating how consumers behave, and adjust their marketing plans accordingly.

Foreign market selection

In too many instances the selection of foreign markets, often for considerable investment, would appear to be an informal process. Since a firm's resources are limited it is essential that enough resource is concentrated in a small enough number of markets to have an effect. Resources spread too thinly will not only fall short of 'critical mass' but will also serve to inform competitors of your intentions. Foreign market selection is applicable to those organizations moving into international business for the first time as well as those organizations looking to extend their operations by moving into new international markets. The problem remains, what should we do, and where? Foreign market selection should be a prioritizing activity based on the three rules of 'potential', 'similarity' and 'accessibility' (see Figure 3.4).

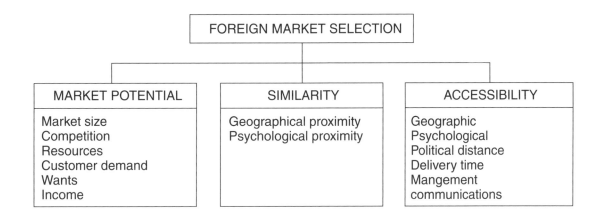

Figure 3.4
Foreign market selection

An organization should resist the temptation to attack too many markets at one time thereby spreading effort and resources too thinly to be successful. The initial effort is often better directed at a single market and extended to other, possibly neighbouring markets later.

Market potential

The first critical measure of foreign market attractiveness is to try to assess the potential of the foreign market for profitable operations. There are a number of aspects to this question:

- *Market size* How big is the market for our intended product or service? Remember that a straight reading of population may not be enough. We are interested in identifying the size of the market which could be potential purchasers for the product or service in question.
- *Competition* How strong is the competition in the proposed marketplace? What is the picture of domestic and international competition either operating or contemplating entry into the marketplace? Will there be enough competition to stimulate growth but not too much competition to restrict profits to a possibly untenable level?
- *Resources* What resources are available within the marketplace to support our entry and operations there? What resources ideally do we need? If the resources are not there at the moment can they be brought in from neighbouring markets at reasonable cost?
- *Customer demand, wants, income, etc.* What do customers actually want? What is the level of demand? What are the softer, societal issues that must be considered in the market (green issues, ethical issues). These can make all the difference in how the organization and its products/services are perceived. To what extent are current needs and wants being met by local or international competition? Is there available income to create profitable demand that the organization can meet? Remember, prospective customers who can't afford to pay is business we can find anywhere in the world!

The textbooks explain the practical approaches to identifying market attractiveness, similarity and potential (see for example, Doole and Lowe and Paliwoda and Thomas).

Activity 3.6

For your company/a company of your choice what criteria did management actually use to select target foreign markets? How would you suggest improving the selection process?

Similarity (to home or other (understood) foreign markets)

In addition to the financial parameters of the marketplace it is important to understand whether the target market is close enough to either our home market (which we ought to understand) or to another foreign market which we understand because we are successfully operating there already:

- *Geographic proximity* Is the intended market geographically close for us to access it with our products or service and with the management expertise needed to satisfy customer needs?
- *Psychological proximity* Do we understand how the people in the marketplace think? Do we have a degree of rapport with the local culture? Will we understand management attitudes and activities in the local marketplace? Will they be able to interact with our organization's established culture and norms of behaviour?

...ility

...to the marketplace? Accessibility can be judged on a number of different para-...of which are equally important to the development of a successful international marketing strategy:

- *Geographic accessibility* Can we physically reach the marketplace and the separate segments or parts of the market within the local marketplace? Can we meet the lead times and delivery times required by the local customers to at least match, if not improve upon, competitive performances? Are there any physical or communication barriers which will stop us achieving these needs?
- *Psychological access* Do we understand the local culture and buyer requirements and needs sufficiently to be able to position the products or service to be relevant to local market conditions? Are we able to meet local buyers at an emotional as well as a rational level? (Remember, the majority of purchase decisions are taken on an emotional basis and not rationally – much as we might like them to be so.)
- *Political distance* How far away is the political system and government ideology and activity from what we are used to dealing with? Do we understand the political motivations and are we able to predict activities in the future? Is there a solid rapport between the home government and the host government and between the host government and other markets in which we operate?
- *Management communications* Any international marketing operation will require a level of local management in order to implement its plans. This may be carried out by local agents and/or distributors or local or expatriate staff employed by the company. In any event, the local management will have to be part of the local culture in order to implement any marketing strategy properly. Management attitudes, behaviours and motivations tend to differ quite markedly among different cultures and it is important that the organization be able to communicate effectively with people on the ground. No international marketing strategy can be successfully implemented without this level of communication.

Country attractiveness

	High	Medium	Low
Low	P	S	T
Medium	S	T	
High	T		

Company's compatibility with each country

P = primary opportunity
S = secondary opportunity
T = tertiary opportunity

Figure 3.5

Questions

As a check on your understanding of what has been covered in this unit, consider the following questions:

Question 3.3

1. What are the key aspects of the 'environment' which affect the foreign customer?
2. What are the eight key aspects of culture?
3. What effects can 'language' have on our international marketing strategy?
4. What effects can 'religion' have on our international marketing strategy?
5. What effects can 'values and attitudes' have on our international marketing strategy?
6. What effects can 'education' have on our international marketing strategy?
7. What effects can 'social organization' have on our international marketing strategy?
8. What effects can 'technology' have on our international marketing strategy?
9. What effects can 'aesthetics' have on our international marketing strategy?
10. What are the two main roles of government in the economy? How will our international operations be affected by foreign governments?
11. What are the main aspects of the international legal environment? How will our international operations be affected by these?
12. What are the key aspects of the international economic environment that the organization should consider? How will these affect our international operations?
13. What role can models of economic growth and development play in the formulation of international marketing strategy?
14. What are the main aspects of the international technological environment? How will these affect our international operations?
15. What are the main aspects of the international competitive environment? How will these affect our international operations?
16. How does business-to-business marketing work in the international environment?
17. What are the three parameters by which we can prioritize and select foreign markets?

Case Study

11th September 2001: A case of the effects of environmental change

The events of 11th September, the attack on the World Trade Centre in New York and the Pentagon in Washington DC, changed the world economic/ political scene in a dramatic way. The knock-on effect in world trade was far reaching. Immediately the number of air passengers crossing the Atlantic to the USA from the UK dropped by 30 per cent. This triggered a 'multiplier'of world proportions. The world airlines, especially the USA carriers, but British and others also, faced reductions in the work force of some 30000 people as aircraft were mothballed due to the downturn in travel. Some 1000 aircraft were taken out of service and routes were cut as airlines struggled to contain costs. Some airlines like Air New Zealand and

Swiss Air could not survive, so shut down, with further loss of jobs. On the other hand, budget airlines, like Easyjet and RyanAir mainly locally or regionally based, experienced a boom as passengers switched to less long haul based tourist locations.

The knock-on effect continues. The tourist industry has been hit around the globe. It is estimated that the UK has experienced £2 billion in lost tourist revenues since 11th September with some 2000 hotels and restaurants hit hard and some of London's West End theatres have had to close. Up to the beginning of 2002, earnings from overseas tourists fell 12 per cent. According to The Association of British Travel Agents,16 tour operators and 20 travel agencies went bust in 2001. Tour operators such as Thomas Cook and Airtours have cut thousands of jobs. Falling numbers of tourists have added to the UK's growing balance of payments gap, standing in the 10 months to October 2001 at £12 billion compared to £9.3 billion over the same period in 2000.

As world airlines cancel options on new aircraft, suppliers to the industry have been hit hard. Rolls-Royce, suppliers of aircraft engines, has recently announced 5000 redundancies world-wide as Airbus and Boeing experience cancellations. The downturn in demand for Rolls-Royce engines has meant less orders for R-R suppliers as the secondary shocks are felt in the supply chain. Even Jaguar cars, which has a large percentage of its sales in the USA, has experienced a downturn in orders. The International supply chain has been heavily hit and it is not over yet.

The fallout does not stop at the immediate supply chain. As workers lose their jobs, demand for other goods and services slows down. The ripple effect is, therefore, felt in a variety of goods and services. The events of 11th September were unpredictable and devastating and show the true effects of changes in the marketing environmentals on global business in a big way.

Source: Various public sources

Extending knowledge

For a more detailed analysis and explanation of customers and their environments, read:

International Marketing Strategy, I. Doole and R. Lowe, 3rd Edition, Thomson, 2001, Chapters 2 and 3, pp. 32–92.

International Marketing, S. Paliwoda and M. Thomas, 3rd Edition Butterworth-Heinemann, 1999. Chapter 2, pp. 42–95.

Global Marketing Strategies, J-P. Jeannet and H. D. Hennessey, 5th Edition, Houghton Mifflin, 2001. Chapters 3, 4 and 5, pp. 77–215.

Summary

In this unit we have considered the various environmental factors which act upon the customer in a given or prospective foreign marketplace. We have seen the heavy impact of culture on buyer behaviour and perceptions as well as the infrastructure constraints delivered by legal, economic and political systems.

Technology, competition and currency are all moving to global stages and are having serious effects on international business worldwide. Although often difficult to predict, these effects cannot be ignored or international profitability will suffer badly.

Finally we considered how to select target markets on the basis of this analysis and the broad parameters required for successful marketing strategy implementation which follows.

Objectives

Knowledge is power. In this unit you will study the key issues relating to gathering information on the international front. The scale of the task is wider and the problems in collecting data multiply as markets and customers differ. The major thrust of the unit is not concerned with the specifics and technical details of gathering information but discusses the management perspective. You will:

- Understand issues relating to scanning international markets to decide initially where we should go in the broadest terms
- Examine models of how to approach the broad tasks of identifying market/product combinations and on to prioritize opportunities
- Study the sources of international data and how to deal with such issues as researching within numerous markets
- Understand the difficulties involved in comparing data across countries/markets, i.e. cross-country research.
- Have a knowledge of the problems and pitfalls of international primary and secondary research.
- Know the basic principles of appointing an international market research agency
- Be aware of technology and its impact on information gathering, i.e. the internet.

See syllabus sections 2.1.6 and 2.1.7.

Having completed the unit you will be able to:

- Explain the difference between gathering data from an international market(s) and a domestic one
- Apply the process of narrowing down broad-scale international opportunities and identify specific countries for further more detailed examination
- Match sources of data to specific problems
- Identify the resource implications of international market research.

NB: A lot of the fine details concerning management information and subsequent market decisions is covered in the module 'Management Information and Market Decisions' at Advanced Certificate Level.

Study guide

International market research needs to be considered stage by stage. It is not feasible for even the major global players to be totally global in their research. Time and the scale of the task dictates a measured approach. Costs are equally important. The unit takes the approach that information searches begin on the broad scale and subsequently narrow down. Initially the question is 'Where should we go?' With as many as 200 countries to select how does one go about prioritizing? Think about the implication of planning and control against this background. Remember as you work through this unit that the biggest problem is not so much obtaining data but being selective about what data is essential rather than 'Let's collect everything we can'. Again, consider the issues surrounding the comparability of data, e.g. specific words are culturally loaded. What is a 'small business'? What does 'healthy' mean or 'leisure', 'home owner' etc.? These words in common use nonetheless mean different things in different countries.

International market research – cross-country issues

As international marketing has developed rapidly in recent years so has the need for information and knowledge. For example, international marketing research, (i.e. research into the application of the 4/7 Ps to a market) is taking an increasingly important role in strategic planning. It is estimated that the 1990s have seen its growth exceed 30 per cent per annum – twice the rate of UK domestic research growth. For example, when Toyota decided to re-design its flagship luxury car, the Lexus, it relied heavily on 'direct perception' research (Source: Healy, J.R., (1994) 'Toyota strives for new look, same edge', USA today, 13 October, 1B–2B). Since 1995 it is estimated that international marketing research has grown by some 32 per cent per annum – twice the UK domestic research growth. At the beginning of 1998, global marketing research revenues by the top 25 global research organizations exceeded US$6 billion.

When discussing the changes taking place in world trading in an earlier chapter it was apparent that information, knowledge gathering and transference attains critical importance in decision making. Peter Bartram, of Applied Research and Communications, identified three key areas of development:

1. Development of improved techniques, data availability and research supplier networks in developing countries (e.g. India and the Pacific Rim).

2. In more developed countries where market research is more established the key competence will be:

    *   Development of pan-regional or global surveys allowing a comparison of data
    *   The identification of niche markets across national boundaries creating clusters of customers with similar motivations and needs
    *   The specialization of research organizations on a regional/worldwide basis. The more detailed your knowledge search, the greater will be the need for appropriate expertise
    *   Rapid if diffusion of new products internationally will dictate faster research delivery.

3. In mature markets the forefront of research may move into the development of database market research via electronic transfers and the deeper involvement of research into 'value' discriminators in identifying segments within markets.

This unit adopts the outlook that the decision has been taken to 'go international' and, furthermore, our view is to concentrate on the information gathering that relates to marketing issues (strategic and tactical).

The scale of the task: personnel and money – operational issues

With around 200 countries to aim at, even the Coca-Cola's and McDonald's of this world would find it a challenge to undertake research everywhere. For those medium-to-large UK companies who in the normal course of events conduct, shall we say, ten pieces of research per annum in the UK, the task of replicating that in Europe alone would require a budget way in excess of most companies' resources to say nothing of the organizational and operational ramifications. Clearly there has to be a systematic approach at conducting international marketing research.

What information?

1. *Where to go?* Having decided to internationalize, the first critical consideration is the need to rank countries in order of priority or attractiveness.

2. *How to get there?* Having decided where to go, the next decision area is how to access the market(s), i.e. exporting, licensing or local production, etc.

3. *What shall we market?* Should we modify our product or service, in what way and to what degree, i.e. the start of the application of the marketing mix, the product P.

4. *How do we persuade them to buy it?* The development of the mix via the necessary Ps (place, price, etc.) and incorporating all four or seven depending on the nature of our offer (product or service).

The information stream

What information should market research provide? The following list sets out the least intelligence needed.

1. *Where to go?*
   - Assessment of global demand
   - Ranking of potential by country/region
   - Local competition
   - Political risk.

2. *How to get there?*
   - Size of market/segments
   - Barriers to entry
   - Transport and distribution costs
   - Local competition
   - Government requirements
   - Political risk.

3. *What shall we market?*
   - Government regulations
   - Customer sophistication
   - Competitive stance.

4. *How do we persuade them to buy it?*
   - Buyer behaviour
   - Competitive practice
   - Distribution channels
   - Media and other promotional channels
   - Company expertise.

Table 4.1 augments this abbreviated list and embraces the point that in today's challenging environment the successful domestic firm cannot ignore international market research for inbound competition is accelerating. This is particularly true within the EU, which should be viewed increasingly as a domestic market.

Research methodology

Scanning international markets/countries

In the initial stage countries are scanned for attraction and prioritization. The search may be extremely wide covering many countries, and three criteria lend themselves to this exercise:

1. *Accessibility* Can we get there? What's preventing us? Trade barriers, government regulations, etc.?
2. *Profitability* Can 'they' (i.e. potential customers) afford our product? Is competition too entrenched? Is the market ready? What is the likely payback? Timescale? Will we get paid? Remember, unprofitable business we can get anywhere!
3. *Market size* Present and future trends.

Differences across countries and regions of interest				
The marketing environment	**The competition**	**The product**	**Marketing mix**	**Firm-specific historical data**
Political context: leaders, national goals, ideology, key institution	Relative market shares, new product moves	Analysis of users Who are the end-user industries?	Channels of distribution: evolution and performance	Sales trends by product and product-line, salesforce and customer
Economic growth prospects, business cycle stage	Pricing and cost structure, image and brand reputation	Industrial and consumer buyers; characteristics: size, age, sex, segment growth rates	Relative pricing, elasticities and tactics	Trends by country and region
Per capita income levels, purchasing power	Quality: its attributes and positioning relative to competitors	Purchasing power and intentions	Advertising and promotion: choices and impacts on customers	Contribution margins
End-user industry growth trends	Competitors' strengths: favourite tactics and strategies	Customer response to new products, price, promotion	Service quality: perceptions and relative positioning	Marketing mix used, marketing response functions across countries and regions
Government: legislation, regulation, standards, barriers to trade		Switching behaviour, role of credit and purchasing	Logistics networks, configuration and change	
		Future needs, impact of cultural differences		
Source: Terpstra and Sarathy (1997)				

As long ago as 1985, but still relevant today, Gilligan and Hird (1985) identified three types of market opportunities:

1. *Existing markets* Markets already covered by existing products/ suppliers making market entry difficult without a superior offering.
2. *Latent markets* Evidence of potential demand but with no product yet offered, making entry easier. No direct competition.
3. *Incipient markets* No current demand exists but condition and trends suggest future emergent demand.

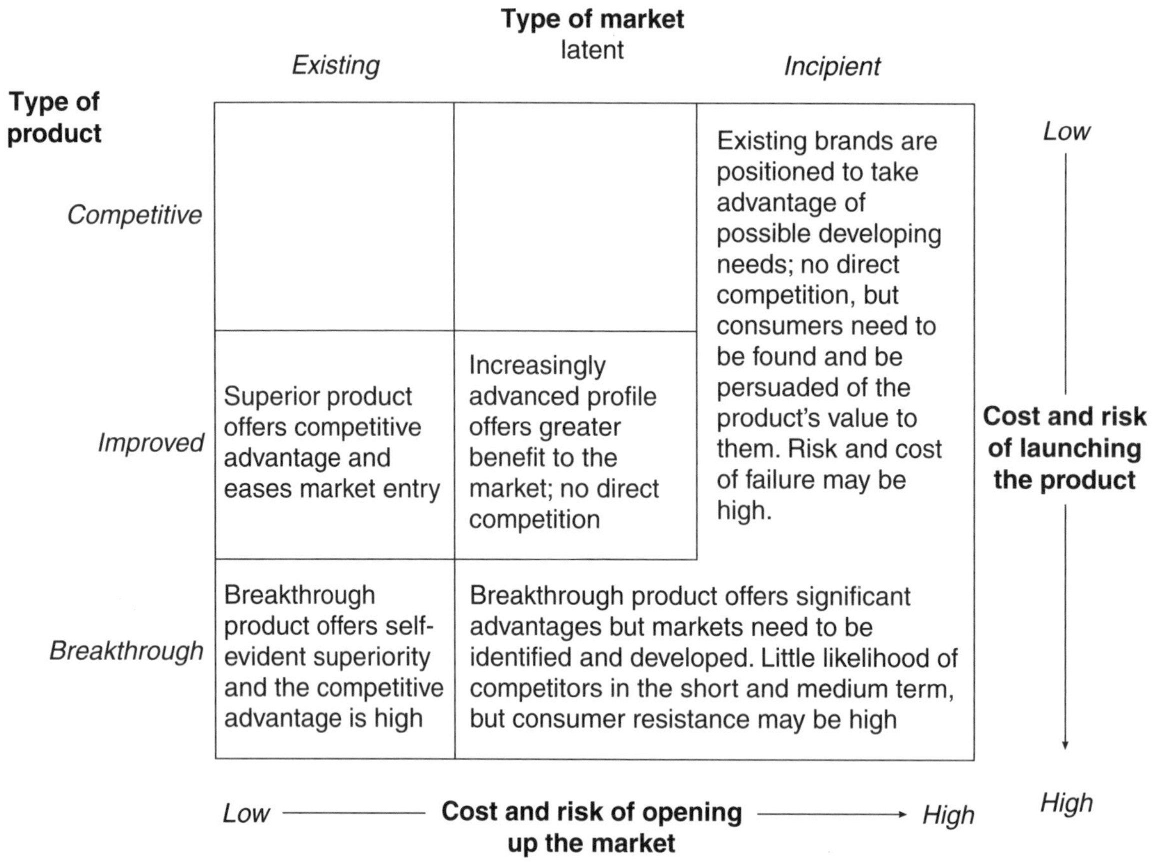

Type of market

Type of product	Existing	latent	Incipient	
Competitive			Existing brands are positioned to take advantage of possible developing needs; no direct competition, but consumers need to be found and be persuaded of the product's value to them. Risk and cost of failure may be high.	**Low**
Improved	Superior product offers competitive advantage and eases market entry	Increasingly advanced profile offers greater benefit to the market; no direct competition		**Cost and risk of launching the product**
Breakthrough	Breakthrough product offers self-evident superiority and the competitive advantage is high	Breakthrough product offers significant advantages but markets need to be identified and developed. Little likelihood of competitors in the short and medium term, but consumer resistance may be high		**High**

Low ——— **Cost and risk of opening up the market** ———→ High

Figure 4.1
Product/market combinations and the scope for competitive advantage on market entry.
Source: Gilligan and Hird, 1985

Figure 4.1 allies the three types of market opportunities to three types of products:

1. *Competitive product* A 'me too' offering with no significant advantages.
2. *Improved product* While not unique has a discernible advantage over present offerings.
3. *Breakthrough product* An innovation with significant differentiation.

Figure 4.1 provides an insight into the nature of the marketing task needed. It forms the basis for further detailed investigation (e.g. the degree of competitive advantage and other dynamics). Although the model is dated, the general principles remain relevant. However, students will recognize that breakthrough products are diffused internationally at an ever-increasing pace, with new technology-led products leapfrogging 'old' infrastructures, e.g. the development and introduction of mobile telephones has made terrestrial 'copper wire' technology unnecessary and redundant in many 'emerging' markets.

There are other more recent methods to help the international marketer identify potentially attractive countries and markets in which to operate. We have already mentioned that 'coarse grained' screening methods like the BERI index (see Unit 1) can be used to assess the political risk in entering new markets. However, this is limited to assessing political risk only and a broader approach is needed. For this a powerful 'fine grained' aid for identifying 'best opportunities' is the application of the market attractiveness/competitive strength matrix. Basically the technique involves the construction of a matrix which, unlike the Gilligan and Hird (1985) model, seeks to combine as many market attractiveness and competitive strength variables as possible. The matrix produces a plot of countries against the market attractiveness and competitive strength dimensions and enables the marketer to identify quickly and easily the 'most' and 'least attractive' countries in terms of potential. For a full description of the approach, see Hollensen, S. (1998), Global Marketing: A Market-Responsive Approach, Prentice-Hall Europe.

Method of scanning in underdeveloped countries

Frequently in international marketing it is not easy to obtain relevant information directly, or without resort to expensive research methodologies. When a broad overview only is required/ sufficient at this stage where concern is mainly to eliminate non-starters other methods of scanning markets, particularly in developing countries, include the following.

Analogy estimation

Given the absence of significant hard data researchers might rely on analogous countries by either a 'cross-section comparison' of economic indicators, disposable income or a 'time series approach' estimating that country B is developing or following a similar pattern of development (and therefore product usage) as country A. The limitations of analogy estimation is to assume linear patterns of development and should be used as a first stage and inexpensive screening. Care needs to be taken and companies should be cautious of taking a literal approach.

Regression analysis

A more sophisticated development of the analogous method involves studying, for example, the relationship between economic growth indicators and demand for specific products in countries with both kinds of data (country A), then transferring it to countries with similar economic growth data, but no product data (country B). For example, if £100 equivalent increase per capita GNP in country A resulted in an increase of 10 cars, 20 fridges, 8 TV sets, etc. per 1000 population, the same might well occur in country B. The limitations of this approach are also obvious as no two countries are totally alike.

Table 4.2	
Level of institution	**Potential markets**
1. Market square	Cloth material (not made up), a village economy.
2. Church, elementary school	Small-form economy, packaged goods, radios, bikes, garage, petrol, etc.
3. Secondary school, police, government building	Urbanization (first steps), social dresses, fridges, plumbing, etc.
4. Higher education, sewerage system	Factories, office supplies and service industries.
Source: Modified from Terpstra and Sarathy (1994)	

Cluster analysis

Using macro economic and consumption data is a popular technique of identifying similar markets, for example:

- *Infrastructure dynamics* energy consumption, urbanization, motorway and other transport facilities such as airports, containerization, etc.
- *Consumption variation* numbers of cars, telephones, educational level
- *Trade data* import and export figures
- *Health and education* life expectancy, number of doctors.

Accepting these measures are crude, in the absence of customer sensitive data they form the basis for first line decisions.

Improvization

This is literally extrapolating data between broadly similar countries and in a way 'second guessing' the potential product need and demand in those countries (Table 4.2).

Finally, there are other methods that may warrant your attention. For example, risk evaluation is obviously important (see political risk).

International market segmentation: prioritization

The scanning method represents Phase 1 in international marketing research. The next stage is to evaluate markets/countries in order to prioritize them for still further investigation. The key issue here is not simply to list countries in terms of priorities, but to group them in clusters or segments. We are searching for *similarities* more than differences. Similarities provide:

1. Economies of scale
2. Optimization in marketing
3. Easier diffusion of products
4. Ease of operation, management and control
5. Greater profitability.

Unfortunately marketers spend too much time highlighting differences between markets/countries and forget to identify the areas of similarity and convergence. It is similarities that determine whether a pan-regional or global approach is possible. This is becoming increasingly critical for companies particularly in the EU, where harmonization is under way. Major international pan-regional players largely reject the notion that each country requires individual products. Convergence is increasingly the name of the game.

The major methodology is to classify countries into categories as illustrated in Figure 4.2. Broadly, countries fall into four groups:

1. *Primary markets* Where high attractiveness coincides with a high degree of company strengths. This might lead to the company investing heavily within the country(ies).
2. *Secondary markets* Riskier but where there is still significant business to be gained albeit through a lower level of strategic investment.
3. *Tertiary markets* Business gained via short-term, *ad hoc* and opportunist activity with no serious commitment in an operational sense. However, good profit may be earned here and it is no reason not to do business providing the level of financial investment and risk to exposure is low.
4. *Avoidance markets* Treated simply as opportunist events i.e. passing trade.

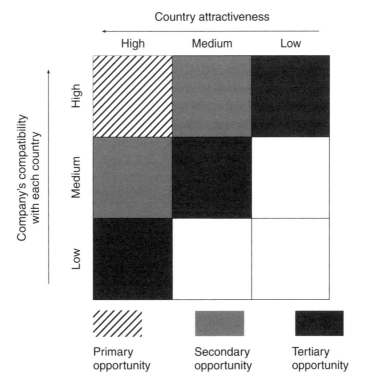

Figure 4.2
Business portfolio matrix (Source: Harrall and Kiefer, 1993)

It has been stated earlier that the principles of the model are extremely sound but exceptions to the rule exist, e.g. technology-led products can have equal appeal across all levels of opportunity – but even so companies frequently need to prioritize their expansion.

Once key markets/countries have been identified and prioritized, further market research is necessary to identify customer segments within the chosen countries using the recognized and standard quantitative and qualitative research techniques – demographics, buyer behaviour, consumer motivation, lifestyle, etc. This further research is critical, for although the international segmentation model described above identifies clusters of countries, the key to successful international marketing is discovering clusters or segments of customers. Country segmentation is therefore often oversimplistic, for it pays insufficient attention to customer similarities across national boundaries.

Kole and Sudharshan (1987) speak of firms needing to achieve strategically equivalent segments (SES) that transcend national boundaries. They contend that to achieve SES companies need to:

1. Identify countries with sufficient infrastructure to support its product and that are lucrative to the company
2. Screen those countries to arrive at a realistic short-list (e.g. those countries with a sufficiently large segment)
3. Develop micro-segments within those countries identified by product characteristics required
4. Identify the key characteristics of the demand of each micro-segment searching for similarities in terms of behaviourial pattern
5. Through cluster analysis identify meaningful cross-national segments which would respond similarly to a consistent marketing mix strategy.

The search is underway to unravel customer behaviour and response similarities across Europe. The major European multinationals (e.g. Volkswagen, Vodaphone) are fast acquiring and developing Euro (and global) brands. To achieve synergies in marketing they are seeking Euro consumers. It is early days but Euro Mosaic is claimed as the first pan-European consumer segmentation system to classify consumers on the basis of neighbourhood having identified ten Euro neighbourhood classifications:

1. Elite suburbs
2. Average areas
3. Luxury flats
4. Low-income city
5. High-rise social housing.
6. Industrial communities
7. Dynamic families
8. Low-income families
9. Rural/agricultural
10. Vacation/retirement.

As can be seen, the segmentation is broad – and, frankly, is at an early development stage. However, in the absence of more sophisticated approach it is a start.

Nielsen has introduced Quartz, its first pan-European research service, which provides simulated market tests based on consumer reaction in five European countries. Procter & Gamble, Nestlé and in total 25 multinationals subscribe to the service. Europanel, a pan-European panel consortium, checks 55,000 households monitoring the movement and consumptions of consumer goods. Ipsos, a French company, evaluates consumers' viewing and reading habits in major EU countries. The demand for quality multi-country research is still in its infancy and we can anticipate rapid growth in, for example, pan-European quantitative and qualititative comparative research across national boundaries.

The international marketing information system

Doole and Lowe (2001) refer to the 12C analysis model for creating an information system:

✓Country

- General country information
- Basic SLEPT data
- Impact of environmental dimensions.

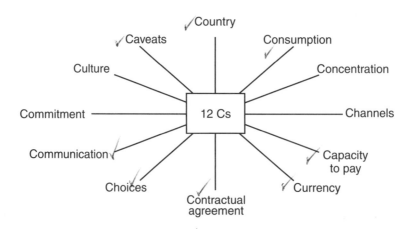

Figure 4.3
The 12 Cs (Source: Doole and Lowe, 2001)

Choices
- Analysis of supply
- International and external competition
- Characteristics of competitors
- Import analysis
- Competitive strengths and weaknesses.

Concentration
- Structure of the market segments
- Geographical spread.

Culture/consumer behaviour
- Characteristics of the country
- Diversity of cultural grouping
- Nature of decision-making
- Major influences of purchasing behaviour.

Consumption
- Demand and end-use analysis of economic sectors that use the product
- Market share by demand sector
- Growth patterns of sectors
- Evaluation of the threat of substitute products.

Capacity to pay
- Pricing
- Extrapolation of pricing to examine trends
- Culture of pricing
- Conditions of payment
- Insurance terms.

Currency
- Stability
- Restrictions
- Exchange controls.

Channels
- Purchasing behaviour
- Capabilities of intermediaries
- Coverage of distribution costs
- Physical distribution infrastructure.

Commitment
- Access to market
- Trade incentives and barriers
- Custom tariffs
- Government regulations
- Regulations on market entry.

Communication
- Promotion
- Media infrastructure and availability
- Which marketing approaches are effective
- Cost of promotion
- Common selling practices
- Media information.

Contractual obligations
- Business practices
- Insurance
- Legal obligations.

Caveats
- Factors to be aware of.

Without doubt, collection of this information is a formidable task – well beyond the resources of all but the largest firms. Even these will find difficulties in drawing the comparison and making the necessary links between countries to assist in the creation of potentially profitable segments. Having made this point a list is useful as a consistent point of reference.

Sourcing international market research

Where and how do we find international information – and the problems involved? Terpstra and Sarathy state that because of its complexity, international market research generates more and different problems than domestic research. Because countries are different, each poses its own set of problems. Furthermore, how does one deal with gathering information from dozens or up to a hundred countries?

The breadth of the task

International market research covers macro economic, micro economic, cultural, political and a host of other variables. Also, because of the drive towards internationalization, markets can no longer be studied individually – they must be screened for similarities to develop pan-regional or even global markets. It follows that the international market researcher (or the division) has a far wider remit than any domestic research organization making the creation of an MIS system even more important.

The problem of numerous markets

Besides such important considerations as cost and because countries are different, the international researchers must take into consideration various problems in designing and interpreting multi-country research. Mayer identifies some basic considerations:

- *Definition error* Countries often define markets and categories differently, e.g. the term 'small business' varies across Europe.
- *Instrument error* Arising from the detail written on questionnaires.
- *Frame error* Sampling frames vary by country. The UK socio-demographic definitions of A, B, C1, C2 etc., will have little direct equivalent overseas. Even within the EU, whilst there is a very broad equivalent the differences remain substantial.
- *Selection error* Problems arising from the way the actual sample is selected from the frame.
- *Non-response error* The cultural variance such as occurs frequently in the Far East where rejection of a question may be considered impolite.

Returning to the issue of costs, how much research can we afford? A sense of realism must prevail, we can't research everything and the organization must refer to its resources and the timescales involved.

Secondary data – acquiring it and problems with it

With so many markets to consider it is essential that companies begin their international market research by seeking and utilizing secondary data, i.e. data that already exists and is generally available at low cost. For those who are unclear in terminology secondary research is frequently referred to as desk research.

Many countries are awash with secondary data but, in general, there is a correlation between the stage of economic development and the availability, depth and accuracy of information. Where it is available it is generally plentiful, cheap and accurate; where it is not its quality is variable, its relevance dubious and its accuracy flawed. As a preliminary stage of investigation secondary research can quickly unearth general background information to eliminate many countries from the scope of enquiries. Such information might include:

- Population, language(s), ethnic differences
- Type of government, political stability and that of neighbouring countries, risk of war, etc., social policies
- Location, geography, topography, climate
- Basic economic data, income and its distribution, employment, industry versus agriculture, policy towards businesses, tax structure, private versus government sector split
- Legal information, regulations, barriers to entry and exit (of profits), member of WTO, etc.
- Overseas trade patterns, with UK, other nations, importance of exports and imports to the economy.

All this material forms a good solid basis for initial screening purposes but falls some way short of providing marketing information to help pinpoint real customer needs and wants. Most of the above information can be unearthed on the majority of countries but it is only in the more sophisticated countries that you might discover the following:

- Size of market (as defined locally), its make-up and structures
- Who are main customers, who buys what (what are the available products) and, very importantly, why they buy (motivations for purchase)
- Competition, scope and practices (marketing mix)
- Promotional practices - availability, sophistication, legal restrictions
- Distribution patterns - where customers buy (supermarkets or market squares), intermediaries (choice and number of stages)
- Pricing, how much customers pay, what the trade structure is in terms of mark-up, margins
- Service element; after-sales guarantees, who fixes the product if/when it breaks.

Note: The list is not complete, it is indicative of the broad range of data services available in the UK.

Problems with secondary data are as follows:

1. The non-availability of data. Westernized countries apart, the rest of the world varies considerably in its statistical output. The weaker economies have weaker statistical services – many do not carry out a population census. In some countries there is only an estimate of the population

2. The reliability of the data. Data may have been massaged by governments to prove a particular point or to gain funds from world bodies. Again the data may be time-lagged or even old and therefore may have limited bearing on the status quo

3. The source of the data will inevitably reflect local/national conditions and may be meaningless to outsiders. Even something as straightforward as pensions both in terms of retirement age and size of payment show considerable differences between for example the UK and France

4. Comparability across markets is difficult. The terms car owner, small business, householder, youth, health, engineer, family, leisure, etc. mean different things in each country. The term middle-class is a good example. We know what it means in the UK cultural terms of reference (but each of us would find it difficult to explain precisely) – but in India it generally means adults with an annual income of £2,000

plus. A considerable difference, but one with broadly speaking similar purchasing powers within each country context

5. Availability of sources either private or public varies enormously. The international major corporation such as A. C. Nielsen (the world's No. 1 researcher) is operating only in 28 countries. It and others are totally absent in more than half the countries in the world. Trade associations, chambers of commerce, all are equally variable in their existence and indeed in their output for they too mean different things country by country. In France, chambers of commerce are very powerful organizations capable of generating income and information, but what information might you expect from Burkina Faso?

Sources of secondary information

The UK and European Union has a rich source of secondary information covering everywhere in the world. We in the UK are awash with information and data sources. Although at first sight the gathering of information seems a daunting task, if set about logically and with diligence it is no more difficult than obtaining domestic data. The method is to accept that 'everything we need to know' is unlikely to be forthcoming but applying Pareto's 80:20 rule will unearth most of the key facts with the remainder to be discovered either via primary research (in sophisticated markets) or by using skilled executive judgement and testing in markets where such information may be less accessible. Set out below is a list of desk research sources. It is not a complete list but gives guidance – for much of the information sought will be industry-specific.

- Specialist trade press
- Quality press, journals and magazines
- Trade associations
- Directories, e.g. Kompass and Euromonitor
- Major university business schools
- Public libraries and specific business libraries
- Chamber of Commerce
- Your bankers
- International consultancies
- Electronic media, e.g. internet including the following sources of general data:

  www.spss.com – for general data bases

  www.mintel.com – for market information

  www.ciao.com

  www.economist.com

  www.thetimes.com

  www.guardian.com

  www.FT.com

  www.google.uk.com

For many useful website references and sources of information see the sites referenced in the recommended text by Paliwoda and Thomas (1999)

- Syndicated or published research
- Competitors' published information
- Export houses and freight forwarders
- Embassies, both UK ones overseas and foreign embassies in the UK.

The internet

This is rapidly becoming the favourite tool for accessing secondary information. Its breadth and depth of searching has really made it feasible for SMEs (small to medium enterprises) to discover previously impossible to access data about overseas customers and competitors, pricing policies, etc. It really is transforming companies' knowledge of the international environment. For further reference to the internet, Unit 4 considers its impact on reconfiguring market entry strategies for SMEs, Unit 7 its importance in managing the interface between customers and companies and Unit 8 assesses its impact on distribution, logistics and the value chain.

But for the majority of UK companies the first port of call for information on overseas markets will be the Department of Trade and Industry (DTI). With its vast database and many years of experience the DTI provides a wide-ranging and excellent service, and even if it does not have the answers can provide new leads. Reasonably priced, its services are invaluable and the staff helpful and accessible by phone/fax/e-mail or personal visit to Victoria Street, London SW1. Students outside the UK would be well advised to discover and know for examination purposes their own range of both government and non-government internet and traditional sources of information.

Primary research – acquiring it and problems with it

In dealing with primary research we are discussing the everyday research techniques utilized in our domestic market to unearth usage and attitude information concerning our company's customers, their choices and preferences, the stimuli that motivate them to behave positively to our products, prices, promotional practices, etc. By the time primary research is to be employed the organization will have narrowed down its choice of potential markets to a few. The complexity and cost of generating new, first-hand information is formidable. For example, a national usage and attitude survey in the UK might cost upwards of £80 000. Imagine replicating this across Europe.

We are not going to discuss the techniques of primary research, which should be familiar to readers. Instead we highlight the problems involved in carrying it out overseas.

Problems with primary research

Countries are different, people are different and respond differently. This makes uniformity of information a potential and often real nightmare from a research standpoint as self-reference criteria (SRC) are imposed. Let us examine some of the more obvious ones:

1. *Costs* Conducting primary research varies. The UK is one of the least expensive, Japan one of the most expensive.
2. *Language* In which language should the survey be conducted? Singapore with a population of about 3 million has four official languages requiring four translations and four different ethnic interviewers:

    • Interpretation of languages (translation) is frequently misleading and even back-translation into the author's language can be flawed. What is required is not translation but transposition of the questionnaire into the respondent's cultural framework. This is very sophisticated and difficult
    • Literacy: pictorials are not easy to understand or interpret. Technical literacy is also a frequent problem, i.e. the non-comprehension of things abstract, for example, time or concepts such as health, leisure, etc.

3. *Sample* in a non-urban or low urbanized country where will you find AB respondents? They may be scattered far and wide. In Muslim countries who do you interview, buyer (male) or the user (female)? Interviewing the latter is rare.
4. *Geography* Where do you conduct the survey? For example, in Nigeria, the north is desert, the south equatorial. Responses in one area may have no relevance in another. Similarly, tribal differences in a country will elicit different responses.
5. *Non-Response* The Japanese always like to please and invariably say 'Yes'. Then they really mean they don't like your product. 'I will consider it very carefully' is Japanese

for no. In other societies being interviewed has connotations of 'agents of the state' or tax inspectors.

6. *Social Organization* In some societies even business-to-business and industrial markets are affected. Unlike the West, companies are often family owned where openness is frowned upon and secrecy is important. Furthermore, Western terminology may have little direct relevance (e.g. cash flow, stock turnover are not everyday terminologies).

7. *Terminology* The point has already been made concerning the interpretation of language as it is bounded by SRC. What do we mean by holidays, well off, health food, live alone, family, youth, middle aged? Methods for classifying consumers are evolving all the time. For example, the shift in factors driving the green market have led the USA based Hartman Group to change the way in which it describes it (see Table 4.3).

Table 4.3
The Hartman group's traditional segmentation (1998) is based on environmental concerns and activities, which resonate with few consumers today, i.e.: • *True naturals* express deeply felt environmental concerns and tailor their actions and purchases to these beliefs. • *New Green Mainstream* are concerned about the environment, but alter their actions and purchases only when it is convenient. • *Affluent Healers* are most concerned about the environmental issues that relate to their personal health. They are less inclined to consider the environment when shopping, but can be persuaded with the right message and product attributes. • *Young Recyclers* are most concerned about environmental issues that relate to solid waste. They are less inclined to consider the environment when shopping, but can be persuaded with the right message and product attributes. • *Overwhelmed* feel too caught up in life's demands to worry about the environment They're unlikely to favour a product for environmental reasons. • *Unconcerned* simply do not pay attention to environmental issues or do not feel that the environment is seriously threatened.
Source: www.demographics.com/publications/ad *27/01/01*

With the shift in factors driving the green market, the earlier surveys based on the above segmentation into unique environmental categories with accompanying demographic patterns, have given way to more recent studies using a gradual core-to-periphery lifestyle model placing consumers on a scale of health and wellness activities. Hartman believes this method is more useful to marketers because it does not place consumers into strict categories of behaviours and demographics. So, while the environmental segmentation can still be helpful to some marketers, those wishing to reach the much larger and wellness market are better served by the lifestyle model.

In conclusion, it is certain that some cultural bias will exist in all primary research activities as SRC are applied depending on the cultural context of the host nation. For example Germany, Austria and Switzerland are described as having a low cultural context, i.e. responses to questions are straightforward. Japan, on the other hand is at the other extreme where the subtly of the response is important, i.e. the manner in which the question is answered is at least as important as the response itself. Figure 3.4 illustrates the contextual continuum of differing cultures. Most will be surprised to see the English and the French so close together. To paraphrase the research, Edward Hall found that some cultures, 'low context cultures', rely much more than others, 'high context cultures', on the actual words used in communication. Communication is complicated in high context cultures by the need to understand more aspects of the context surrounding the message, e.g. social setting, status etc. Usunier devised a contextual continuum of differing cultures, in which in the UK and the US are found to be similar in terms of the importance of context to the understanding of communication. It is also evident that SRC will exist between the client company and the organization(s) conducting the research if they are from different cultures.

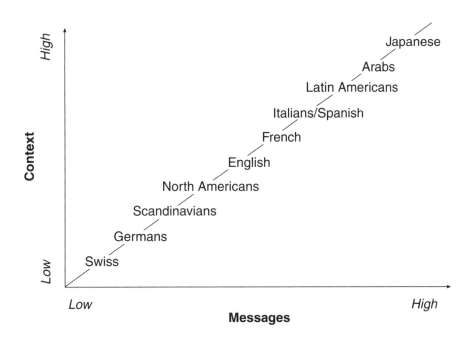

Figure 4.4
The contextual continuum of differing cultures (From Usunier, adapted from Edward T. Hall)

Attempts are being made to create order out of across-country research by using structured questionnaires, telephone interviews and postal surveys, but again infrastructure variables and cultural differences interfere. For example, some countries have a less than perfect postal service and telephone ownership is restricted to the elite. Furthermore such techniques are applicable only to certain areas.

Finally, the key to minimizing the variable response in primary research is superior research design, transposition of words and concepts in its cultural reference, an understanding (by the researcher) of the problem involved and the skill in interpretation of data into information and knowledge. With close to 50 per cent of the world's primary research being conducted in Europe there is clearly a long way to go.

Planning and organizing for international market research

We are going to focus on the medium to large firm as it is apparent that small firms will have too many restrictions to engage in multi-country primary research and will rely on gathering secondary data. Additionally, they will rely on channel intermediaries for their information. However, it must be noted that large organizations, e.g. Toyota also rely on global research agencies.

The extent to which medium to large firms will engage in international market research will similarly be guided by the nature of the market and its customers, company resources, its marketing expertise and the scale of the task. A major consideration is whether to conduct the research in-house or to appoint external agencies. It is absolutely essential, for example, that in countries such as China local research agencies must be used both to get close to the market and get round government red tape. An industrial scenario might be handled in-house (there being few customers and each being identifiable) whereas a consumer goods scenario lends itself to the use of external research agencies. There are, of course, many sources of information and in some cases, financial aid, open to organizations of all sizes. For example, the Department of Trade and Industry in the UK, has run many initiatives to aid exporters gather research data, including, in some cases, the provision of financial assistance and expert advice to carry out international research.

In choosing an agency, Doole and Lowe suggest six options:

- An agency local to the chosen market
- A domestic agency with overseas subsidiaries
- A domestic agency with overseas associates
- A domestic agency with subcontracted fieldwork
- A domestic agency with competent foreign staff
- A global agency.

The choice will depend on the variables in the market(s), the desired strategic level of marketing involvement on the part of the client company and the scale of the marketing task to be undertaken eventually. Further consideration includes:

- Language issues and other expertise
- The level of 'specialist knowledge of the market'
- The budget or cost. For example, it is estimated that attitude surveys in the Pacific Rim countries are cheaper than in Western Europe, on the other hand in-house product tests are more expensive in Pacific Rim countries. (For further examples of across-country cost comparisons and other very useful international research applications see ESOMAR, the European Society for Opinion and Marketing Research, Amsterdam, The Netherlands)
- The level of interpretation post-research
- The 'track record'
- Length of time it has been in business
- Clients it has worked with
- If cross-border considerations are important, the willingness of the agency to be flexible and a team player
- Communications ability
- Possible conflict of interest with other clients.

This suggests that there is no one solution and that companies select agencies appropriate to the task. There are directories and other aids which help in the choice of research agency. For example in the UK, the Market Research Society produces an annual directory of research agencies, including their capabilities. In the USA, Marketing News produces an annual directory of international research organizations. Examples of some of the world's largest international research organizations include A. C. Nielsen Corp. (USA), Cognizant Group (USA) and The Kantar Group (UK), the first two being the largest with a current turnover in excess US$1 billion. It is vital to brief the agency(ies) carefully and to maintain a close relationship throughout. Piloting the research may be essential if comparative data is required. Care in analysis and interpretation of the data is equally important. This is particularly important in coordinating research between global headquarters and local subsidiaries. Basically it revolves around the argument of standardization, favoured by Headquarters, and customozation, favoured by subsidiaries, the so called 'emic' (favouring individual country peculiarities) and the 'etic' approach (favouring universal behaviour). In cross cultural research the 'etic' approach is favoured as similarities are sought. To cater for local peculiarities a combination approach may be the best. The management role in organizing and coordinating international marketing research is not to be underestimated, especially if the findings are to be disseminated from one country to another in assisting marketing planning decisions. An excellent example of how coordination was achieved in an across Euoropean context is provided by BMW. In order to achieve coordination on a positioning study across borders it made sure all parties were involved, all contributed funding wise and results were both standardized and customized were necessary. (See Horst, K., Wagner, H.-C. and Hassis, R. (1990) 'European aspects of a global brand: the BMW case', *Marketing and Research Today*, February, pp 47–57.)

International marketing and the internet

E-information

Given the enormous amount of data available to e-business from their special operations, it is surprising that this area needs to be covered at all. But the problem still seems to be the same one – what do you need to know?

Non-e-business has always fallen over at this hurdle by confusing 'data' of which they have warehouses full – and 'information' which is as scarce as hen's teeth in most businesses. What e- and non-e-businesses often have is lots of demographic or description data that tells them *what* customers and prospects do and buy. This is fine, as far as it goes. What businesses need, but rarely have, is motivational data that tells them *why* customers behave the way they do and what they want/need.

In theory, e-business should be much better placed to collect and make sense of the motivational data that they need so badly. But that depends on e-business people knowing what they don't know – before it's too late!

There are many web-based sources of information which can be consulted and provide lots of information on every international topic which you care to mention. As well as numerous dot com sources a particularly good reference source for numerous website sources of data is given in the Appendix – global marketing research/ decision support system in Hollensen, S. (1998) Global Marketing: A Market-Responsive Approach, Prentice-Hall, Europe.

Other excellent sources include:

- ciber.bus.msu.edu/busrea.htm Michigan State University's Center for International Business
- web.iderect.com/-tiger/supersit.htm World Class Supersite including detail on markets, news, money, trade, learning, networking and world beaters
- www.Worldbank.org The World bank
- europe.eu.int The European Union
- www.eiu.com The Economist Intelligence Unit
- www.euromonitor.com Euromonitor providing market information
- www.nexis.com A superb source of international information (subscription necessary).

Activity 4.1

Select one or more of the websites listed above. Try and locate the following information and write it down. It will prove very useful for revision purposes:

- Market detail of a less developed country, an emerging country, a developed country and a post-developed country
- Detail of at least six global organizations, size, product range, country(ies) of operation etc. Choose at least one organization from a different product/market area, e.g. service, not-for-profit, commercial, business-to-business.

Questions

As a check on your understanding of what has been covered in this unit, consider the following questions:

Question 4.2

- As the international marketing manager for Coca-Cola how would you monitor reactions around the world to a major competitor such as Pepsi?
- Identify the advantages and disadvantages of both secondary and primary data in international marketing
- Why is it so difficult to assess demand for a product in multi-country research?
- Explain how screening can be used to prioritize international markets. Illustrate your answer by the use of models
- Select a product category (e.g. shampoo). What criteria might you apply to evaluate information internationally?
- Identify a major international firm in your locality. Establish what kinds of help in terms of marketing information assistance are available in the UK
- Contact the DTI (or the equivalent bureau in your country) with a view to obtaining marketing information for a specific country.

Case Study

Creative use of marketing research: Japanese manufacturers.

Some Japanese manufacturers, like Toyota and Hitachi, have used a different, yet creative approach, to product development. In the USA, by the creative use of marketing research. Toyota, used a team of anthropologists in the late 1990s, to help develop new vehicle features. Using California as a leading indicator of lifestyle trends, the anthropologists observed people in their homes as an environment in which people express their preferences. By observing volume levels on the television, colours of paint and wallpapers in living rooms etc, it enabled Toyota to anticipate the future design of vehicle interiors and exteriors.

Hitachi used the same type of indirect analysis in the development of household appliances. By observing that more and more Japanese women were going out to work, and observing that most washing was, therefore, being done in the early morning or evening, Hitachi invented a quieter machine. Further observations of the limited Japanese housing space and the trend against hanging clothes out to dry, led Hitachi to gaining a competitve advantage in inventing a combined washer and dryer.

Not all marketing research goes right! The classic example is the Ford Edsel, which was researched from every angle, in fact, perhaps over-researched, in the sense that when it was launched it was to appeal to everyone. As it happened, it appealed to no-one! Other examples abound.

Sources: *Contemporary Marketing Research,* C. McDaniel and R. Gates, South Western Publishing, 1999 and other published sources.

Extending knowledge

For additional supporting information read:

International Marketing Strategy, I. Doole and R. Lowe, 3rd Edition, Thomson, 2001. Chapter 4, pp. 93–135.

International Marketing, S. Paliwoda and M. Thomas, 3rd Edition Butterworth-Heinemann, 1999. Chapter 2, pp. 42–95.

Global Marketing Strategies, J.-P. Jeannet and H. D. Hennessey, 5th Edition, Houghton Mifflin, 2001. Chapter 6. pp. 214–256.

Summary

All too frequently organizations fall back on one of two strategies when dealing with information issues on the international front. Self-reference criteria, i.e. foreigners are just like us and if we licked the problem 'here' we can do it overseas or, alternatively, use guesswork. Both approaches invariably result in grief. It is clear that if information = knowledge = power, then it is even more important that we have the facts in dealing with environments beyond our normal range of experience. Knowing where to start and how to go about gathering information on overseas nations and customers must be the fundamental benchwork that underpins all our thinking.

Unit 5
Planning for international marketing

Objectives

This unit is concerned with the ways in which the firm can exploit defined marketing opportunities in international markets and how best it can organize itself. In studying the unit you will:

- Understand the concepts of international marketing planning
- Come to terms with the importance of planning and the changing frameworks as companies deepen their involvement

  See syllabus section 2.2.1 and 2.2.2.

- Review the key planning models and match marketing variables to strategic international decisions

  See syllabus sections 2.2.3, 2.2.4 and 2.2.6.

- Understand the basic options in determining the international market entry plan

  See syllabus section 2.2.10.

- Recognize that control systems are even more important internationally than domestically
- Identify the key organizational issues that concern international development and the employment decision.

  See syllabus sections 2.2.7 and 2.2.11.

See also the Planning and Control syllabus of the Diploma in Marketing for further details of the planning process relevant to this section.

Having completed the unit you will be able to:

- Cross-reference planning with strategic issues
- Evaluate the suitability of specific market entry strategies
- Identify the elements of an international marketing plan
- List the stages of the control process and establish key principles of a control system
- Explain the different methods a firm might employ in creating and developing its international organization
- Explain the variables that affect organizational structure
- Evaluate the roles and conflicts of HQ versus local management structures.

Study guide

This unit is concerned with planning in an international environment. Students must familiarize themselves with the planning process before addressing this unit. Therefore you must first have read one of the recognized texts (e.g. the *Strategic Marketing Management* coursebook in this series) which will inform you on additional reading. Most students are unfamiliar with international planning and therefore it is especially important you read the texts in the 'Extending knowledge' section at the end of the unit.

Strategic planning and control

It is not the intention to cover Planning and Control issues in depth as the benefits of Planning and the models we employed in the planning process are dealt with fully in the *Strategic Marketing Management* coursebook in this series, authored by Fifield and Gilligan. The models of strategies are equally applicable internationally as they are in the domestic marketplace. However, it is important to recognize that planning and control are inescapably linked. The former is a structure (or series of structures) devised to develop a strategy and utilizing the capabilities of the organization against the background of the environment. Control is the process of monitoring and evaluating the implementation of the chosen strategy so that it can be developed to meet changes in the environment.

State of country development

When considering global planning it is essential to consider the country stage of development. Planning between less-developed countries and other less developed countries and between less developed countries and developed countries is likely to be very different. These differences are likely to be on the basis of import requirements and export product or services. A lot of less-developed countries may be planning to import goods and services which ultimately will lead to import substitution. In terms of exports, less-developed countries will more likely be planning exports of commodities, where value is added elsewhere, than technologically advanced finished products. Of course, as the LDC's become more economically advanced, they will move through the classic stages of development and eventually import and export those technologically advanced products and services associated with post-industrial societies. The differences in trading emphases between less-developed countries and post-industrial countries is given in Table 5.1.

Table 5.1 Trading emphases according to stage of development	
Regime	**Trading emphasis**
1 LDC to LDC	Commodity or lesser tech trading. Trade pacts
2 LDC to EMC	Commodity or semi-added value products. Trade pacts
3 EMC to LDC	Added value products or commodities
4 L(E)DC to DC	Commodities, low/high value added products or services
5 DC to L(E)DC	High value added, high tech products or services
6 DC to DC	High tech/value added products and services
7 PIE to PIE	Knowledge-based trading
LDC = Less Developed Country EMC = Emerging Country L(E)DC = Less Developed or Emerging Country DC = Developed Country PIE = Post-Industrial Economy	

It is obvious from these different emphases in trading that planning activities will take on different approaches according to country development. For example, in planning to export perishable commodities from an LDC to a DC, the emphasis must be on speed of delivery throughout the supply chain, the necessity of a contract between supplier and purchaser and government support, i.e. infrastructural and 'red tape' reduction. A good example is the export of horticultural produce from Zambia or bananas from the Caribbean. On the other hand, in exporting financial services from say the USA to the UK, planning activities would take on a very different complexion. In the main all infrastructure and technology will be in place and the emphasis will be on contractural and delivery arrangements.

For a further discussion and some excellent cases on this aspect of planning see Quelch, J.A. and Bartlett, C. A. (1998), Global Marketing Management, 4th edition, Addison Wesley Longman.

Activity 5.1

Referring to Table 5.1, think of an example of a product or service traded between the different types of country. What changes in emphasis in international planning activities must be effected when trading between the different types of country?

The learning organization – issues in international planning

In marketing domestically the marketer can readily apply his or her SRC, confident in meeting customer desires. Internationally this is rarely possible as customers, their culture and the environment changes by degree. Table 5.2 shows the issues involved in domestic versus international planning.

The difficulties of planning internationally are shown in Table 5.3.

What these tables illustrate is that companies need to consider carefully the process of developing an international plan. The question of the level of involvement, superficial on the one hand to global reach at the other extreme does require differing experience levels, knowledge and resource capabilities. The nature of the overseas market, the product category and the competition, all impact on the planning decision. What is certain is that moving from a domestic to an international operation requires that companies think before they act, plan carefully and learn as they go along the continuum. Having said that it is possible in some market categories to move directly to a global position, e.g. using the internet to access niche markets as is the case with Amazon.com in the world book market. In the immediate future we will see a proliferation of internet activity creating global niches in such activities as music and, interestingly, education (electronically delivered CIM programmes and distance learning MBAs). But this avenue is not open to every product category or customers who have to interface by more conventional means.

Table 5.2 Domestic versus international planning factors	
Domestic planning	**International planning**
1 Single language and nationality	1 Multilingual/multinational/multicultural factors
2 Relatively homogeneous market	2 Fragmented and diverse markets
3 Data available, usually accurate, and collection easy	3 Data collection a formidable task, requiring significantly higher budgets and personnel allocation
4 Political factors relatively unimportant	4 Political factors frequently vital
5 Relative freedom from government interference	5 Involvement in national economic plans; government influences affect business decisions

6 Individual corporation has little effect on environment	6 'Gravitational' distortion by large companies
7 Chauvinism helps	7 Chauvinism hinders. For example, the word British has negative connotations in parts of the globe. Hence British Telecom is now BT and British Petroleum is now BP
8 Relatively stable business environment	8 Multiple environments, many of which are highly unstable (but may be highly profitable)
9 Uniform financial climate	9 Variety of financial climates ranging from over-conservative to wildly inflationary
10 Single currency	10 Currencies differing in stability and real value
11 Business 'rules of the game' mature and understood	11 Rules diverse, changeable, and unclear
12 Management generally accustomed to sharing responsibilities and using financial controls	12 Management frequently autonomous and unfamiliar with budgets and controls

Source: William W. Cain, 'International planning: mission impossible?', *Columbia Journal of World Business,* July–August 1970, p. 58. Reprinted by permission.

Table 5.3 International planning problems Adapted from Jeannet and Hennessey (1998)

Headquarters	Overseas subsidiary
Management	*Management*
Unclear allocation of responsibilities and authority Lack of multinational orientation Unrealistic expectations Lack of awareness of foreign markets Unclear guidelines Insensitivity to local decisions Insufficient provision of useful information	Resistance to planning Lack of qualified personnel Inadequate abilities Misinterpretation of information Misunderstanding requirements and objectives Resentment of HQ involvement Lack of strategic thinking Lack of marketing expertise
Processes	*Processes*
Lack of standardized bases for evaluation Poor IT systems and support Poor feedback and control systems Excessive bureaucratic control procedures Excessive marketing and financial constraints Insufficient participation of subsidiaries in process	Lack of control by HQ Incomplete or outdated internal and market information Poorly developed procedures Too little communication with HQ Inaccurate data returns Insufficient use of multinational marketing expertise Excessive financial and marketing constraints

Economic transcience in global operations

Globalization confers many advantages for the firm. However, there are pitfalls. To be global requires a stable strategic involvement in the local markets/countries. But as we can see in the business press, markets can become unstable both politically and economically. Profits can disappear virtually overnight as countries' economies implode. Much of South-East Asia descended into serious 'negative growth' to use the economists' terminology as currencies collapsed. Thailand, South Korea, Malaysia, the Philippines and Indonesia all suffered declining economic fortunes, as has Japan in the late 1990s. Those companies investing heavily in these countries, particularly companies involved in infrastructure programmes (externally or internally, i.e. building hotels for local customers, or building their own factories) have been hit badly. It is incumbent upon corporate planners and strategists to create a balanced portfolio of international business activity in order to avoid the worst effects of economic global fluctuations. Having your eggs in a single basket invites a roller coaster future of profit and loss.

The international planning process

There are many different planning paradigms in international marketing. These range from transactional and emergent through to muddling through and expert systems. They are meant to be complementary rather than contentious or substitutable for each other. Ambler and Styles (2000) provide a succinct yet comprehensive review of the different planning paradigms, summarised in Table 5.4:

Table 5.4 Different international planning approaches		
Type	**Origins**	**Features**
1 Transactional	1960s	Involves four key stages-analysis, planning, implementation and evaluation and control *Examples: Doole and Lowe, Paliwoda and Thomas.*
2 War	1980/90s	Beat the competition-exploitation of core competences, competitive advantage *Examples: Porter, Prahalad and Hamel, Hooley, Saunders and Piercy*
3 Relationship	1990s	Empathy, customer relationship building, strategic partnerships, networking, e- commerce *Examples: Gronroos, Christopher, Chaffey, Mayer, Johnstone and Ellis Chadwick*
4 Organizational learning	1990s	Identifying relationships with 'actors', cultural interpretations through discourse analysis, commitment to organizational memory, renegotiate or affirm with key 'actors' *Examples: Halliday, Prasad and Ghauri, Hampdon-Turner*
5 Expert systems, online real time	1990s	Database approaches, use of software, strategy devolution to 'operational staff' *Examples: EXMAR, EASY VIEW (Carter and Scheuing)*
6 Biological	2000	Based on 'feel' rather than 'think', turning social information into organizational knowledge *Examples: Ambler and Styles*
Source: After Ambler and Styles (2000)		

The principle difference between the approaches is the degree to which the organization 'gets closer to the customer' and builds a lasting relationship. For example the transactional approach, with its emphasis on information processing and rational decision making is less conducive to relationship building than, say, the customer relationship approach. Approach 6, the 'Biological approach', is the most recent and, unlike the other approaches is based on 'I feel' rather than the rational. The transactional approach finds its origins in the USA in the early 1960s and fundamentally sees the customer to 'be won' through target marketing and the 'correct' deployment of the marketing mix. The Nordic School was responsible for the development of the relationship marketing approach, challenging the marketing mix as the prime focus for reaching customers in favour of a more negotiated relationship-building approach. The biological approach challenges the previous approaches to international marketing in that it views most paradigms as built on information processing and rational decision making, devoid of the human element. The approach suggests that paying attention to social information from the marketplace, coupled with the 'animal spirits' (i.e. passion to succeed) of the management and turning this into organizational knowledge, is a good foundation for success.

You should familiarize yourself with these different approaches and consider their merits and demerits in different international marketing situations. To this end you should read the recommended text Ambler, T. and Styles, C. (2000), The Silk Road to International Marketing, *Financial Times* Prentice-Hall.

The rest of this Unit concentrates more on the 'transactional' approach to global Planning.

Despite many difficulties, planning remains an essential activity if the organization is to succeed. Moreover, planning demands structure and this becomes even more important internationally, dealing with a variety of markets/countries. As stated previously, we are not reviewing the models of portfolio analysis but we remind students that the most widely acknowledged methods are:

1. Boston Consulting Group (BCG)
2. General Electric/McKinsey (GE)
3. Profit Impact of Market Strategy (PIMS)
4. Arthur D. Little
5. Scenario Planning
6. Michael Porter's work is also extremely important and the 'Planning and Control' module of the Diploma syllabus with its accompanying reading list.

Students are expected to be knowledgeable in the constructs of the models, their application, relevance and shortcomings. Once again, cross reference can be made with the *Strategic Marketing Management* Coursebook.

At the strategic level the organization has six key corporate decisions to take when moving into the international arena, beginning with the question 'Should we go?' and ending with 'What organization structure should we adopt?' Against these six key decisions they need to apply the marketing planning variables. Table 5.4 shows the interface between marketing planning and the key corporate decision to form the basis for strategic market planning.

Activity 5.2

Go through Table 5.5 in depth. Select some product categories and then apply what you might consider to be the planning variables. In other words, get some simulated experience of marketing planning in action.

Table 5.5 Strategic options and marketing planning: marketing planning variables						
Key international decisions	Marketing environment and scale of marketing	Competitors	Objectives	Marketing mix variables	Marketing budgets	Expected outcomes
Should we go international?						
Where should we go?						
How should we get there?						
What should we sell?						
How should we market it?						
How do we organize?						

Exam Hint

The matrix in Table 5.5 could be invaluable in examination terms. It allows you to get to the heart of planning immediately, saving you several pages of writing which means saving time. The transactional approach for the development of a marketing plan for any situation will follow the basic principles underpinning all marketing planning:

1. Who are we?
2. Where are we now?
3. Where do we want to be?
4. How might we get there?
5. How do we ensure we get there?

Following on from this the individual country plan should consider the following stages:

1. An evaluation of shareholder/stockholder expectations, together with ambition and resolve of key implementers
2. An audit of the firm's capabilities
3. An assessment of the environment – present and future
4. A statement of vision, mission, corporate objectives
5. An evaluation of strategic alternatives/options
6. An assessment of market/competitor responses
7. The selection and justification of a strategy

8. Effective implementation – involving the range of business functions and not just marketing
9. Monitoring and control procedures
10. Development of organizational systems to ensure effective international co-ordination.

Managing and controlling in-house and external resources

The wider the range of international penetration, the greater will be the need and requirement for control. The establishment of an effective control system is interrelated to the organizational systems (people and procedures). The purpose of control is so that the business (not just marketing) activities can be measured. Measurement can only be achieved and proper assessment made if the plan contains clear objectives. No plan goes totally smoothly and deviations from expectations always occur, but without effective monitoring corrective action cannot be implemented. Control is the basic building block of management – not an afterthought. Future plans depend on control, for control is information and information is power. The issues that affect control are:

1. The scale of the task, the size of the firm
2. The diversity of markets, the number and range of markets/ countries
3. The method of entry – which may vary by country
4. The availability and accuracy of data and information
5. The distance from the home market and the sophistication of communication, qualitative and quantitative.

Key factors in controlling international markets

The starting point is the marketing plan itself and the objectives it sets out to achieve. In basic terms the key control mechanisms are:

1. Establishing standards
2. Measuring performance against the standards
3. Correcting deviation.

Many methods are appropriate in addressing the first of these two points, not least the establishment of common benchmarks and values across multi-markets. The task is extremely complicated and it is only the largest and most sophisticated organization that can consider a complex intermarket comparison of standards. But all firms can determine standards for individual markets and take the necessary action (see also Unit 9).

Organizing for international and global marketing

Managers are the company's scarcest resource and therefore their most valuable. It seems odd therefore that practically all the accepted textbooks on international marketing place the chapter on organizing for success at the end. People are very much a key resource and the model in Figure 5.1 places Company Objectives and Resources at the top of the linear sequence. Furthermore, planning for international expansion cannot take place in a vacuum, it needs the full consideration of the management of the company.

How an organization can structure itself to exploit overseas opportunities is a matter of considerable debate. As in the case of a 'plan' there is no one correct way. If there is a balance to be struck it should be as follows:

1. The organization should be structured in a way that best meets the task of servicing the customers' needs
2. The structure must take full account of the environment, domestic and international, and the skills and resources of the organization.

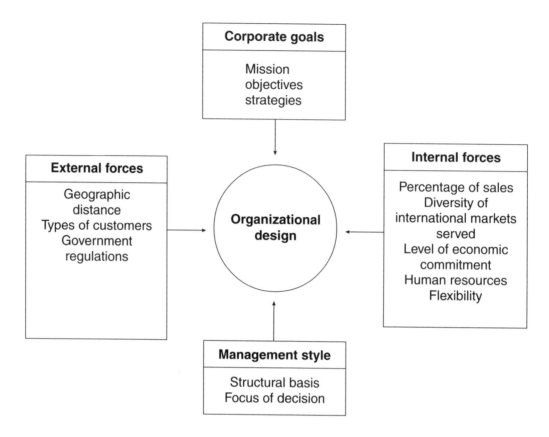

Figure 5.1
Factors affecting organizational design. Source: Jeannet and Hennessey, 1994

For companies to be successful it is necessary to arrive at the appropriate balance.

It is not easy, for tensions exist simultaneously between the need for diversity and decentralization in terms of servicing customers in different markets and the corporate requirement of evaluation and control. The ideal organization structure should incorporate both – a goal rarely realized.

We must also recognize that customers, markets and environments are dynamic, ever-changing and never static so the organization and its structural interface with the customer/market must also change. Some companies are already anticipating the shape and nature of global competition and planning for it. Most are reactive to the changing situation.

Who to employ – expatriates or local nationals?

At several points in this coursebook we discuss the relevance of the decision of manning and staffing the overseas function. The philosophies of ethno-, poly-, regio- and geo-centric approaches are developed. The decision is a major planning one and establishes the policy, ambition and vision of the organization well into the future. Balancing the benefits against the disadvantages is a twofold process. The first and most important is the 'close to the customers' one, i.e. what is most appropriate in customer and competitive terms. The second is largely a function of corporate strategy/philosophy which often reflects the nature and history of the organization. This topic is also discussed in Unit 7.

At all times the focus of the organization should be to develop a structure that provides the framework to 'optimize' the relationship between planning, strategy and control. Terpstra and Sarathy (1997) identify some of the variables in this process:

- Size of the business
- Number of markets
- Level of strategic involvement in the markets
- Corporate objectives
- The level of international experience
- The nature of the product category(ies)
- The scale of the marketing task.

Types of international organizations

Domestic-led companies

Later in this unit, we see that it is possible for domestically orientated companies to operate in overseas markets receiving enquiries from overseas buyers. Domestic staff will respond as if they were home-based customers – which some may well be. Such companies will have few or no additional costs but they will gain relatively little from the exercise – lacking expertise or scale to profit greatly.

Domestic company with an export department

As the overseas opportunity grows companies begin to employ international specialists and create an export department. This brings advantages in expertise, faster response and the beginnings of a proactive international policy with the export department exploring new country opportunities. But the scale of search for overseas services will be relatively low-key and restricted largely to pockets of opportunity. Furthermore, the tendency will be to market unmodified products thus failing to optimize the potential even where the product is sold. Generally, sales per country will be modest. This format typifies the position of both the small- or medium-sized business making its first foray into overseas development.

Developing the international division

Jeannet and Hennessey suggest that companies should move to this phase when international business represents 15 per cent or so of the company's total. At this scale it is necessary to increase the level of involvement in overseas markets – paying close attention to consumer needs, attacking competition, modifying product and the marketing mix to create business proactively. This requires the development of an international division reporting at a senior level and capable of coordinating the business functions across country boundaries.

In terms of considering the appropriate stages of internationalization, Doole and Lowe have identified four stages through which the international strategies of most companies evolve:

- Developing the core strategy, usually for the home country first, on the basis of an identified sustainable competitive advantage
- Internationalizing the core strategy through an international market extension strategy
- Integrating the specific country strategies into a worldwide strategy on a multi-domestic basis
- Rationalizing the integrated strategies to develop a regional or global strategy.

Worldwide organizational structure

Companies recognize the need to coordinate the operation spread geographically to cover large areas of the world. There are five recognized approaches:

1. *Country and regional centres* This structure allows companies to delve even deeper into the dynamics of consumer behaviour and the environment within a country or region. The difference is essentially a matter of size. On reaching a certain size a market (country or region) will require management – staff located within it to maximize the business opportunity and creating a physical presence in the market, possibly for political as well as business reasons. It is very likely that production may be based within the market. Apart from the limits of economies of scale it allows greater sensitivity in building consumer relationships and understanding the culture, responding faster, being more flexible than operations centralized around HQs. Presently, many organizations are creating European centres to coordinate business functions such as R&D, production, distribution, marketing and finance. This regionalization in attitude is being rewarded with the creation of Eurobrands. For example, Unilever have created a European organization, Lever Europe, eliminating diverse brand names such as Jif, Viss and calling them Cif. Likewise, we have seen the demise of Marathon chocolate bars – renamed Snickers! The same 'hub and spoke' approach is being adopted in South-East Asia with Singapore often being the hub, i.e. regional headquarters.

2. *Functional operation* This structure is best suited to companies with a narrow product base with relatively homogenous customers around the world. Thus organizing worldwide on a functional basis is an option open only to a few companies. The structure itself is simple with senior executives having worldwide responsibility for their specialized function be it finance, R&D, marketing, production, etc.

3. *Product structuring* This is most common among companies with a portfolio of seemingly unrelated product lines where each product group may have its own international division. A difficulty with this structure is that conflicts will emerge between product groupings and therefore management problems arise with clashes of culture usually at the source. Similarly, a lack of coordination or of cross-fertilization of ideas often occurs. In an attempt to minimize the conflict, companies may provide functional coordination for customer-related activities such as marketing communication and after-sales service.

4. *Matrix structuring* Very popular in the late 1970s but less so nowadays, this organizational structure appeared to offer solutions to the one-dimensional approach of the three previous methods. Matrices are created by combining two (or more) dimensions of equal importance in the decision-making process. Thus an organization has a dual chain of command. The two most popular dimensions are product and market (country/region). Despite appearing to resolve conflicts and giving greater control and flexibility (responsiveness), the matrix system has largely fallen by the wayside – a victim of its complexity as each axis of the matrix attempts to consolidate or indeed optimize its position within the organizational hierarchy. Sadly, matrix structures show up the weakness and fallibilities of human relationships creating power struggles. Matrices can and will work only when organizations can admit to conflict and are capable of resolving conflict positively by adopting an influence system rather than an authoritarian system of management. Philips

was in the vanguard of introducing a matrix structure in the mid-1970s but has abandoned it in favour of global product divisions.

5. *Strategic Business Units* (SBUs) These are currently in vogue and consist of dividing the global organization into defined businesses, each addressing an identified customer base either by country/region or even on a worldwide basis. The advantages are corporate flexibility in disposing of an SBU or, alternatively, the company can refocus the overall business more easily. The integration of new acquisitions is easier and from a financial and operational control perspective SBUs make for good sense. However, the downside is that the company is not optimizing its economies of scale in world markets and it makes acquisition of the company itself by predators easier, so the unwanted SBUs can be disposed of more readily.

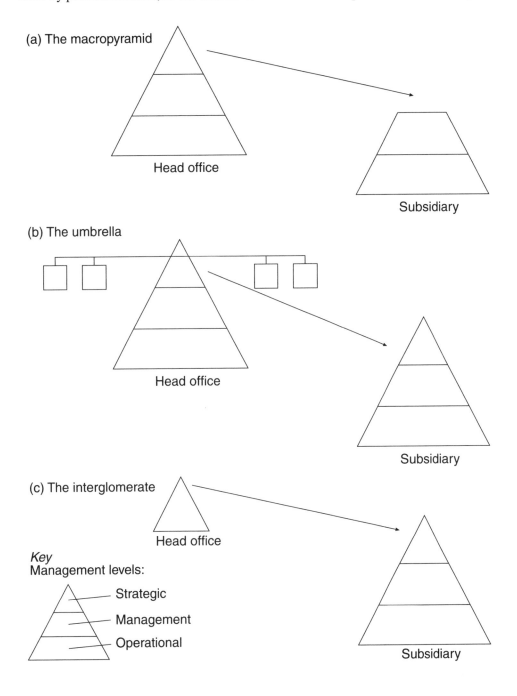

Figure 5.2
Possible head office/subsidiary organizational structures

Trends in global organizations

With more firms moving into the international arena and with the growing importance and power of the mega corporations, it is inevitable that cultural differences need to be considered carefully in creating the 'optimum' organizational framework. There are a number of alternative philosophical positions a multinational/transnational may adopt. The one chosen will reflect the strategic predisposition of the firm which will be guided by the value, long-term objectives and the extent of its 'globalization'.

- *Ethnocentric* This positioning is when the strategic position and the key managers in the majority of the overseas subsidiaries are from the home country. In other words, headquarters personnel and culture dominates and pervades internationally.
- *Polycentric* Here the culture of the subsidiary countries take the lead. Headquarters set the agenda in terms of return on investment, etc. leaving local managers to devise appropriate strategies and implementation.
- *Regiocentric* A mid point, so to speak, attempting to coordinate a geographic region, e.g. EU, or perhaps more appropriately utilizing a country such as Singapore as a regional hub. Managers tend to come from the region and strategic decisions are taken to develop pan-regional marketing and production. A good case is the appointment of an Indian national to lead Nestlé South-East Asian region. He was previously General Manager of Nestlé Indonesia.
- *Geocentric* – Simply the attempt to manage and integrate strategy globally. Managers are appointed on the best person for the job basis. An Indian national is the head of Mckinsey's, the leading management constancy; Tony O'Reilly (Irish) headed up Heinz worldwide until recently, Alex Trottman (Scottish) was CEO of the Ford Motor Company, a position now held by Jac Nasser, an Australian of Lebanese descent.

It is worth noting that no one method is the correct one – the one that reflects the strategic intent matched to the objectives is the most appropriate.

It is abundantly clear that the management issues surrounding international organizations are extremely complex. There are a number of trends to add to the already lengthy discussion:

1. Organizational structures are becoming 'flatter' with individual managers having wider responsibility and more subordinates
2. Correspondingly, responsibility and authority are being pushed closer to the relevant point of contact with the customer
3. The trend will therefore be towards the macropyramid format with the centre deciding the global corporate decisions relating to the direction the company should take but the marketing decisions will be made increasingly with the subsidiaries
4. Transnational organizations – the latest thinking in international management is that being global is not enough. Kenichi Ohmae, a disciple of globalization curiously argues against rigidity, believing that as the world increasingly develops around the Triad economies the global company must be equidistant from each of the three major trading blocs yet simultaneously position itself as an insider within each. This renaissance corporation should exploit whatever economies of scale, technology or

branding it has within the Triad. Ohmae's argument is that while tastes may vary, the broad motivations among consumers are similar

5. Shared vision The task of moulding an organization to the needs of an ever-changing world marketplace involves building a shared vision and developing human resources. For example, Coca-Cola's vision is simple – 'To put Coca-Cola within arm's reach of everyone in the world'.

To succeed, the company must employ all its talents and avoid the pitfalls of adopting the narrow vision of ethnocentric management employing both a polycentric style yet recognizing the importance of the regiocentric and geocentric contributions.

Bartlett and Ghoshal (1992) broadly confirm the view that renaissance companies must be composed of specialist managers who network across countries/regions. They explain the management implications as:

- Global managers need to be multi-disciplined providing leadership and innovation
- The country manager is a pivotal character, being closest to the customer and understanding the finesse required in building customer relationships
- Global product group managers have the responsibility for quality control and efficiency and driving down costs. Additionally, they will be the architects for worldwide resourcing.

Activity 5.5

Return to Unit 1 briefly and see how the points made here match the challenges outlined. There should be a direct correlation. No aspect of international planning/organization acts independently of its environment.

Market entry methods

Once the organization has pieced together its plan for its international markets the first practical step has to be taken – international market entry. By this stage the organization and its managers will have decided:

- To market internationally
- Where to market
- What to market.

The key decision now is to decide the best way of entering the chosen markets.

No ideal strategy exists – one firm may choose a variety of methods, appropriate to each country/market situation. In the same way, entry methods change over time. But underpinning the decision are the firm's objectives, attitudes and commitment to successful exploitation of overseas opportunities. The level of involvement referred to in the text (and also in the introduction to the Coursebook) is the key factor in determining the correct strategy.

International market entry strategies

Having previously identified where we wish to go in developing overseas business and having addressed our basic marketing strategies, the next step is deciding how we might get there – the market entry strategy. This is of critical importance for it sets the agenda for future battles. It signals to competitors the scale of our intention and, with it, our commitment.

There is no one ideal way of entering an overseas market. There are options to suit all sizes of firms and all situations. There are no barriers preventing the smallest firm from taking the first tentative steps overseas, for international marketing is not the exclusive preserve of large companies. Indeed, large companies do not pursue a rigid policy in exploiting opportunities but often seek to take the most appropriate route for each market judged as an entity. Du Pont operates with wholly owned or joint-venture operations in 40 countries, with marketing subsidiaries in 20 and with distributors in 60. McDonald's has a mixture of wholly owned and franchised operations. No route is the correct one.

However, the chosen entry method requires the greatest of care. Once selected and resourced, it may not be easy to change or withdraw from the market. (Exit strategies are also important, especially in high-risk markets.) Similarly, the extent to which the company's marketing strategy can be employed is also dependent upon the decision. So the alternatives must be weighed most carefully and should be viewed by the international marketer over the longer- rather than the shorter-term horizons. A straightforward exports orientated company can take a short-term tactical approach but international marketing involves dialogue with consumers, understanding their needs and wants, creating appropriate satisfactions and managing the relationship between the company, its intermediaries and its consumers.

Entry strategy alternatives

If international marketing is about relationships with overseas customers/consumers then the starting point in considering market entry alternatives is a strategic not a tactical one and revolves around the question of 'level of involvement', or, putting it simpler 'how close do I need to be to the consumer in order to succeed?' As in all marts, closeness to the consumer is the discriminator of success. Refer here to the International Business Process model in the Introduction 'What is international marketing?' for guidance and reinforcement of the point.

Level of involvement

This is dictated by the following:

- *Corporate objectives/ambition/resources* These will shape the market entry strategy in terms of narrowing the options but will not necessarily constrain the organization to a single-entry choice.
- *Nature of the markets/product category/competition* The scale of the market, the number of markets, the nature of the product category and the level of competition will influence market entry strategy.
- *Nature of consumer culture* What customers buy, where they buy, why they buy and how often will certainly focus thinking.
- *Coverage of the market – breadth, depth and quality* Again, this is largely dictated by consumer needs. The product has to be available where the customer expects to find it. The basic choice of market entry strategy is influenced by the required penetration demands.
- *Speed of entry* The nature of the product, where it is on the product life cycle, the rate of new product innovation diffusion and the pace of market development will have a profound bearing on our choice.
- *Level of control* What feedback is required? What research information do we need on customer purchasing to assist future planning and to effect current and future controls?
- *Marketing costs and commitment* Consumer demands and competitive pressure will influence this. Clearly, the greater the marketing cost, the higher will be the level of involvement.
- *Profit payback* This is related to corporate aims and objectives but varying by company and by country. The general rule is that paybacks are longer overseas. Sony, when entering the UK market, took a corporate decision not to take profit for the first 10

years, but to invest it in the development of its market share. At the other extreme, a leading question might be 'Can I get my money out?'. This, too, will colour the approach to market entry.

- *Investment costs* The deeper the involvement, the higher the costs; inventory, finance, credit, management, etc.
- *Administrative requirements* Documentation, detailed knowledge of legal requirements, foreign taxation.
- *Personnel* This obviously increases with greater involvement; management, training, language, cultural assimilation are all factors to consider.
- *Flexibility* Learning from doing; testing the situation before heavy involvement, political risk, multi-market entry are just some of the factors to take into account in planning the entry strategy.

Activity 5.6

What does level of involvement mean? Take a small firm and compare it with a major multinational. See how this equates with cost.

Exam Hint

Practically every examination paper has questions on entry methods either in the mini case or in the Section B part of the examination. It is extremely rare that the subject is not included in the paper. Therefore it is essential you have a very thorough grasp of the subject.

With entry strategy alternatives two basic routes present themselves:

1. Exporting – defined as 'Making it here, selling it there'
2. Overseas Production – 'Making it there and selling it there' (not necessarily the same country).

Figure 5.3 sets out the strategic alternatives under both headings. The choice is extensive and we propose to comment briefly on all of them. But before doing so it is important to recognize that the level of involvement increases in descending order and that overseas production requires greater involvement than exporting.

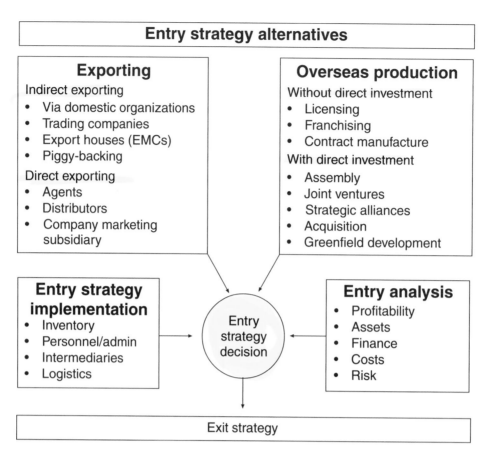

Entry strategy alternatives

Exporting

Indirect exporting
- Via domestic organizations
- Trading companies
- Export houses (EMCs)
- Piggy-backing

Direct exporting
- Agents
- Distributors
- Company marketing subsidiary

Overseas production

Without direct investment
- Licensing
- Franchising
- Contract manufacture

With direct investment
- Assembly
- Joint ventures
- Strategic alliances
- Acquisition
- Greenfield development

Entry strategy implementation
- Inventory
- Personnel/admin
- Intermediaries
- Logistics

Entry strategy decision

Entry analysis
- Profitability
- Assets
- Finance
- Costs
- Risk

Exit strategy

Figure 5.3
Market entry alternatives

Exporting

Indirect exporting

This deals with exports as if they were domestic sales. No specific overseas knowledge is required as the work is done by others. New opportunities can be opened up but control is limited and profitability generally low (others are taking the risk, doing the work). Various methods exist:

- *Overseas organizations with buyers in domestic markets* Major retailers have UK buyers (e.g. Macy's in New York has buying offices in 30 countries). The Body Shop procures products from obscure sources (e.g. the Kayapo Indians deep within the Brazilian rainforest).
- *Multinationals' procurement offices* The major multinationals source widely.
- *International trading companies* With their roots in the colonial era and consequently of fading importance, nevertheless ITCs are important in gaining access to many Third World countries. United Africa Company, a Unilever subsidiary, is the largest trader in Africa. The Japanese Sogo Shosha, as their ITCs are known, are major international players embracing Mitsui and Mitsubishi. The Sogo Shosha handle the majority of Japanese imports today. The advantages of ITCs are wide market coverage and fast, easy access to markets. However, they will carry a wide portfolio of products, often competitors, and therefore there will be a dilution of effort. Additionally, a feeling of

resentment may persist in some countries due to the historical legacy of colonialism. Burma and Egypt have nationalized ITCs to rid themselves of foreign influence. In summary, sales are less stable and there is little company control.

- *Export houses (Export management companies – EMCs in American textbooks)* This is by far the most important method of exporting (numerically) with around 800 operating in the UK. Ranging from generalist to specialist (by industry and country), they provide the performance of an export department without direct involvement and generally allow the company some (if small) degree of cooperation and control. Most suitable for the small to medium firm. Further advantages include: instant market contact and knowledge (particularly local purchasing practices and government regulations). They are paid on commission and therefore are motivated to develop the business (ensuring that the product is attractive to sell). Additionally they offer freight savings by consolidating shipments and, if selling complementary products, can enhance the representation. Disadvantages include: the country coverage by the export house may not coincide with the company's objectives, and they may carry too many products (including competitive ones) thus diluting the effort.
- Therefore care must be taken in choosing the appropriate export house. The company's trade association is often a helpful source of advice.
- *Piggy-backing* This is essentially a form of cooperation in exporting where one company uses its facilities to sell another's product. It is more common between US multinationals and exporters than in Europe. Generally, piggy-backing involves longer-term involvement and it is certain that partner choice requires great care. The advantages are introductions to new markets via an organization established and respected in the country together with savings in infrastructure costs covering warehousing, marketing and sales.
- *Note*: *Piggy-backing is often included under direct exporting as this utilizes the resources of an intermediary based in overseas countries.*

Activity 5.7

Study some trade magazines in more than one industry (e.g. fashion, electrical equipment, etc.). What avenues and approaches are there for small firms to export?

Activity 5.8

Contact a trade association, see if you can obtain a list of export houses or alternatively via a trade telephone directory, contact an export house direct. See what they offer small firms.

Direct exporting

This is exporting using intermediaries located in foreign markets. In doing so the exporter is becoming more involved and committed to the new marketplace, adding investment, time and management expertise. The benefits of greater involvement are more influence, greater strategic leverage (variable) control (also variable) and, of course, profit. The step from indirect to direct exporting should not be taken lightly as the costs and expertise levels rise sharply and therefore the company must be sure it has the capabilities of managing this significantly higher workload and knowledge requirement. Mahon and Vachini (1992) suggest that a 'beachhead' strategy be employed initially, thereby testing overseas markets (small countries or niche markets) prior to a full-scale abandonment of indirect exporting.

Factors for success

- Top management commitment
- Confidence
- International marketing skills
- Detailed planning
- Commitment to quality
- Research and development
- Reliability/relationship building.

Factors for failure

- Failure to research the market
- Inadequate funds/financial backing
- Failure of commitment/perseverance
- Under-representation in the market
- Failure to understand cultural reference
- Inexperienced management and personnel.

Once individual countries have been selected the first decision is how the company will be represented. The size of the market, the nature of the product category, the level of involvement and contact with the consumer pre- and post-purchase will influence the degree of contact between the company and the market (e.g. a full-time staff in residence at one end of the spectrum to a home-based export sales manager liaising with intermediaries or, alternatively, simply communicating by telephone, fax and e-mail at the other end).

Exam Hint

Throughout the book we stress the importance of using examples. However, don't just quote ours – think of ones of your own. Originality will be rewarded in the examination.

Agents

These represent the lowest level of direct involvement in exporting. Their distinguishing feature is that they are country/territory bound (be sure your contract states this to avoid parallel exporting/importing). Paid on commission for orders obtained they, as a norm, represent non-competing manufacturers with sole rights. The critical fact to keep in mind is that agents do not take title to the goods (although there are exceptions). Their advantage lies in that they are paid by results, there is limited risk involved, they can tap into existing contacts, they have a cultural and linguistic affinity. Furthermore start-up costs are low. Their disadvantages stem from quality of service, coverage of the market, conflict of interest (dilution factor), lack of control over them. They are difficult to fire due to legal complexities, stretched resources, communication (both inward and outward), motivation, distribution and their financial competence, i.e. you getting paid! Great care needs to be taken in drafting the agreement and agents are usually chosen when high-price, low-volume goods are ordered – business-to-business or industrial products.

Distributors

These differ considerably from agents in both the level of involvement and the relationship. Distributors represent the major (most popular) form of international distribution numerically.

They are used by small and large firms alike for entering markets where a marketing as well as a sales presence is required. This marketing input accounts largely for the deeper level of involvement. Distributors differ from agents also by buying the goods themselves and selling them on – usually at their own determined price (although company considerations and cooperation in pricing the product is important). In other words, distributors 'take title to the goods'.

It is apparent that success in the market is largely dependent on the performance of the chosen distributor (the selection process is critical). The challenge then becomes 'how to motivate the distributor'. The key is through building intercompany relationships; by continually rewarding the distributor to do as well, treating them as if they were in your own organization. Recognizing such perfection is unlikely, the company should take all necessary steps to create distributor loyalty, e.g. ensuring an adequate payment structure, developing training programmes, determining agreed targets and other performance standards; and evaluating those performance levels regularly at the same time as maintaining an efficient communication system.

The distributor is not your employee but your business partner and often your sole representation in a country. Treat the arrangement on a mutually (equally) beneficial one, for an unhappy or disgruntled distributor can inflict great damage. Gaining success breeds confidence and greater cooperation. Finally, the advantages and disadvantage of distribution broadly coincide with those for agents.

Activity 5.9

Examine the question 'When exporting, you are only as good as your distributor'. Draw up a plan for forging a positive relationship.

Other direct export methods

These include management contracts and usually relate to large-scale undertakings, e.g. the running of international hotels, turnkey projects, etc. Also included is the growing field of direct marketing via freephone (0800) numbers and/or direct mail brought about by advances in information technology and convergencies in consumer lifestyles.

Operating through an overseas sales/marketing subsidiary

It is often the case that companies set up overseas sales/marketing subsidiaries either to operate within the market via expatriates or to manage a local sales force. Additionally, an overseas subsidiary might provide technical back-up in terms of after-sales service to distributors, contract manufacturers or licensees.

The advantages of an overseas presence are closer contact, specialized know-how and faster/more efficient control. The disadvantages include higher initial costs and a time-lag in becoming estabished, no initial local contacts, cultural disharmony and a risk to company reputation if failure is the result. Re-establishing the company's presence in the marketplace may not be straightforward re-entry.

Activity 5.10

Do some digging. Identify firms, by example, who are involved in each of the identified methods of entry. This will serve you well in examination terms.

Overseas production

This is the starting point for serious involvement – making the product overseas. For most companies the determining factor in manufacturing overseas is the size of the market and the profit potential. The greater the opportunity, the more is the likelihood of production overseas. However, before discussing the alternatives it is important to point out that overseeing production in foreign markets is a vast step upwards in terms of company commitment and involvement from the previous entry strategies. Although labour and buildings may be cheaper, the additional costs involved in transferring technological know-how, quality control and the management of the operation together with the finance involved should not be underestimated. Usually the additional 'pressure' is placed on the domestic production and operational staff who are transferred overseas to supervise the new start-up, often with regressive performance on domestic quality and supply. Reasons for producing overseas include:

- Size of market and perceived profitability
- Tariff barriers reduce competitiveness in the chosen market
- Government regulations (e.g. India, Egypt) demand production be located there for some categories of product
- A major client company moves into overseas production. Japanese subcontractors moved into the USA when Honda set up production
- Government contacts and support to inward investment
- Regionalization – being an 'insider' within the EU is important and, as a result, Toyota and Nissan have opened plants in the UK
- Speed of response, delivery, feedback and after-sales service.

Having decided to become involved in overseas production it is possible to hedge the limit of that involvement from licensing at one extreme to building a manufacturing plant on a greenfield site at the other.

Foreign manufacture without direct investment

Licensing

This requires a low level of direct investment. It confers the right to utilize a company-specific patent, trademark, copyright, product or process for an agreed fee, in a given country, over a prescribed timespan. The benefits to the licensor i.e. the company giving the licence are:

- No capital outlay, considerable cost savings
- Attractive to small and large firms alike
- Multi-market penetration quickly, especially important when dealing with 'products' with a short life-cycle (e.g. movie merchandising, fashion goods, computer games, etc.)
- Access to local distribution
- Payment by results.

It is easy to see how licensing has emerged as one of the frontrunners in penetrating global markets speedily. Furthermore, licensing is attractive where markets are politically sensitive, the risk is high, the tariff barriers are prohibitive or government regulations forbid company control in the market. The disadvantages are:

- Limitations on control of licensee
- May be establishing competition at end of the agreement
- Limited returns – the licensee is doing the work and will seek the major reward. Licensing fees can vary from 2–3 per cent for industrial products to 30 per cent for faster-moving short life-span products, e.g. computer games
- Quality control and assurance. Given these circumstances, it is hardly surprising that the company's home standards or quality levels may have limited relevance.

Managing the licensing agreements

With these pitfalls in mind:

- Careful selection of the licensee is essential, especially in the area of quality control
- Careful drafting of the agreement is necessary (domestic language and legal systems whenever possible)
- Retain control of key component/formulation. Coca-Cola is a licensing operation worldwide. The essence is produced in Atlanta, shipped everywhere to which 99 per cent local product is added (i.e. water!). However, they can still get it wrong, e.g. contamination in both Belgium and French factories in 1999, the reason for which is still not clear
- Don't license latest state-of-the-art technology – license yesterday's technology (dependent, of course, on the market)
- Limit the geographic area of the licence
- Register all trademarks, patents, copyrights, etc., in licensor's name
- Finally, make the agreement attractive to retain.

Franchising

This has similarities with licensing but is more complex and involves greater management commitment and expertise as the franchiser makes a total production, operational and marketing programme available. Usually the franchise includes the full process of overseas operations and all the factors involved are prescribed.

Generally, franchises involve a service element and well-known international franchises include The Body Shop and McDonald's. Franchising, too, is expanding rapidly. It is a fast track to internationalization for many organizations. As the franchisee pays into the franchise the capital outlay is reduced and the financial risk lies mainly with the franchisee.

For the franchisee the arrangement enables small, independent, entrepreneurial individual(s) to enjoy the benefits of belonging to a large organization with all its power of economies of scale and marketing expertise.

Franchising is very fast-growing but not without its problems which centre on standards of efficiency and service levels and reflect cultural expectations. Even McDonald's has bowed to cultural values, and Kentucky Fried Chicken (KFC) in Japan has succeeded (after initial failure) by adapting to Japanese cultural values and expectation of what a US product should feel like. Similarly, The Body Shop sets its overriding corporate standards but the management and the delivery of the 'product offer' are left largely to locally determined values.

Contract manufacture

This is manufacturing by proxy, with a third party producing the product under contract. Besides obviating the need for investment and therefore entailing less risk, it avoids labour problems but enables the company to advertise 'local made'. Differing from licensing in that the end product is usually turned over to the company for distribution, sales, marketing, etc., contract manufacture is usually undertaken where political risk is high, the country is economically unstable, sales volumes are relatively low or tariffs are high.

In seeking contract manufacturers the company should give consideration to quality control issues and not produce where there is only one manufacturer, seeking to offset alternative producers. Finally, proxy manufacturing should take place where the marketing effort is of crucial importance to the success.

Exam Hint

In the same way as candidates mix up agents and distributors, they do the same when considering licensing and franchising. Make sure you know the differences. Return to the text and check this point now.

Foreign manufacture with direct investment

In moving toward direct investment the company is again increasing its level of involvement.

Assembly

This typically involves the last stages of manufacture and usually depends on the ready supply of components shipped from another overseas country(ies). The key figures in this practice are the world's major car manufacturers who have created integrated component supply and assembly from CKD (Completely Knocked Down) operations, often referred to as 'screwdriver plants' to extensive deconstruction arrangements with specialized components, gearboxes, engines, etc. being made in highly automated plants and then shipped to a common assembly point - usually within a region (e.g. the EU). A good example of this is the production of the new Mercedes-Benz C Class motor car, the right-hand drive version of which is being manufactured soley in South Africa. We wonder if UK buyers will be made aware of this?

Often local governments force manufacturers into assembly operations by banning the import of fully made-up vehicles. BMW, Mercedes and others are assembled in Thailand and Malaysia. The success of Proton cars, the indigenous Malaysian producer, partly reflects barriers and taxes on imported vehicles.

Other reasons for establishing foreign production include:

- *To defend existing business* Fearing US government intervention against Japanese imported vehicles, Honda started the move to produce within the USA. Other Japanese vehicle producers have followed this trend
- *Moving with established customer* Once Honda moved to producing cars in the USA its Japanese suppliers soon followed to maintain the relationship and partnership bonding at the same time preventing US suppliers from cutting in on 'their market'. Suppliers here include banking and financial services and not just vehicle component suppliers
- *To cut costs* With total quality management (TQM) becoming increasingly global, manufacturers no longer feel so insecure about moving production overseas to benefit from lower labour costs, fewer restrictions or less taxes. The massive inward investment in China, India and Indonesia reflects this move and it will further accelerate.

Joint ventures

In joint ventures two companies decide to get together and form a third company that is co-owned (not necessarily equally). The third company then is an entity in itself and the proceeds (and pitfalls) are jointly shared according to the proportion of ownership. Generally, the two parties contribute complementary expertise of resources to the joint company. Joint ventures differ from licensing in that an equity stake exists in the newly formed company.

Increasingly, joint ventures are an attractive option for international companies. Factors accounting for this include:

- Technological development is prohibitively expensive but necessary to achieve breakthroughs. Companies collaborate increasingly on this front
- Rapid internationalization of many markets is beyond the resources of many major companies. Cooperation on production, distribution and marketing have brought benefits
- Complementary management or skills and especially finance deals have led to new companies being jointly formed
- Many countries restrict foreign ownership. China, India and South Korea are among those who insist on a form of joint venture.

Many hi-tech companies are now forging joint venture links to cut the costs of development and speed up market development. Those companies moving into Russia or Eastern Europe are nearly all doing so via this route. In the early 1990s Russia saw 150 joint venture deals signed, McDonalds and Pepsi among them. Obviously, partner choice is important. McDonalds and Pepsi chose the city of Moscow as a partner; Procter & Gamble's chosen partner in Russia is the University of St Petersburg. The partners are preferred to the normal commercial arrangement partly because none of any substance or reputation exists.

On a negative note there is always the possibility of joint venture divorce which is invariably messy. Some points for consideration before entering into the arrangement are:

- The venture must develop its own culture
- Venture partners must be prepared to share the problems, not try to blame the other party
- The venture managers must have access to top management of both parties
- The venture should receive sufficient capital and finance to develop
- The venture should not be overcontrolled by central bureaucracy.

Strategic alliances

A strategic alliance has no precise definition but is different from a joint venture in that there is often no equity involvement, no separate organization is created. Loosely described, a strategic alliance is a 'swap shop' between two or more organizations who agree to cooperate strategically to the mutual benefit of both or all parties to the arrangement.

The development of strategic alliances is continuing apace. Hardly a month elapses without one or more being announced. May 1996 saw Disney and McDonald's cooperating for a ten-year period to exploit Disney characters worldwide. The forces underpinning the creation of strategic alliances include:

- High R&D costs
- Pace of innovation and market diffusion
- Concentration of firms in mature industries
- Insufficient resources to exploit new technological breakthroughs
- Government cooperation
- Regionalization
- The fast-developing global consumer – the fundamental and most important reason
- Self-protection against predators
- Access to otherwise difficult markets.

Like joint ventures, strategic alliances need to be considered carefully before entering into the agreement. They should either be seen as a short-term, stop-gap arrangement or as a long-term partnership. Divorce is always messy and reneging on strategic alliances often brings repercussions at a later date.

***

Activity 5.11

Read the quality press, cut out examples/articles of joint ventures and strategic alliances – they are happening weekly. Create a file. Build your knowledge. It could be vital in the examination.

***

Wholly-owned overseas production

One hundred per cent ownership representing the maximum level of commitment, complete management control and maximum profitability. This option optimizes international integration – but is exposed to foreign problems and could face higher risk. Two main routes present themselves:

1. Acquisition
2. Development of facilities from a 'greenfield' situation.

Acquisition is the quick way in, direct in approach with a clear picture of what is being bought – trained labour, management, sales, market share, distribution and an immediate return on the investment. However, many acquisitions come to grief due to existing management leaving and clashes in cultural approach with management. Firms buy in haste but repent at leisure for, in buying an overseas firm, the company may be taking on board everything that is culturally at odds with the home way of doing things. Selecting the right company to acquire is difficult. It is easy to buy up a weak or 'poor firm' but turning it into a high-performance competitor is difficult. Volkswagen struggled for years to come to terms with Seat (its Spanish subsidiary's inability to match Volkswagen standards of output and quality). Good-quality firms are not always available for purchase and are difficult to acquire – often requiring paying 'over the odds'. When Nestlé acquired Rowntrees in 1984 for £1.4 billion (at the time this was 30 per cent of the projected cost for constructing the Channel Tunnel) *The Economist* remarked: 'What price for 2 ft, (60 cm), of Supermarket Shelf-space - £1.4 billion!'. Nestlé were not just buying technology, factories, management – they were paying £1.4 billion for brands, primarily Kit Kat, the UK brand leader in chocolate snack bars, and in doing so were eliminating uncertainty and risk in their market growth and search for pan-European brands and the development of a world brand.

With *greenfield* development, of course Nestlé would have chosen the option of building its own factories, developing its own brand over time. But time is a premium in today's marketplace and success in new product introduction is often ephemeral – few achieve it. Cadbury's spent years and a fortune in creating and developing Wispa (a chocolate bar) – a success but nowhere near on the scale of Kit Kat.

Having said that the benefits of greenfield developments are also significant. Nissan and Toyota deliberately located their new UK plants in locations away from exposure and experience in motor car construction so as to inculcate new employees with modern Japanese work patterns. (Acquiring firms means that you acquire their bad habits as well as their good ones.) Honda, BMW and Mercedes chose the southern US states for their greenfield developments when moving production to North America. Incidentally, the Mercedes M Class 4 is manufactured only in the USA.

In summary, the pendulum has swung towards acquisition, particularly in the world of modern developments such as information, technology, multimedia and other communications (e.g.

satellite stations and entertainment industries). Some mega examples of late 1990s mergers are Daimler/Chrysler, Glaxo Smith Kline and Vodaphone's takeover of Mannesmann.

Activity 5.12

Who's merging or taking over whom? Again study the quality press – something big is happening regularly. Create a file of examples. Additionally, consider the benefits accruing from each example you discover.

Entry strategy implementation

This aspect of the model has been covered comprehensively in the section dealing with channel distribution and logistics.

Entry analysis

A simple method of examining the options can be found in Terpstra and Sarathy; and also in Cateora. It is brief but does give the reader insight into some of the variables of choice (Table 5.6).

Table 5.6 Matrix for comparing alternative methods of market entry							
Evaluation criteria	**Entry methods**						
	Indirect export	Direct export	Market-ing subsi-diary	Marketing subsidiary-local assembly	Licen-sing	Joint venture	Wholly-owned operation
1 Number of markets							
2 Market penentra-tion							
3 Market feedback							
4 Inter-national marketing Learning							
5 Control							
6 Marketing costs							
7 Profits							

8 Invest-ment							
9 Admini-stration							
10 Foreign problems							
11 Flexi-bility							
12 Risk							

Jeannet and Hennessey have assembled a more complex model analysing the data required to assist the company in selecting its entry mode (Figure 5.4). It is complex for the variables are many. Getting it right is important. There must be a clear relationship between the benefits accruing from the method chosen and the implication for the firm. Table 5.6 provides a method for evaluating the different market entry strategies. The left hand column indicates the evaluative criteria against each method of market entry. The implications for strategy are clarified by using such a matrix approach, for example, if the number of markets are few, marketing costs may be high and, therefore, potential profits will be difficult to realize. As a result a more hands off entry strategy will be more appropriate. The choice in this case will be direct exporting or joint venture with a local organization. A good example of this is in the mini case which was part A of the June 2001 examinations. Go to www.marketingonline.co.uk or www.bh.com/marketing to access Specimen Answers and Senier Examiner's advice for there exam questions. Such were the risks and potential low return for Indeco (Pvte) in Zambia that it was best to export direct or enter into a joint venture with a local organization.

Financing global operations

Global operations require finance, they don't just happen. There are many sources of finance both internal and external. Internal sources include accumulated surpluses and cash. External sources include the international stock markets, commercial and private banks, factoring and forfeiting, discount markets, leasing, hire purchase, venture capital, joint financing (dealers, distributors and principals) and bilateral and multilateral aid in cases of international development, for example, the World Bank. Each source has its own merits and demerits but, obviously, internal sources are best as interest is non-payable. Borrowing money on the international money market can be very expensive, especially if the organization is located in a country prone to drastic devaluation. Sometimes, as in the case of less-developed countries, foreign currency may be in short supply or at a premium. In this case money can often be obtained from the international money markets by 'off shore lending' from anticipated future sales and earnings in foreign currency. A good example of this is the tobacco crop in Zimbabwe. Farmers obtain inputs – fertilizers and seed – from abroad using foreign obtained capital, provided on the prospect of the tobacco crop being sold overseas with the resultant inflow of foreign, hard currency. The input costs are deducted before final crop payments are made to the farmers. Some organizations are so cash rich that they seek ventures to invest in. Such an organization is GE Venture Capital.

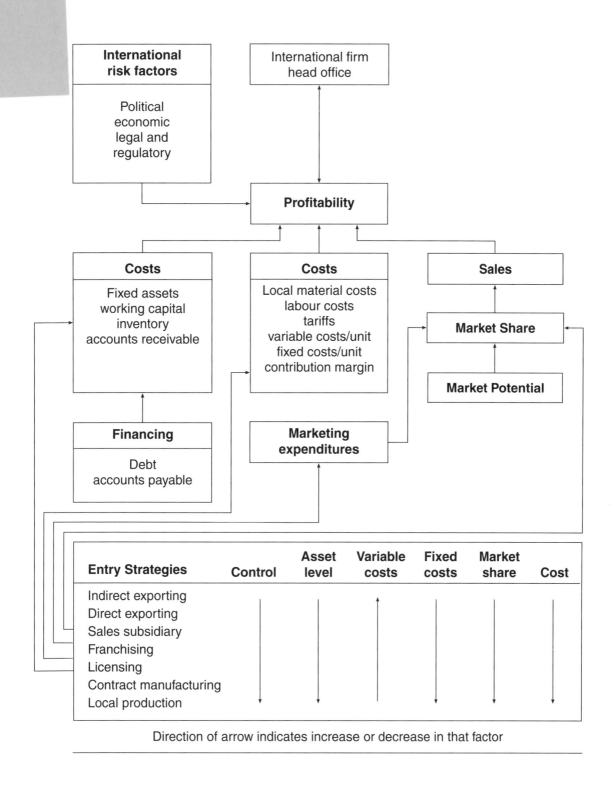

Figure 5.4
Considerations for market entry decisions (Source: Jeannet and Hennessey)

Exit strategy

Painful as it may be, companies are sometimes forced to leave a market(s). The conclusion is that with foresight, firms may dispose of their assets profitably (occasionally) and consideration should always be given to the possibility of having to evacuate a lost-cause position taking the plunge and entering a market.

Political reasons

Changing political situations sometimes force companies to exit markets. Expropriation is often a risk in some countries and companies are advised to plan their exit strategies accordingly. Coca-Cola departed the Indian market rather than sell its controlling interest to local investors as required by local laws.

Business failure

Before entering any market, consideration should be given to the cost of failure. Peugeot, Renault and others have left the US market with their fingers burned. Volvo similarly pulled out (at the last minute) of a strategic alliance with Renault before being eventually acquired by Ford. Lancia have withdrawn from the UK car market. Abandonment of a market, especially a major one such as the USA is very expensive and can be damaging to the global reputation of the organization.

Exam Question 5.1

It has been suggested that the best way for developed countries to market into developing countries is via another developing country. Using examples, explain the reasoning behind this proposition and its implications on the organization and resources of a developed country based multinational. (December 1999. Question 5)

Go to www.marketingonline.co.uk or www.bh.com/marketing to access Specimen Answers and Senior Examiner's advice for this exam question.

Exam Question 5.2

Analyse the strategic implications of a major global bank deciding to withdraw its operations in a less developed country. (December 2000. Question 3)

Go to www.marketingonline.co.uk or www.bh.com/marketing to access Specimen Answers and Senior Examiner's advice for this exam question.

Implementing international/global marketing across differing cultures

When implementing international/global marketing across different countries many factors have to be taken into account. In Unit 3 the relevance of, and importance of, assessing environmental factors was stressed, and this is particularly important when marketing occurs across different cultures, as these environmental factors are likely to differ from country to country. Similarly Unit 5 stressed the importance of assessing the state of development of the country when considering global planning, especially in different countries with different states of development. As the examinations frequently ask you to market a product or service across different cultures it is essential that you learn the strategic, tactical and operational implications of so doing. For example in a less developed country (LDC), 'the government' and politics are likely to play a major role. A good example of this is in countries in Sub Saharan Africa and South America. In

Tertiary countries, the government is likely to be less of a factor and 'competition' and 'rules of entry' are likely to be very important as is the state of technological development. These nuances must be appreciated when implementing global strategies across differing cultures and countries.

Questions

As a check on your understanding of what has been covered in this unit, consider the following questions:

Question 5.3

1. In creating an international plan what basic elements might you consider important?
2. What are the difficulties in adapting headquarters' broad plan to local countries?
3. What impact should competition play in affecting international marketing planning?
4. What are the benefits of choosing region, product or function as the basis for organizing the firm on an international basis? Headquarters hinder local market development. Discuss.
5. What control elements do you consider appropriate in multi-country marketing planning?
6. What is the purpose of control systems? What distinguishes a good one?
7. What is a marketing audit and what are its strengths and weaknesses in developing international markets?
8. What is the relevance of the BCG model in planning for international markets?
9. What decisions are best left to local managers?
10. Itemize and justify six characteristics you consider necessary for an organization to compete successfully in a global market.
11. Strategic alliances often fail. Can you explain why?

Extending knowledge

International Marketing Strategy, I. Doole and R. Lowe, 3rd Edition, Thomson, 2001, Chapters 5, 6 and 8, pp.141–213 and 247–278.

International Marketing, S. Paliwoda and M. Thomas, 3rd Edition, Butterworth-Heinemann, 1999 Chapters 3 ,4 and 9, pp. 96–187 and 352–391.

Global Marketing Strategies, J.-P. Jeannet and H.D. Hennessey, 5th Edition, Houghton Mifflin, 2001 Chapters 8, 9, 16 and 17, pp. 301–373 and 636–698.

Summary

This unit has covered two strategic aspects of international marketing: first, the line of marketing planning and second the organizational implications. Both involved a high degree of personnel issues. The unit discussed briefly the importance of models in developing strategy and also considered the marketing planning variables set against the key international decision areas. This particular matrix is of considerable help in defining quickly your options (from the perspective of the examination) and the issues revolving around control.

Likewise, the manner in which the company organizes itself to best deal with its international development establishes the level of involvement and the intensity of its competitive impact.

There is a wide variety of choice. Finally, the unit discussed developments that will shape the competitive challenges in the future.

Choosing the appropriate entry strategy is probably the most perplexing decision that companies have to make. A survey among CEOs of American companies suggested that they spent more time deliberating this question than any other in international business. Once the decision is taken it determines the rest of your strategy – financial, managerial as well as marketing. Moreover, it establishes the terms of engagement in the war for sales in a chosen marketplace. Such decisions are not taken lightly. But success in the future is not for the slow or the timid. Companies are going to have to become more ambitious and radical in their approach to the question – joint ventures, strategic alliances, complex partnerships between firms and governments are becoming the order of the day. The pace of advancement, customer demand and technology are forcing developments. Yet exit strategies are also important considerations. So the final thought is that flexibility will prevail over rigidity in the future.

Objectives

Globalization as a strategic option open to the international organization has been a major topic of discussion since Theodore Levitt wrote his mould-breaking article in 1983 (Harvard Business Review). Globalization, in essence, is about treating the world as one market both for marketing and for production purposes. In this unit you will:

- Understand what globalization means
- Consider the factors which drive an organization towards a globalized strategy
- Understand the factors which may affect or inhibit a drive towards globalization
- Be aware of when a globalized strategy is appropriate for an organization and when it is not

See syllabus sections 2.2.2 and 2.2.5.

Having completed this unit you will be able to:

- Consider the viability or otherwise of globalization as a strategy for the international organization
- Understand the implications of a globalization strategy upon the organization, its marketing, its production and organizational structure
- Understand the effects of a globalization strategy upon the international marketing mix.

Study guide

This unit is important to an overall understanding of international marketing strategy. Although globalization represents only a very small part of the syllabus (5 per cent), the effects of following a globalization strategy will be felt throughout the entire operation and implementation of the international marketing mix. Decisions taken at this level will also affect how activities are evaluated and controlled in the international marketplace.

Globalization as a strategy offers significant potential savings through economies of scale but is also clearly an inappropriate strategy in certain situations. The key to understanding globalization is being able to differentiate the times and occasions when it is a suitable strategy for the organization and when it should be avoided in favour of other, more local, approaches to markets.

As you work through this unit remember that good strategy must be thought out carefully. The international market, as always, must be the inspiration for good marketing and when local needs are so divergent in their nature as to make a standardized (globalized) approach inappropriate the international marketer needs to be able to direct strategy accordingly.

What is globalization?

Globalization as an issue came to the fore in 1983 with the publication of Theodore Levitt's article in the *Harvard Business Review*. Levitt's initial article on globalization put forward the view that there was simply no such thing as local markets, that all markets tended towards a universal standard and that organizations indulging themselves in producing many variants in overseas markets were simply wasting resources on a grand scale. He suggested that organizations would be much more efficient and effective if they were to standardize their marketing approaches to overseas markets. They should not only market themselves and their products on a global basis but also consider production and service on a globalized basis. Since Levitt's first article a number of articles have appeared by various authors both for and against this basic premise. Indeed, Levitt himself joined the fray a few years later, saying that wasn't exactly what he meant and that in some instances 'think global, act local' was the right and proper policy for international markets.

> ### Definition
>
> **Global marketing** – can be defined as 'the process of focusing an organization's resources on the selection and exploitation of global market opportunities consistent with and supportive of its short- and long-term strategic objectives and goals'. (*Source: Toyne and Walters, 1989*).

It is relatively easy to see Levitt's original inspiration for the globalization concept. If we consider the North American market, although it is called 'domestic' by US companies, it is far less homogeneous than most other domestic/national markets with which the organization has to deal. While in the domestic marketing situation most US companies will look for similarities among quite often varied market needs, as soon as these same organizations consider overseas markets they start by looking at differences rather than similarities. While there is obviously much fluency in the globalization argument it is equally difficult to understand how it will be universally applicable to all organizations in all situations.

International or global?

Definitions in textbooks abound to describe the different types of international operations. A simple checklist is:

Domestic marketing

Marketing directed at the domestic or home market only.

Export marketing

Making the product or service in the home markets and selling it in international markets.

International marketing

Moving beyond exporting, the organization often still makes the product or service in the home market but has its own representation for sales, marketing and distribution in the foreign market(s).

Multinational marketing

The next stage of growth and involvement. The organization has a greater proportion of its assets in markets other than its domestic base. The domestic market is now one of many markets all approached mainly on an individual basis. Sometimes called a *multidomestic* strategy, the organization puts local market considerations first.

Multiregional marketing

In an attempt to find economies of scale in their operations, the organization has started to standardize its international marketing strategies around regional groupings of markets.

Global marketing

Some authors, (e.g. Douglas and Craig 1995) describe this process as the 'EPRG' Framework. This stands for Ethnocentrism (domestic/export marketing orientation), Polycentrism (international marketing orientation), Regiocentrism (multinational marketing orientation) and Geocentrism (global marketing orientation). Source: Douglas, S.P. and Craig, C.S. (1995) Global Marketing Strategy, McGraw-Hill.

The organization defines a single strategy for a product, service or company that can be followed in all markets in which the organization operates. Typically, senior management will set general strategic guidelines and local offices will develop these at local market levels.

As it is described above, global marketing can be seen as the latest stage in the development of the organization into international markets. Clearly globalization is not appropriate to all organizations, nor does an organization necessarily have to go through all the stages described above to get to globalization. The best way to understand globalization and its applicability for any given organization is to understand the factors which drive globalization and those which may inhibit its implementation in an organization's marketing strategy.

Factors driving to globalization

There are a number of factors in today's modern world which may drive an organization toward a global marketing strategy. Some of the most important are:

1. *The international flow of information* Predictions of the 'global village' were being made 10 and 15 years ago and they are now starting to come true. The flow of information across national boundaries is becoming both faster and greater in quantity. People also are much more able and willing to travel than a decade ago. This increased flow of international information and customer awareness means that consumers and suppliers nowadays are much more aware of products and services that are available in often very distant markets. With this increased flow of information and awareness comes demand, and markets for products and services grow on a global scale.

2. *The international spread of technology* As with information, technology is now flowing much more freely across national boundaries and frontiers. With the international spread of technology the ability to design, develop, manufacture and market products and services of all descriptions is available on a much more global scale than 10 or 20 years ago.

3. *Size of investment required* Driven by the spread of international information and technology, the minimum production batch size is starting to decrease as enabling technology spreads. Consequently, the size of financial and human investment required in developing new products or services has grown. In a number of markets, for example motor cars, military hardware and pharmaceuticals, the absolute size of the investment required to develop the next generation of new products has outstripped the ability of any one single market or company to pay back on the investment. In these industries (among others) investment has to be based on the likely future demand in more than one market, if possible for global application, in order to make such investments financially viable. So we see that developments such as the Ford world car (Mondeo) and the European fighter aircraft are now developed by and for more than one marketplace.

4. *Reduction of trade barriers* As the world develops into a smaller number of larger economic and political regions (EU, LAFTA, NAFTA) the number of small, independent markets with their own regulations and legislations requiring adapted or specialized products reduces. As trade barriers and restrictions fall away, the marketplace opens up for much more standardized products and services and makes a globalized international marketing strategy more viable for many organizations.

5. *Relative global peace.* Most conflicts these days are intense but local, for example the Gulf War. Coupled to this, is the growing influence of multinational peace keeping. These factors, and others, have created a relatively peaceful world since the last global conflict of 1939 to 1945. It is within this scenario that global operators feel relatively confident to continue their operations and encourages those contemplating to go global to continue with their plans.

6. *Evolution of global market segments.* In recent years, with the parallel growth of international information technology and communications, the phenomenon of the 'global consumer' has emerged. A good example of this is the global cosmetic user. Across the world you can see a customer demanding, purchasing and using one certain brand of cosmetic wherever they may be, for example, Estee Lauder. This evolution of the global consumer has encouraged the globalization process.

Factors inhibiting globalization

As well as the easily identifiable factors which encourage organizations to take a more globalized international marketing strategy, there are a number of factors which can be identified that may make such a strategy inappropriate or impractical. Some of the more common factors are as follows:

1. *Customer tastes* The key concept upon which globalization is based is that of a broadly standardized approach to international markets. Before any form of standardization can be applied it requires that customers' tastes in various markets are also standardized. In many cases this is simply not the case. If customers actually want or need or require different products or services from a neighbouring or other foreign market and if competition is such that their needs can be met, they will not buy the standardized (globalized) products or service. Even where tastes converge, many organizations have found that other elements of the product or marketing mix may need to be varied on a local basis in order to gain acceptability. For example, many American adverts on TV might be visually acceptable but may be have to be dubbed in to the local language – including English!

2. *Culture* As we have already seen from Unit 2, culture is a major force in determining customer and buyer behaviour. In the same way, culture can be a major barrier to globalization strategies. Culture is a major factor in everybody's life and people (and organizations) will seek out products and services which enable them to reinforce their sense of belonging to a given culture and will avoid those products and services that are seen as transgressing particular cultural rules. Certain products and services are evidently the product of an identifiable culture. For example, McDonald's, Coca-Cola and Harley-Davidson are seen as products of US culture. In these cases, they will still be purchased as people wish to sample that culture as well as consume the product. In other cases such as Phileas Fogg snacks, the organization may find that while the concept behind the snacks is valid on a worldwide basis the actual products required to deliver the company's promise differ from culture to culture and need to be modified accordingly.

3. *Local market conditions* As well as the strictly cultural variables at play when considering globalization strategy, there are a number of other variables that also need to be taken into account. These will vary from organization to organization and from

product to product but may include issues such as the local market's need for particular national or regional identity, the role of individualism in the target market and the degree of nationalism inherent in local purchase behaviour. In these instances a degree of globalization may be possible but also some degree of adaptation to local requirements may be required.

4. *Pressure Groups.* Recently there has been growing pressure by various groups opposed to the global operators. This has taken the form of protests at government economic summits, including those of the G8.The principle objection of the groups is to the perception of excessive profits gained at the expense of mainly developing countries, especially the notion of promoting a 'sweat shop'culture. Other objections centre around the need to give a fairer opportunity to developing country manufacturers. In some ways this has triggered global operators to enhance their ethics and social responsibility programmes.

Exam Hint

The debate between total globalization and adaptation to local market needs continues to be waged in the pages of marketing journals. You should be aware of the arguments on both sides. You should have an opinion and be prepared to justify it.

Activity 6.1

Select a company that is generally thought of as being a global operator. (McDonald's, Coca-Cola, Pepsi, Ford, International Harvester, Compaq, etc.). What degree of standardization are they actually able to achieve? What adaptation in the marketing mix can you identify?

Global marketing strategy

If, depending on the organization, its competition and its target customers' needs, globalization is deemed a valid international strategy, then there will be many consequences for the organization and its marketing. Globalized organizations need to develop and refine the ability to consider business, markets and competition all over the world and to distil this (often conflicting) data into a practical marketing plan. Global marketing strategy is not the same as domestic marketing strategy applied all over the world. The skills and management required to develop and implement global strategies are different.

'Think global, act local' requires a constant knowledge of where the line lies that divides globalization from multinational marketing. Striking the balance between standardization and adaptation is difficult. Setting central, global strategic guidelines for local, tactical, implementation requires precise strategic skills. The ability to think above the detail is rare. All elements of the international marketing mix will be influenced by the global strategy. Balancing local requirements against the wider global benefits may not always be popular in local operating units.

Policing (monitoring and controlling) products, services and global brands in diverse markets needs tact, diplomacy and interpersonal skills native to the international marketer.

Extending knowledge

The Diploma examinations are strategic. Examiners are looking for evidence of candidates' ability to think for themselves about issues that really matter. Globalization, too, has its critics. One, Sir James Goldsmith, was decidedly anti-free trade. He said:

'The doctrine of free trade, if applied globally, will be a disaster.'

'Economies should not be self-serving structures, but directed at promoting the stability and contentment of the societies within which they operate.'

'Europe faces a future of unemployment, poverty and social instability.'

'Britain will become the Mexico of Europe.'

'A reason for this is our quasi-religious belief in free trade. A moral dogma which was born when Britain was the manufacturing centre of the world.'

He suggested the future should be based on:

'Country preference.'

'A world of fenced-off regions with economies that reflect local conditions, cultures and needs.'

You can read more – and make up your own mind – *The Trap,* J. Goldsmith, Macmillan, 1994.

Cross-cultural dimensions of global strategy

From the previous section on culture it should be recognized that some products and services are more culture-bound than others. In other other words, some marketing activities are seen as affecting the target markets' cultural values more than others. Cross-cultural dimensions of the globalization are extremely important in planning to go global. There is much written on 'culture' and you are well advised to read the syllabus recommended text by Usunier (1999), *Marketing Across Cultures*, Prentice-Hall. You should acquaint yourself with the concepts of High versus Low context Cultures (Hall, 1977). Low context cultures put the emphasis on the written or the spoken word, for example Germany, whereas high context cultures, for example Japan, put the emphasis on context. This is very important in the design of advertising messages for example. The work of Hofstede and his culture classification scheme is another concept that you should be familiar with. This is fully described in the set text, Doole and Lowe. Hofstede's classification of cultures on the dimensions of 'power distance' and 'uncertainty avoidance', is seminal and are a very useful base for planning the emphasis of the elements of the marketing mix. There are other cultural studies worth consideration, for example the work of Von Trompenaars.

Some, or all, of the cultural models may be affected by global marketing strategies and the effects cannot be ignored. Obvious examples are religious or social taboos which can be flouted by ill-advised marketing and the international textbooks abound with such examples. The more aggressive the cultural 'gaffe', the more visible the response. Unfortunately, less severe mistakes are not necessarily so visible but the global organization simply fails to penetrate the market and never really finds out why.

Business-to-business markets tend to be less culturally sensitive but fundamental differences do exist and the 'standardize-everything' brigade should take care. Even in this world of e-mail and e-commerce some differences remain fixed in the culture and the different sizes of US (quarto) and Europe (A4) paper sizes remain fixed.

As with most aspects of marketing, emotion plays a greater role than logic and the global player needs to pay attention to the illogical needs and wants of its marketplaces. We are about to see one great battle played out on the streets of the UK in the coming years: Starbucks has acquired the Seattle Coffee Company, Whitbread has acquired Costa, and

Nestlés taking the Nescafé brand to high street coffee shops. Will the British believe that coffee is American or Italian?

Key aspects of cross-cultural analysis include:

- How do we account for cultural diversity, complexity and sensitivity?

It would be ideal if international marketers could treat all countries as one culture e.g. 'British' or 'American'. However, this is far from the case. In the UK whilst 94% of the population may be white, the balance is made up of people whose descendents may have emigrated to the UK many years ago. In the UK the balance is made up of black Caribbean, African, Indian, Pakistani, Bangladeshi, Chinese and other people of different ethnic backgrounds. In Malaysia, the proportions are even more dramatic, with 60% of the population made up of Bumiputra's and the balance made up of people of Chinese and Indian origins. This diversity makes it difficult for international marketers to treat populations as one culture.

Similarly, cultures can be exceedingly complex. Switzerland has a population made up of four different languages and cultures – French, German, Italian and Swiss Romansch. Imagine the results which would ensue from a UK-based telephone marketer who, in selling to Switzerland, employed a salesman who had 'O' level French only! Fortunately most Swiss speak English!

Even within cultures there are sub cultures. Marketers have to be alive to these, many of which can be transient in nature. Young people often adopt a hero culture from film characters presenting global marketers with global merchandising activities. However, many of these are short lived. How long did it take to replace the 'Star Wars' culture with the 'Harry Potter' culture? There are subculture based on gender, age, attitudes to work and a host of other variables.

Marketers need to be extremely culturally sensitive. Cultural identity can be changeable due to the rapid changes in the socio-political environment. Cultural identities are negotiated, co-created, reinforced and challenged through communications. Cultural stereotypes can be extremely dangerous. A classic example is that portrayed by some DC's to LDC's. Dakin (2001) found that the negative image of some UK leather importers to Zimbabwean shoe manufacturers was hindering trade between the two countries. A mutual 'distrust' existed – the UK importers held a preconceived image of Zimbabwe and the Zimbabwean exporters were guilty of doing little to dispel the myth. A simple 'getting together' would have gone a long way to dispel the misunderstandings on both sides.

There are many theories aimed at trying to aid the understanding of inter-cultural communications. These include 'Episode Representation' (Forgas, 1983), 'Constructivist Approach' (Heider, 1958), 'Expectations', 'Anxiety/Uncertainty/ Management (AUM)' (Gudykunst, 1988), 'Cultural Identity Negotiation', 'Ellingsworth's Adaption', (1988) and 'Network' theories. See 'Extending Knowledge' at the end of this section for further reading.

The concepts of cultural diversity, complexity and sensitivity are very important to marketers. It is essential that they are taken into account in the marketing planning and implementation stages, to ensure inclusivity, especially in planning the Marketing Mix and deciding on cross border organizational issues.

- How does the culture see the benefits of the product or service being offered?

Different cultures can perceive the benefits offered by products and services in different ways. For example, in Malaysia or Hong Kong, the mobile phone is seen as a neccesity for all types of application, business, social and so on which is readily acceptable. It is acceptable in the UK, except there is a backlash against its use in certain cicumstances, for example we now see 'quiet coaches' on trains. Presumably this backlash is due to the English sense of 'personal space', a trait not in universal evidence.

- How does the local culture affect the decision-making and the purchasing of the product or service?

This is particularly important in many cultures. For example, in a number of Islamic countries, the sale, purchase and consumption of alcoholic products is forbidden.

- Which aspects of the cultural map are particularly strongly triggered by the offering?

This is a very important question. For example, we are all familiar with the dangers of the translation of brand names or slogans into different cultures. Pepsi's well known slogan 'come alive with Pepsi' when translated into German, becomes 'come out of the grave'!

In order to overcome this, James Lee's (1996) 'self-reference criterion' (SRC) (see Doole and Lowe for a full description) can be used to overcome the unconscious reference to one's own cultural values. He suggested a four-step approach to eliminate SRC:

1. Define the problem or goal in terms of home country culture, traits, habits and norms
2. Define the problem in terms of the foreign culture, traits, habits and norms
3. Isolate the SRC influence and examine it carefully to see how it complicates the problem
4. Redefine the problem without the SRC influence and solve for the foreign market situation.

Source: Lee J (1996) 'Cultural analysis in overseas operations', *Harvard Business Review*, March–April, pp. 106-14.

It is essential to see culture in the context of that country and better to assume that it is different from rather than better, equal or worse than your own. With this approach the risk of failure is at least minimized.

- What aspects of the marketing mix might make the offer culturally sensitive (e.g. promotion, people, service, etc.)?

A nother crucial question and one easily ignored in its totality. McDonald's produce mutton and veggie burgers in India, not pork or beef, so as not to offend the Hindu and Muslim populations. In the UK cigarette advertising is banned on most television. Dell computers take a less aggressive approach to selling their products in Japan than in the USA. Again Lee's SRC approach can help in the formulation of the marketing mix.

- What alternatives already exist for the proposed product/service, how are these related to the local culture?

This is an interesting question and one which relates significantly to less developed countries. For example, a roof tile is common enough in developed countries, but price wise may well be out of reach of the rural poor, say in India and Africa. The answer? It is not uncommon to see flattened cooking oil cans acting as roof tiles on many a rural home. The can serves two functions, to contain cooking oil and, when empty, flattened and used as a roof tile. Now if this was seen on an estate in Middle England all manner of aspersions would be cast at the occupants! In the culture of India and Africa this is acceptable. In this case, a viable, affordable alternative to an internationally marketable product is both culturally and locally acceptable.

Exam Question 6.1

As the Category Manager of a major global bank, write a report to the Marketing Director explaining, with reference to specific examples, why in a global context it is difficult to find a truly global product (June 2001, Question 4)?

Go to www.marketingonline.co.uk or www.bh.com/marketing to access specimen Answers and Senior Examiner's advice for this exam question.

Exam Question 6.2

Choosing any international or global brand of your choice, write briefing notes for the Marketing Director on the role 'culture' plays in global marketing planning. (December 2001, Question 4)

Go to www.marketingonline.co.uk or www.bh.com/marketing to access specimen Answers and Senior Examiner's advice for this exam question.

Conclusions

Any discussion on globalization cannot take place in a vacuum. As you consider this concept of a standardized international approach to marketing and production you need also to bear in mind the customers (Unit 3), the infrastructure within which international trade is carried out (Unit 1) as well as the implications for product policy (Unit 8). It is probably fair to say that, given their choice, most organizations would prefer that they provided a completely standardized global product and marketing programme and would ideally have only one major worldwide centre for production. The financial and human resource economies that such an approach would produce are undeniable. However, the international marketer needs to realize that the world simply is not like this. Apart from a few companies who have truly global markets, most organizations have to come to grips with the fact that the world is still not homogeneous and needs to be catered for on a local basis. Obviously, it is a question of balance. To what extent can we standardize our approaches to overseas markets and to what extent do we have to make modifications in order to achieve customer acceptance and acceptable sales levels in overseas markets? Significant economies can come from standardization but if the standardized product or service is too far from local requirements, sales volumes and revenues may suffer as a result.

In any event, the importance of conducting careful market research (see Unit 3) into the needs and requirements of overseas markets cannot be overemphasized.

Questions

As a check on your understanding of what has been covered in this unit, consider the following questions:

Question 6.2

1. What is meant by 'globalization'?
2. How practical is a strategy of pure globalization?
3. What factors actively promote globalization?
4. What factors will inhibit a globalization strategy?
5. How close to a true global strategy can an organization plan?

Case Studies

You are invited to explore the following websites which give extensive details of truly global companies. Analyse the material and write a mini case study for yourself covering the following points:

1. What are the origins of the organization?
2. How big is the company now?
3. What was the evolutionary path from domestic to global operation?
4. What are the key drivers to the company's global strategy and operations?
5. What global cultural factors have enabled the organization to become a global operator? What cultural factors, if any, are hindering the organization from implementing a truly global operation?
6. How does it act in a socially responsible way and why?

   www.disney.com

   www.un.org

   www.toyota.com

   www.IBM.com

   www.bp.com

Extending knowledge

For a more detailed analysis and explanation of globalization, read:

International Marketing Strategy, I. Doole and R. Lowe, 3rd Edition, Thomson, 2001, Chapter 7, pp. 214–246.

'Managing in a Borderless World', K. Ohmae, *Harvard Business Review*, May/June 1989.

Global Marketing Strategies, J-P. Jeannet and H.D. Hennessey, 5th Edition, Houghton Mifflin, 2001. Chapters 7 and 8, pp. 260–352.

Communicating across Cultures, M. Guirdham, Macmillan Business, 1999.

Summary

In this unit we have seen that globalization is a major force in international marketing strategy. The benefits from a globalized marketing approach are significant and offer major economies from a standardized approach to foreign markets.

There are a number of reasons globalization is coming to the fore and many international marketing variables are stimulating interest in this area. There are also a number of factors which may stand in the way of an organization successfully globalizing its operations, and most of these are concerned with local tastes, requirements and perceptions.

In any event, the organization considering globalization should:

1. Not be dazzled by the rare instances of successful pure globalization
2. Carefully research and understand overseas markets before moving to globalization
3. Look for similarities as well as differences in overseas markets before planning
4. Carefully evaluate the savings to be made from a globalized/standardized approach against the likely loss of sales from not fully meeting local market requirements.

Objectives

This unit is concerned with issues pertaining to managing international business/marketing. The issues covered straddle other complementary ones which are mentioned in a variety of areas in the study guide. In studying the unit you will:

- Recognize that, with the changing nature of international business and customers, the successful company must develop a learning culture

  See syllabus section 2.2.4.

- Recognize that economic transience affects all firms and that strategies need to be developed to cope with change and uncertainty

  See syllabus section 2.2.6.

- Understand the principles involved in controlling in-house and external resources

  See section section 2.2.7.

- Understand that the management and development of global human resource management, planning, training and creating a global mindset are essential prerequisites for success

  See syllabus sections 2.3.6 and 2.3.7. This element is developed in detail in the next unit, 'Managing the International Mix'.

Study guide

This unit is to be read in conjunction with the preceding unit dealing with international planning and is also closely connected with managing the mix and operational implementation.

The international firm – the learning organization

We have discussed on several occasions the fact that today's business is ever increasingly global. Life today for most organizations is fundamentally different from even five years ago. The economic landscape and the accelerated pace of change will ensure that successful organizations have only one option – to be a continuous learning organization. It is believed that continuous learning is *the* sustainable competitive advantage. Virtually everything else is relatively transient. As a consultant of many years' experience it is rare to come across a company that has a genuine strategic sustainable competitive advantage (the exception being specific patents and guaranteed government protection – both increasingly elusive). The outcome of the fundamental changes, dealt with in Unit 1, is that the majority of tomorrow's successful companies will have to think globally just to survive. Business futurologists are of the opinion that the mega changes in business finance and economics taking place today are just a warm-up act and that the corporation of the year 2020 will be largely unrecognized today – indeed many of them have not even been formed.

To compete in this new economic and business scenario companies must learn to both adapt and be flexible in their approach to business. Kenichi Ohmae, the Japanese futurologist, speaks of companies becoming insiders or 'insideration' as he refers to it. Companies need to be operating inside all the major spheres of economic influence and fewer and fewer are located solely in their country of origin. Being operationally involved in the very least the Triad economies is a prerequisite for success. Those companies which ignore the USA and key Asian economies will find themselves at a significant disadvantage. They will simply fail to keep pace with intellectual and technological development, for it is across the Triad that the real competitive edges are created. The Japanese, long considered to be myopic from a diversification standpoint, i.e. concentrating on exporting from the home market, have largely abandoned this stance philosophically as well as from a practical perspective. Many leading edge Japanese corporations now have around 40 per cent plus of their employees outside the home country. They are rapidly becoming insiders everywhere. The advantages from this business strategy are simple:

Companies learn more by learning together!

Learning through cooperation

The trend towards the creation of strategic alliances has been dealt with earlier. What is being discussed here is both internal and external cooperation. Traditionally strategic alliances (external cooperation) have been largely centred around research and development activities and the literature abounds with celebrated examples. Note: students have been advised to prepare their own list of current/recent strategic alliances. Sharing knowledge and information provides considerable leverage to the firms involved which might be summarized as:

- Jointly learning new techniques
- Sharing costs involved
- Reduction of financial risk (technology and research are expensive and there is no guarantee that they will result in universal acceptance)
- Improving and streamlining supplier and distributor value chains
- Forging superior relationships with all parties thus delivering speedier solutions and often creating beachheads for mergers and acquisition.

These factors are equally relevant within international organizations. Knowledge gained in one subsidiary can be leveraged across other international subsidiaries and back to the home operation, if such a thing exists. Motor component suppliers have factories in many countries. I know of one operating in Japan, China, the UK and Mexico with a home base in Germany. It has a vice-president responsible for knowledge transfer whose departmental role is not just concerned with benchmarking the industry's best. He has to ensure that any breakthrough, however small, which happens in any of the international factories, is transferred across all factories speedily bringing increased competitiveness to the entire organization.

Simple rules for creating learning

Rule 1 Eliminate obstacles

Leadership and change don't have to come from the top of the organization but the philosophy does. So start by creating a learning organization by insisting on the removal of unnecessary barriers. No more 'them and us'. Everyone is on the winning side and there are no losers. So if something is known, share it.

Rule 2 Exploit the advantage

To know something different is one thing, to exploit it is another. Create a belief that no matter how small or seemingly insignificant a solution might appear in one division of an international organization, it might have important ramifications in another. Open a web site and encourage exchange of ideas and how they might be exploited commercially. UK organizations are famous for developing new ways/ideas but equally famous for not bringing them to commercial reality, profitably.

Rule 3 Look outside your industry

Remove myopia and examine the changes elsewhere, in other industries, related sectors and overseas markets. Call in universities to come inside your organization. Ask their opinion on change. If necessary talk to eccentrics, individuals who are capable of thinking 'outside the box', those who have rebellious attitudes. You might not want to employ them and they very likely wouldn't want to work for you anyway. But don't ignore them. It may be an apocryphal story but Steve Jobs (founder of Apple) was called in by Rank Xerox to look at some quirky creation. Jobs incidentally worked at Stanford University at the time. What he saw got his mind working and he created computer icons. Maybe Xerox should have hired him?

Rule 4 Understand the company's true competence

No firm can be 'best' at everything. It is frequently the case in multinationals that individual subsidiaries develop separate competencies and know-how. There may be advantages spinning off from this approach but nowadays as firms move along the path to globalization greater benefit can be accrued from leveraging core competences worldwide. Should some international subsidiary discover something special that could be leveraged globally, then it should be done.

Rule 5 Move fast

Change is accelerating in many directions and 'getting to the future first' is rapidly becoming a prerequisite for business success. In real life the tortoise rarely beats the hare.

Relationship Marketing

In unit 5, page 64, and in other parts of the text, reference has been made to 'Relationship Marketing'. Its origins stem from the late 1980s and is attributed to the 'Scandinavian School' with authors like Gronroos and Gummerson. However, it is not an exclusively Scandinavian phenomenon with authors like Christopher, Buttle, Morgan and Hunt of the UK and USA also contributing to the debate. For a detailed reading on the concept see the 'Extending Knowledge' section at the end of this unit.

In a very simple way, Relationship Marketing can be seen as a new Marketing paradigm of the late 80s and early 90s in contrast to the 'Transactional' paradigm with its origins in the 1960's and its emphasis on seeing customers as 'targets' and bombarding them with the '4P's' for both the benefit of the organization and consumer satisfaction. This approach is seen as short term and unsustainable with the advocates of Relationship Marketing preferring the longer term approach of developing a lasting relationship where transactions between buyers and sellers are not seen as one offs, in spite of the mutual satisfaction that they may bring, but capable of mutual continuation. This process can be seen in Figure 7.1

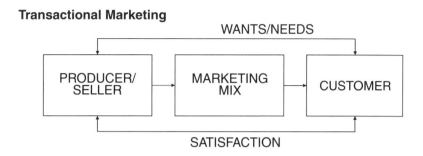

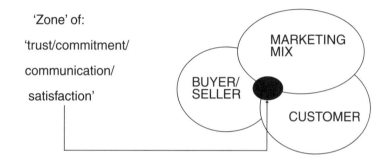

Figure 7.1
Transactional and relationship marketing

In other words, Relationship Marketing is a means of 'getting closer' to the customer through both proactive and reactive marketing.

There has been a lot of recent debate on whether customers actually want to build a relationship with producers/sellers (except in business to business marketing) and whether Relationship Marketing has really been the new marketing paradigm it has been lauded to be. Many financial services providers have seen the growth of the internet as a means to build a 'one to one' relationship with customers and, to some extent, this has been achieved. However, customers have evidenced less than full trust in the internet as a secure medium for doing business with, witness the number of credit card payment frauds over the net recently. Similarly, despite protestations to the contrary, the internet provides marketers with the ideal opportunity for cost cutting rather than the building of customer relationships.

The key success factors in building Relationship Marketing are 'trust', 'commitment'and 'communication'. If trust and commitment can be successfully built, with the appropriate stream of communications, then Relationship Marketing can work well. A good example of this is the company Saga, the conglomerate of services for the over 50's in the UK. Once a pleasant experience has been had with one of the services, Saga are very adept at building further transactions through cross marketing. Should one purchase Saga's car insurance, for example, they then politely enquire if one would like a house insurance quote at the appropriate time. Should the quote be competitive and you take it and you are satisfied with it, then other services are gently introduced. Once happy with the price and benefits of the original car insurance quote, the trust and commitment is being built up via good communications, for the introduction of further products and services.

The Relationship Marketing School has contributed a very powerful complementary approach to the transactional approach to marketing. In an International Marketing context, as described in Unit 1 in the section on 'What is International Marketing', the development of strategic networks and supply chain partners is very important and Relationship Marketing has certainly contributed to a further and deeper understanding of the need for mutual and proactive marketing activity.

Customer relationship management – benefiting from e-business

At various points in the coursebook we have described the growing importance of e-business in international marketing. If the 1990s were about 'precision marketing', i.e. marketing a product or service offer to the customer needs as expressed in Rogers and Pepper's *The One to One Future* then the next decade will see the growing development of customer relationship management (CRM).

CRM is already big business and it is forecast to reach $16.8 billion by 2003 (see Figure 7.2).

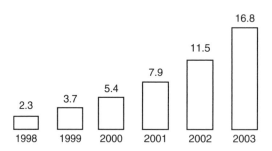

Figure 7.2
Total global CRM revenue 1998-2003 (Source: AMR Research)

The development of CRM is in its infancy – despite growing at 50 per cent per annum – and at this moment it is defined in very broad terms. To some it is precision marketing, to others it is about call centres, to some it is the need to create a 'single, cohesive view' of customers whether they choose to react with the organization in person, by mail, internet or telephone, others focus on the customer database, with CRM seen as the driver for major investment in data warehousing systems.

To leading edge technology corporations CRM is seen as a major driver of future business revenue flows.

It accounts for 40 per cent of revenues at IBM's business intelligence unit, and some forecasters predict that in modern post-industrial countries CRM will employ more persons than farming or education combined (*source:* Datamonitor).

This is all very interesting and will have an impact for many companies (small and large) in their international development but a 'health warning' should be attached. CRM is not applicable or relevant to large areas of the world. For example, Nigeria, Africa's most populous nation with about 122 million residents has around only 50,000 registered websites and is very likely to be more advanced than its neighbours.

In the world of integrated call centres Datamonitor predicts the global market to be $8.5 billion by 2003 and additionally forecasts:

- Global spending on software to support web-enablement will grow six-fold between 1999 and 2003 to reach $1.6 billion
- Software for multimedia call centres (combining voice and data transactions) will grow from $120 million in 1999 to $850 million in 2003

al call centres (with agents networked) will grow steadily. By 2003 there will be 3200
USA and 450 in Europe.

Europe, the distribution of call centre outsourcing in 1999 is as follows:

- ms – 24 per cent.
- Financial services – 20 per cent.
- Consumer products – 16 per cent.
- Technology – 13 per cent.
- Utilities – 10 per cent.
- Travel/leisure – 5 per cent.
- Government – 4 per cent.
- Others – 8 per cent.

Source: Datamonitor 1999

Creating and defending the customer relationship

Here are some basic rules that could guide the process. These, together with other pointers, are
to be found in the *Financial Times*, Mastering Marketing Series, in this case, 28 September 1998.

1. Make learning a priority
   - Constantly carry out pilot tests and in-house scenarios
   - Learn what target customers really value
   - Exploit learning throughout the marketing team
   - Retain key people long enough for them to have a real impact.

2. Engage the entire organization
   - Create and support a learning culture
   - Capitalize on the belief that all parts of the programme (not just marketing) can
     contribute to success.

3. Tighten organizational alignment
   - Success or failure will be directed by the weakest link
   - Scrutinize every element for improvement
   - Pay the team by results measured in terms of retention rather than acquisition of
     customers.

4. Refresh and maintain databases and rewards
   - Once created a database will decline in value. Consider that 20 per cent of US
     households move address every year. Keeping up to date is a tough task yet it is
     very important for, in two and a half years most of your potential customers may
     have disappeared – maybe for good.

Exam Question 7.1

Evaluate the impact and opportunity of 'electronic commerce' developments (e.g.
internet, etc.) on the marketing strategy of a global consulting organization. What are
the potential dangers of electronic commerce? (June 1999, Question 5)

Go to www.marketingonline.co.uk or www.bh.com/marketing to access specimen
Answers and Senior Examiner's advice for this exam question.

The effects of economic transience on global marketing

No firm is an island. It cannot control its destiny. All it can do is to develop a winning formula and keep going. The firm can never win. It has to continually balance its performance to be in some kind of harmony with its environment – suppliers, customers, competitors and the non-business infrastructures. This is not a simple task even in the domestic market. Achieving harmony in the international environment with all the inherent instabilities is almost impossible. Yet companies are required to balance their activities across the boundaries of instability and change (both of a positive and negative nature). The financial implications are dealt with in the appropriate unit and all students of international marketing must be fully aware of the implications of the mega changes such as the economic meltdown in South-East Asian economies in 1997/98; South America in 1998/99; and currently Russia. Right now, the talking point among European economists is the implementation – of the Euro, since its introduction in January 2002, which lost around 11 per cent between its launch in January 1999 and May the same year. Evidence to date shows that some countries are finding they have 'lost value' as the Euro has not gained in value since its introduction. While the smaller exporters can be tossed around on this tempestuous sea, the larger multinationals, while battered, can survive by balancing their subsidiaries on a portfolio analysis, managing transfer pricing, switching production to optimum locations, implementing operational efficiencies, even closing facilities and buying new ones, etc. Multinationals generally operate at the hub of a wide-ranging network or clusters. They generally have long-term relationships with partner organizations. The partners may be suppliers, competitors even (in R&D) and frequently governments. Through these long-term relationships multinationals can leverage power in moments of crisis and instability enabling them to weather the storm although not making them immune to the winds of change.

Managing and controlling in-house and external resources

As firms become more international in their dealings, the management issues multiply. Production, distribution, finance, human resources, operations as well as marketing all take on a heightened significance. For many companies it simply isn't feasible or desirable to conduct all business functions in-house. Back in the 1980s, companies attempted to streamline their organization into strategic business units (SBU) in order to understand better and plan for the future. Today's 'holy grail' is outsourcing with leading corporations focusing their talents and resources on what they describe as core competences and outsourcing just about everything that is a non-essential. The reasons they give for doing this are varied but essentially it comes down to concentrating on delivering the appropriate level of satisfaction/solution to meet the demands of their customers; who literally search the world for the 'best' product, price, technology, delivery and service solution. As no firm can be 'best' at everything it is logical to partner with organizations that are. In this way companies such as Hewett-Packard form solution ventures with Federal Express. HP is among the world's best makers of printers, Fed-ex the leading delivery provider. Such marriages deliver superior customer solutions.

Issues dealing with the management and control of in-house activities internationally are dealt with elsewhere and in great depth in the recommended texts. The management of external resources – outsourcing – is a new addition to the syllabus and is therefore explored in some depth.

Global sourcing and production

The reasons for global (re)sourcing are many. What follows is a list and it is incumbent upon examination candidates to find examples from the current business press that fit the reasons. *The Economist*, *Financial Times* and other quality papers are rich in their examples, practically on a daily/weekly basis.

- Labour rates are often cheaper. Virtually anything that is a process can be outsourced. From the production of Nike shoes to typing up doctor's patient examination notes. Doing a letter in Bangalore costs roughly one thirtieth of the cost in the USA
- Same quality, lower price. India is rapidly becoming the world's number two in software development and production
- Better access to technology, innovation and ideas. Silicone Valley, California is where much of the world's leading-edge IT work is conducted. So make the links and solve your technical problems
- Local market pressures. Either promoted as 'made locally' or, for taxation and tariff reasons, it sometimes pays companies to outsource to foreign markets. The process and creation of a position of insiderization can be enhanced
- Economics of scale is an obvious reason to outsource
- Flexibility and speed of change. In a world of unpredictability it can be a positive disadvantage to have the company's capital tied up in factories especially if the core competence is design, innovation and marketing. For this reason Nike outsource production leaving the company to focus its intellectual capital on its core competence of understanding the needs of customers and designing and marketing appropriate offerings (not simply products).

Of course there are other reasons why companies outsource, e.g. financial and political risks, so this is therefore not the full list.

Advantages conferred from outsourcing

The advantages conferred from outsourcing include:
- The development of collaborative arrangements creating enhanced customer value through synergy
- Lowering the cost for everyone in the value chain
- Superior channel arrangements
- The creation of a partnership as opposed to an adversarial culture and with it mutual bonds of trust where suppliers are wedded to a long-term future and as such can share the risks openly. This is increasingly a source of new product innovation.

Ultimately outsourcing can only be truly effective if it is planned and supported as a long-term partnership function that is geared to delivering on cost, quality, delivery and flexibility. To attempt outsourcing based on short termism, lack of trust, integrity and honesty in terms of the development of strategy invites confusion, unnecessary complications, mistrust and disaster. The message is, do it well or not at all. Understanding the partners, the culture and the society is the key.

Further factors for consideration

Outsourcing has its downside. While exponents cite its virtue, detractors point to the draw-backs. First, outsourcing is not for everyone. It requires knowledge of the implications if anything goes wrong. Second, many believe that outsourcing represents hollowing-out and the loss of skills. It can result in the loss of transferable skills. It can create an atmosphere of hostility in the workforce, i.e. are our jobs next to go? The time and resources required to plan and manage outsourcing cannot be under-estimated. To the customer it is the company that it relates to, not the outsourcing extension. A recent example appeared in *The Times* when a correspondent applied for a BA (British Airways) credit card and was declined on the grounds of having a PO number address, albeit in Aspen, Colorado. On contacting Bob Ayling, the then CEO of BA, whom he knew personally, he was told it would be rectified. Months later and nothing had been done. Communication between BA and whichever outsourced company handled the credit card operation was obviously not of the highest order. The disgruntled customer wrote up his experience in *The Times* with a circulation of one million up-market readers. Be warned!

Exam Question 7.2

As the Marketing Manager of a global retailing chain, contributing to the Board debate on whether to 'make or buy', explain, with examples' how global marketers add value to customers through outsourcing products and services and global partnering. Put your argument in a briefing memo format. (June 2001, Question 6)

Go to www.marketingonline.co.uk or www.bh.com/marketing to access specimen Answers and Senior Examiner's advice for this exam question.

Global human resource management (expatriates – national and global managers)

The topic embracing the role and importance of human resource management has been considered in several sections of the study guide. It comes under people in managing the mix and also under promotion. It is further discussed in the unit dealing with market entry strategy.

Management is essentially about 'getting things done through people'. It's extremely difficult and often demands preoccupation within a domestic context where language, culture and societal frameworks are familiar to all involved. Carrying out a similar task internationally involves a very much more complicated mindset. Yet it has to be accomplished if the international organization is to succeed.

We have considered the different philosophical approaches by international firms:

1. *Ethnocentric* – where the key managers are mainly expatriates and where strong leadership and control are exercised by headquarters.

2. *Polycentric* – where local nationals rule the roost and where decentralization is the order of the day leaving headquarters to set the broad agenda.

3. *Regiocentric* – where a hub and spoke arrangement predominates with leadership coming from within the geographical region, e.g. an Indonesian as general manager of the Malaysian subsidiary with the regional centre established in Singapore headed by an Indian national.

4. *Geocentric* – simply the best person for the job irrespective of nationality.

All four philosophic standpoints have their strengths (and weaknesses). It is equally the case, in reality, that the vast majority of international firms have expatriates in management roles in overseas subsidiaries.

Expatriates

Nearly 80 per cent of medium to large corporations send domestic managers to positions of responsibility overseas. It is therefore an important consideration that organizations get it right, yet sadly the majority of them get it wrong. They may not optimize the opportunity and in doing so lose the business that might have been gained and all too often lose the manager on their return from the mission. Why this is the case is self-evident. Companies underestimate the complexities involved and fail to plan in advance before dispatching managers to overseas posts and then equally fail to rehabilitate them when they return from the 'tour'. Yet having an international management team isn't a luxury these days, it is a necessity. The days when head office knows best and everyone else can do as they are told have vanished. It is incumbent upon modern corporations to train and develop domestic managers to be international in their tasks. Of course the reverse is true in that 'local' managers need to absorb skills and knowledge by widening their international experience.

However, none of this comes cheap. Although estimates vary by country and by industry sector on average it costs two and a half times the domestic equivalent in terms of the package of benefits the expatriate manager would expect to receive. Often it costs a great deal more. In Singapore for example the hire of a suitable house may be £10,000 a month with a further £3,000 per month for car hire (Mercedes E class). This is inflated by school fees, corporate entertainment, membership of relevant clubs, etc. A fully topped-up package might well exceed £250,000 for a regional CEO. With all the expense involved you would think that companies would consider very carefully the process involved in locating and relocating executives. Yet many don't.

Conventional wisdom suggests that many executives return home before their allotted time. Black and Gregerson (*Harvard Business Review*, April–May 1999) state that between 10 and 20 per cent of all US managers sent overseas returned early, almost one third under-performed and 25 per cent of those who completed their tour left their company shortly after returning to headquarters. This represents an enormous wastage, roughly double that of domestic managers.

Getting it right involves three general factors:

1. Make it clear why managers are being sent overseas and set clearly stated objectives, which are usually twofold:
    1. they are sent to leverage and create knowledge or...
    2. they are sent to develop their global leadership skills
    3. although not mutually exclusive executives need to be told what their assignment involves. This avoids disappointed returnees who are frequently not rewarded with enhanced job responsibilities (i.e. they are not sent to develop global leadership skills).
2. Only send executives on an overseas posting if they have cross-cultural capabilities. Superb management technicians will invariably under-perform if they cannot adjust to the culture. Remember our definition of culture is 'the way people do things around here' and our definition of management is 'getting things done through people'
3. The end of the overseas assignment needs to be planned carefully, well in advance. A detailed repatriation programme assists in reintegrating managers to what may have become an unfamiliar, even threatening, environment. At today's pace of change companies are very different places of work over a two to three year period. Settling in again with unfamiliar colleagues, new schools for children, old friends having moved on, can be a daunting experience. Worse still is being undervalued on return and left with a feeling of unfulfilment. Career guidance and planning are very important to avoid losing valuable talent and with it, the loss of the heavy investment in management time and money. All too frequently disaffected managers go to work for the competition. Use and develop the experience and expertise gained by expatriates to build an international marketing team.

Global managers

What has just been said about expatriates is equally applicable to all managers in an international organization. Strengths can be gained from exposing managers to international cultural diversity with the dual aim of creating and leveraging knowledge together with global leadership. There is only a limited point in developing headquarter marketing management with international experience. Top firms nowadays train and develop international managers across all business functions.

Set out below is a checklist for the development of global management:

1. Decide how internationally extensive the organization should be over period. Set down the goals.
2. Decide and plan how this international/global presence is going to be ach should the global presence be built
3. Establish where the optimum cost locations are likely to be over the period. Balance these against quality issues
4. Understand where the value is added in the process of creating and delivering the product or service
5. Decide what to do about the sub-optimal locations
6. Develop a global mindset for the top management team. If you can't, your organization will forever be a follower and not a leader.

The 'people' element in international marketing cannot be underestimated. The next unit in this study guide deals with this in detail. However, it is important to stress that 'people' include internal and external personnel. The preceding sections have dealt with these in some detail in terms of the organization and its employees globally and its partner institutions. There are, however, other 'people' which have to be considered. These include global contractural transaction agencies like market research, advertising and insurance agencies which an organization may have to deal with. Obviously this raises issues concerning cultural diversity but also raises questions relating to differences in service standards, ethical considerations, ways of doing business, etc. A good illustration of this is a global manufacturer who may develop in the UK what is seen as a world class standard of customer service, say for photocopying equipment. Now implementing the same standard of service globally may be very difficult. For example, an independent agent of the global manufacturer in country x may be experiencing difficulties in obtaining foreign currency to purchase parts and may not enforce the same standards of training for its service personnel. In this case, the independent agent may be unable to deliver the set global standard of service. This can cause great resentment amongst customers and damage the original equipment manufacturer's reputation. Cases of this, unfortunately are not uncommon in less developed countries. Other examples may include difficulties in customs clearance and theft in transit. The use, in this case, of reliable and renowned freight forwarders can be an advantage.

The solution to this problem is not easy. Other than making it a condition of contract that the same global standards must apply, enforcing this can be difficult. Activities that can be put in place are:

- Check for reputation
- Making sure that, before an agent is contracted, the terms and conditions on upholding standards are very clear
- Encouraging end users to report any dips in service
- Having 'award' schemes and other incentives
- Regular visits to agents for 'health checks'
- Employing 'mystery shopping' techniques
- Building trust and 'trickle down' encouragement to improve standards
- Initial and recurrent training with, if necessary, shared costs.

Obviously an organization will not be able to apply these to all transactional agencies but adaptions and derivations can be devised to suit. It is well to remember that organizations do not do business with organizations, they do business with people.

Extending knowledge

International Marketing Strategy, I. Doole and R. Lowe, 3rd Edition, Thomson, 2001, Chapter 5, pp. 141–177.

Global Marketing Strategies, J.-P. Jeannet and H.D.Hennessey, 5th Edition, Houghton Mifflin, 2001, Chapter 17, pp. 669–698.

Summary

Successful firms of tomorrow will have to leapfrog the mindset of the domestic organization. Literally thinking global will be one of the crucial management skills. Leadership, vision, flexibility and cross-cultural diversity are prerequisites. The day of the manager with a lifetime's experience in one country only may soon be a thing of the past.

Objectives

International marketing, like domestic marketing, ultimately depends on satisfying customer needs and wants. To do this the organization must use the full range of the marketing mix. Using the 7Ps* mix, this unit, and the next unit, will consider:

Note: The international place policy is dealt with separately in Unit 10, embracing distribution, operational and implementation issues.

- The international product mix

  See syllabus sections 2.2.8 and 2.3.1.

- The international pricing mix

  See syllabus section 2.3.2.

- The international promotion and physical evidence mix

  See syllabus section 2.3.3 and 2.3.6.

- The international people mix

- The international process mix.

See also section 3.4 of the Planning and Control syllabus Diploma paper and the Integrated Marketing Communications syllabus Diploma paper.

Having completed this unit you will be able to:

- Evaluate the factors which drive decisions in the international mix
- Identify the optimum product range through international portfolio analysis
- Apply the tools of international marketing communications to a given set of circumstances
- Develop the physical evidence of international operations
- Discuss the debate on international branding
- Integrate pricing into the other elements of the international marketing mix.

Study guide

International marketing mix management is fundamental to international marketing success. Strategies are only worthwhile if they are implemented.

The marketing mix (implementation) takes up a considerable portion of the syllabus and is an essential reading for the student. All case studies include an implementation element and this section must be studied closely.

This unit cannot be studied alone and it needs to be considered in conjunction with the units on Customers, Globalization and International Planning.

While marketing mix aspects will be key to a number of examination questions, it cannot be the starting point for your understanding of the subject. In marketing, the customer is the natural starting point and product, price place, etc., follow from customer needs. Study of this unit is important but cannot be understood out of context.

International product policy

As you work through this unit remember that product is far more than just the physical product, the technology or the functional features offered to the customer. You will see from Figure 7.2 that the product needs to be considered in deeper terms than just that. The packaging and support services component of physical products and of services are becoming much more important in the competitive environment of the 2000s.

In addition, it has been argued in many papers that the intangible aspects of physical products as well as services are crucial to competitive success. As technology becomes more widespread and cheaper for many organizations to harness, a certain degree of standardization becomes inevitable. If you consider for a moment the case of motor cars, computers, washing machines or bedroom furniture there is little nowadays to choose among the actual functionality of various products. However, the differences perceived by customers in areas such as status, brand, design and styling are key features which lead to the ultimate choice of product or service.

The value chain

Before discussing the international marketing mix it is worth considering the concept of the value chain. The detail of the concept is fully explored in the Planning and Control syllabus of the Diploma, section 3.3.2. Basically the concept involves breaking down the constituent parts of the total chain from inputs supply to inputs conversion to marketing to the end customer into distinct areas where value can be added. Having done this, the marketer can then identify how, using superior technology, service, personnel or other marketing factors he can add value to gain competive advantage. In fact, the marketer may identify that it is better to concentrate on one link in the value chain and do it better than a competitor or an established full chain operator. A good example of this is the computer industry. Giants like IBM and Apple may decide to operate in many sectors of the value chain providing not only the complete range of hardware, but exclusive dealers or agents providing servicing requirements to customers. On the otherhand, Microsoft for example, concentrates on the software section of the value chain only, to great effect.

In international marketing the value chain is an important concept. The international marketer can use the elements of the marketing mix to add value to the customer. Using superior production technology can, for example, make products cheaper, thus creating a possible competitive advantage. Similarly in the service sector, employing more highly trained and knowledgeable personnel, may give the organization a competitive advantage and add value to the end customer. Rolls-Royce, for example, the global aero-engine manufacturer based in the UK, spends some £700 million a year on R & D. This has contributed to its superior product performance enabling it to rise to number 2 in the world's aero-engine manufacturing league and in some cases pushing to number 1.

 This concept of adding value via astute use of elements of the marketing mix is one that you would be advised to learn.

Developing the international product policy

During the discussions of product policy in this unit we will be considering both physical (manufactured) product as well as services. Services differ from physical products in a number of ways. Most importantly:

- Intangibility – we are unable to see, touch, smell or feel services
- Perishability – services cannot be stored and those left unsold today cannot be sold tomorrow
- Heterogeneity – services are very rarely identical from one delivery to the next
- Inseparability – the consumption of the service normally takes place at the same point at which it is created, therefore being inseparable from the source of that service.

(For a more detailed explanation of the nature of services and services marketing c[...]
International Marketing Strategy by Doole and Lowe, or *The Marketing of Services* by [...]
Cowell, Butterworth-Heinemann.)

There are five key areas of analysis in international product management. They include the question of standardization/adaptation – to what extent can or should the international product be standardized for overseas markets? Second is product–promotion mix – how do standardized or adapted products blend with standardized or adapted promotional practices? Third, we will consider the question of image, branding and positioning of products in foreign markets. Fourth, we will describe the special factors influencing packaging decisions in foreign markets. Finally, we will consider the application of portfolio analysis to international product range decisions.

Activity 8.1

Refer back to Unit 4 and the different types of marketing strategy that were described there. In each case can you explain the effects that these will have on international product policy?

Product standardization and adaptation

As we have also seen from our study of globalization the advantages to be gained from a standardized product range marketed throughout the countries of the world are significant. In today's highly competitive environment, savings that can be made in areas of production, research and development and marketing could be a valuable source of competitive advantage to the international organization. On the other hand, there are a number of reasons why a standardized approach to all overseas markets is unlikely to be feasible for all organizations. From Table 8.1 we can see a resume of the arguments made which illustrates the various factors that can be identified as either driving or restraining the organization from a significant move towards a standardized approach to product policy.

Table 8.1 Product standardization	
'Drivers'	**'Restrainers'**
Economies of scale in production	Differing use conditions
Economies of scale in R&D	Government factors
Economies of scale in marketing	Culture and language
Consumer mobility	Local market needs
The 'French'/'American' image	Local tastes
Spread of technology	Company history and operations
Flow of technology	'Not invented here'
Flow in information	
Cost of investment	
Reducing trade barriers	

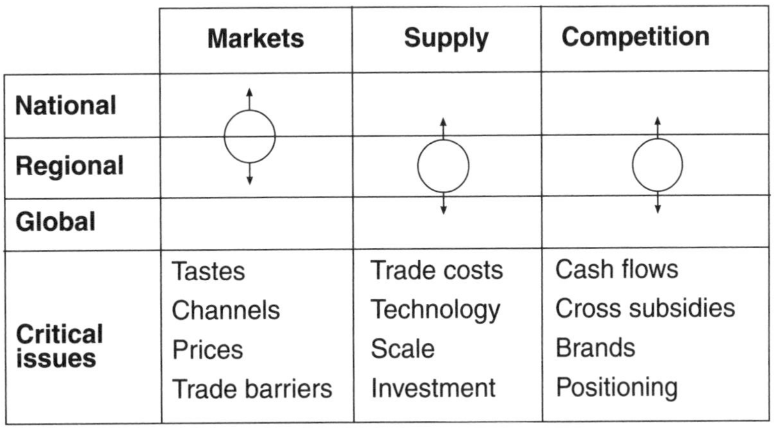

	Markets	Supply	Competition
National			
Regional			
Global			
Critical issues	Tastes Channels Prices Trade barriers	Trade costs Technology Scale Investment	Cash flows Cross subsidies Brands Positioning

Figure 8.1
Factors influencing standardization adaptation

In Figure 8.1 we attempt to identify the situation which faces most organizations operating internationally. Although conditions will vary from one organization to another and from industry to industry, generally the current situation for markets, supply and competition are as follows.

Markets

Most markets generally are between either the national level or the regional level (i.e. EU, LAFTA, NAFTA, etc.). Driven by tastes, available distribution channel, prices and predominant trade barriers, the majority of markets (especially consumer) exist either on a national scale or a regional scale. There is also a marked tendency for polarization here. Some markets by their nature are becoming more national and even sub-national as people search for products and services which reinforce their own local identity. Other markets, meanwhile, are becoming more regional than national in their nature as consumers respond to the significant economies of scale that are available from a standardized product. Examples of these two forms of polarization would include motor cars tending towards the regional market size while snack foods are tending to polarize more towards the national and local market.

Supply

Supply conditions generally tend towards the regional. This is driven by technology, by economies of scale and by the increasing costs of investment. We also see from Figure 8.1 that the supply is being drawn both towards the global, for reasons of scale and ever-increasing investment costs, and towards the local in order to satisfy increasingly individualistic/nationalistic needs.

Activity 8.2

For your organization (or an organization of your choice) can you identify the major trends in markets, supply and competition? What implications does this have for your marketing strategy?

Competition

Competition faced by most organizations is predominantly regional in nature. The larger international and multinational organizations operating globally or in regions such as Europe, North America or the Pacific Rim are the driving force behind most competition in the 2000s. However, there are also signs here of polarization towards competition of a much more local nature as markets driven by a sense of fierce individualism as well as global competition in those industries and industry sectors which are driven by scale and investment decisions.

From this discussion it would seem that the world appears to be facing a polarization of most economic variables. This should not necessarily surprise us and if we consider the international trading environment we can see the two trends being equally successful. The global trend to production of standardized products for worldwide consumption at highly competitive prices is meeting a section of the market's needs. At the same time, organizations and consumers are feeling an increased need to demonstrate their own local or national identity and sense of individuality. As both these trends accelerate, often within the same individual or organization, purchase patterns will continue to polarize.

Product adaptation

Where globalization or standardization of product is not possible, knowing why to adapt products and how products need to be adapted to meet local market requirements is often the key to international marketing success. Before we consider the nature of product adaptation it is worth reminding ourselves of the constituent parts which go to make up the 'product'.

From Figure 8.2 we can see the classical approach to product components. From the customer's point of view the product or service which they eventually decide to purchase is much more than simply the physical product or functional features which go to make up a product or service. Customer choice revolves around the packaging and support service elements of a product offer as much as (if not more than) the actual core component itself. For example, the ultimate choice between two competing brands of washing machine or machine tool can equally be made upon the question of guarantees and after-sales service as they can upon the actual product features inherent within the core product component.

The question of adapting products or services for overseas markets can logically be extended from this understanding of product components (see Figure 8.3). This diagram builds on the previous figure (Figure 8.2) and attempts to identify a number of the characteristics in foreign markets which might possibly drive the producing organization to adapt or modify its total product offer in some way.

To explain the diagram in slightly more detail: a company considering marketing, for example bicycles in a foreign market, might look at the local pressures in the core component and consider that lower local income and isolation from points of service would drive it to 'de-engineer' the basic bicycle marketed in the home market in favour of one which had both less parts to go wrong and also was cheaper to produce. A cosmetics company might look at the packaging component and consider that transportation and distribution networks in the foreign market linked to differences in consumer tastes would drive it to a completely different form of packaging and presentation of the product than they would use to present the products in, for example, the perfume department of a major department store like Selfridges. When considering questions such as adaptation within the context of the CIM examination this diagram produces a useful checklist which can highlight areas of market differences that demand changes or modifications in the basic (domestic) product or service offer.

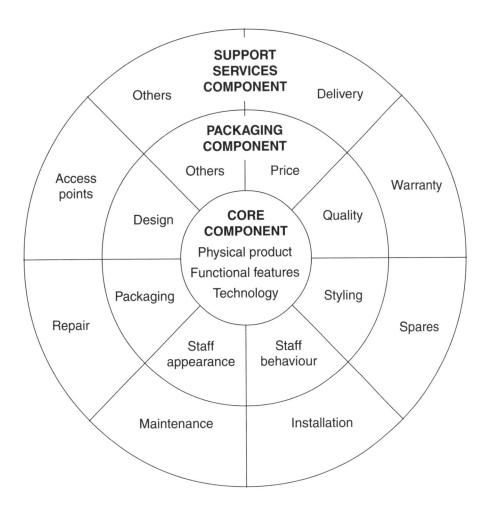

Figure 8.2
Product components

The product–promotion mix

Having decided upon the optimum standardization/adaptation route for the product or service which the organization markets, the next most important (and culturally sensitive) factor to be considered is that of international promotion. Product and promotion go hand in hand in foreign markets and together are able to create or destroy markets in very short order. We have considered above the factors which may drive an organization to standardize or adapt its product range for foreign markets. Equally important is the promotion or the performance promises which the organization makes for its product or service in the target market. As with product decisions, promotion can be either standardized or adapted for foreign markets. Figure 8.4 demonstrates the options available to the organization when it considers blending its product and promotional mix.

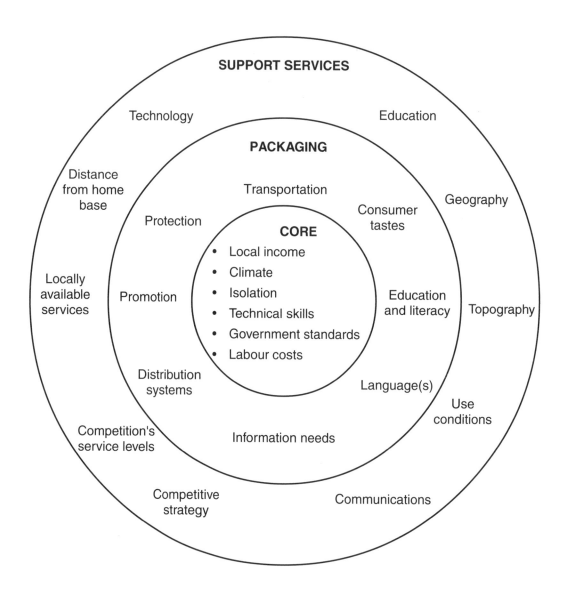

Figure 8.3
Product adaptation

Product

	Standard	Adapt
Standard	Global	Product extension
Adapt	Promotion extension	Dual adaption

Promotion (row label, left side)

Figure 8.4
Product–promotion matrix

We can see from Figure 8.4 that there are four options open to the organization. The top left-hand position is that of standard product and standard promotion to overseas markets producing the global approach (e.g. Intel). Other examples include BP, Gillette, Philips's image campaign, Sony and Bausch and Lomb in Asia. The top right-hand box will be an appropriate strategy for organizations which find they need to adapt or modify the product in order to deliver the same perceived benefits on a market, national or cultural basis. A good example of this approach would be Phileas Fogg snacks or 'After Eight' mints.

Examples of the standard product but adapted advertising include The New Zealand Dairy Board using the brand name 'Fern' in Malaysia and 'Anchor' in Westen Europe for its dairy products and Pepsi's core commercial featuring Tina Turner with local rock stars added according to local markets. An example of both adapted product and adapted promotion is H.J. Heinz. In Greece the ketchup product is shown pouring over pasta and eggs whereas in Japan it is promoted as an ingredient.

Activity 8.3

Choose a product or a product class that you know or use. Try to identify the particular product–promotion mix strategies that are used in various markets. (A good holiday hobby!)

The bottom left-hand box in Figure 8.4 demonstrates the strategy appropriate to an organization that will produce a standardized product for overseas markets but requires an adapted promotions approach, often to support a different position in different foreign markets. An example of this strategy would be that used by bicycle and four-wheel drive vehicle manufacturers. A broadly similar product may be perceived as a transportation or utility item in some markets and a leisure product in others. The final box is that of dual adaptation, where both the product and the promotional approaches are also varied on a market-by-market basis. Many food items fall into this category with products such as sausages, soup and confectionery items being both different physical products and occupying different positions in the customers' perception.

Product positioning

The question of image, branding and positioning is culturally a highly sensitive area and it is true to say that real global brands are still surprisingly rare. Product and company positioning, we should remember, is not something we do to a product – it is something we have to do to the prospect's mind.

A company's 'position' is made up of two interrelated elements – the product's physical or 'objective' attributes (size, shape, colour for example) and its image or 'subjective' attributes, (cool, the best for example) mainly formed through advertising. Without these two elements complementing each other, then disaster may not be far away. For example Virgin's Richard Branson may have the image of the people's hero ('subjective' attributes), reinforced by an excellent airline service, but recent problems with the train part of his organization, i.e. late and/or cancelled services ('objective' attributes) may have somewhat dented his image even though most of the time the problems may not be of his causing. Similarly what makes British Airways claim to be the 'World's Favourite Airline' or Thai Air claims to be as 'Smooth as Silk'? What's more, how is this used to lever their core competencies globally and gain competitive advantage? Do these claims have global appeal? How? Why? Where? You should be able to provide an answer to these important questions.

Extending knowledge

For a more detailed explanation of product positioning and differentiation see the companion coursebook: *Strategic Marketing Management 1999–2000* by Fifield and Gilligan (Butterworth-Heinemann).

Product positioning is a key element to the successful marketing of any organization in any market. The product or company which does not have a clear position in the customer's mind consequently stands for nothing and is rarely able to command more than a simple commodity or utility price. Premium pricing and competitive advantage is largely dependent upon the customer's perception that the product or service on offer is markedly different in some important and relevant way from competitive offers. How can we achieve a credible market position in international markets?

The standardization/adaptation argument raises its head yet again. Depending on the nature of the product it may be possible to achieve a standardized market position in all or most of the international markets in which the company operates. On the other hand, the market characteristics and, most importantly, customer needs and values may be so different as to make a standardized position impossible. Examples of reasonably standardized market positions do exist (for example, Nescafé instant coffee) where the organization attempts to create and maintain a standardized position in all the markets in which it operates. To do this does not necessarily mean that the product itself is standardized. (In fact Nescafé offers a range of blends and roasts in order to achieve a standardized market position.) In other markets this standardized position is just not available. For example, one of the leading Japanese car makers in the North American market is perceived as Honda. If they were able to achieve a standardized position in all markets then one would expect them also to hold the number 1 car position in the Japanese market – where, in fact, they are number 4. What is the reason for this difference? Quite simply if you ask an American, what Honda means he or she will respond with the word 'automobile'. If you ask a Japanese the same question the reply will be 'motorbike'.

Of course, existing, and possibly different, positions in various international markets does not mean that the organization cannot reposition in one or more of its markets to achieve a standardized international position. If this is deemed to be a profitable route for the organization to take then classical strategies on repositioning are appropriate in all international markets.

Branding

Closely linked to market positioning is the question of brands and product image. Brands are the names and personas which we give to our products and services and anything which involves language is liable to cause problems for the international marketer. There are a number of branding strategies and the four most commonly used are:

1. Corporate umbrella branding
2. Family umbrella names
3. Range branding
4. Individual brand names.

(See Doole and Lowe)

We meet the question of standardization/adaptation again in the area of international product and service branding. Should brand names be internationalized to the extent that they can be used everywhere that the company operates? To what extent is such standardization possible or even desirable? As with the discussion about products and the standardization approach, there are many benefits to be achieved from maintaining standard brands across a number of markets. On the other hand, there are a number of reasons why organizations have tried and found this a difficult route to follow. The principal reason why international standardized branding is difficult resides in the area of cultural and linguistic differences between markets. Many brands, brand names, brand marks or brand concepts simply do not travel well and need to be modified in order to gain local market acceptance.

Branding is a major strategic issue and needs to be understood. There is a lengthy debate about how to build in the obvious value of brands on to an organization's balance sheet to give a true representation of the organization's worth. Internationally the issue is accentuated. When Nestlé pays so much money for Rowntree that only 15 per cent of the purchase price is covered by balance sheet assets, we have to ask about the remaining 85 per cent of the purchase price. Major brands like Kit Kat are obviously the answer. It is estimated that the biggest global brand (Coca-Cola) is worth in the region of US$ 44 billion, and that the total value of 'brand equity' globally is US$ 1 trillion – all of it off the balance sheet! Brands have also been described as the world's number 1 intellectual property.

Much of the debate about brand equity centres around how brands are and should be valued. There are a number of methods. The Interbrand method is one of the most popular and attempts to measure a number of dimensions, both hard and soft. Common to all methods, though, is the importance given to what the Interbrand method calls 'reach' or degree of internationalization within the brand. In other words, the more global the brand the greater its value – I think the message is clear. (See also *Strategic Marketing Management 1999–2000* coursebook, Fifield and Gilligan, 1999).

A relatively recent addition to the language of branding is co-branding, the bringing together of two (or more) brands to create greater customer value. The best example of this is Intel whose 'Intel inside' campaign creates alliances with many major PC builders. Co-branding is also used in the airline business designed to add heightened service levels to business travellers making international/global connections, e.g. the creation of One World in March 1999 bringing together British Airways, American Airlines, Cathay Pacific and Qantas to build a seamless solution. The idea is no matter where you are flying simply contact www.oneworldalliance.com if you require service.

Packaging

Packaging for international markets also creates a debate on standardization and to what extent adaptation will be required. As well as the obvious communications and presentation/promotional aspect of packaging which may or may not be standardizable for foreign markets, packaging also needs to consider any transportation and logistics problems. The decisions relating to international packaging might be dependent upon aspects such as:

- *Local distribution considerations* How are products or services distributed within the marketplace? Are there understood and well-configured channels of distribution? Are there middlemen or intermediaries in the channel and what are their requirements? If retail distribution is an important feature, are they served or self-service outlets?
- *Climate* Is the local market subject to extremes or climatic swings? Will there be extremes of heat, cold or humidity which the packaging must withstand?
- *Geographical* How far will products or services have to travel? What is the logistics pattern that must be followed?
- *Economic* What is the predominant economic structure of the target market? To what extent will packaging be used after the primary product has been consumed? (Metal and plastic containers may be put to other, secondary, uses after purchase.)

Activity 8.4

Choose two imported products in your home market. Can you identify those elements of the packaging that have been driven by your local market requirements? What factors in your market have made the changes necessary?

Portfolio analysis

Standard portfolio analysis has been used by a number of international and multinational organizations to help them to identify priorities in their international marketing operations. The four most commonly used methods are the Boston Consulting Group approach, the GEC/McKinsey approach, the Arthur D. Little approach and Product Life Cycle Analysis.

Students will be aware of the current discussion surrounding the use of portfolio analysis and some of the limitations which relate to its application. The same arguments apply to portfolio analysis within the international context as within the domestic marketing situation. Portfolio analyses of various sorts have been used over the past 20 years to consider options for both products and for markets that the organization might address. In international marketing the problems associated with portfolio analysis are probably even greater than in domestic marketing due primarily to the complexity of the data and the analysis required to produce a sensible result. If the evaluation of a portfolio within a single market produces problems then comparing the potential of portfolios across a range of markets becomes even more difficult.

As in domestic marketing, portfolio analysis is a good way of dealing with the product market match in conceptual terms – however, its use as a mathematical model must be viewed as suspect.

Questions

As a check on your understanding of what has been covered in product policy, consider the following questions:

Question 8.1

1. What are the basic 'components' of the product? How will this understanding help your development of international product policy?
2. What are the special aspects of services?
3. What are the five key aspects of international product policy?
4. What are the observed trends in markets, supply and competition?
5. What are the benefits arising from a standardized product approach to international markets?
6. What are the factors which might drive the company to adapt its product offerings to different markets?
7. Explain the meaning and importance of the 'product-promotion' mix?
8. How are products 'positioned' in international markets?
9. How are brands managed in international markets?
10. Can a company develop and maintain a global brand?
11. What affects a company's international packaging decisions?
12. Can portfolio analysis be applied in international product policy? What are the limitations on its use?

International pricing policy

Pricing policy generally is one of the most important yet often least recognized of all the elements of the marketing mix. If we stop to think about it, all the other elements of the marketing mix (both domestic and international) are costs. The only source of profit to the organization comes from revenue, which is in turn dictated by pricing policy. Internationally as well, the way in which an organization fixes and regulates prices in its foreign markets will have a direct effect on profits and profitability.

Establishing the right price for international markets is no easy matter. There are a number of factors involved in the decision process and a number of stages which it may be worth reviewing before the organization sets its price or establishes any precedents in a foreign marketplace. Figure 8.5 shows a logical flow process through the eight major questions which confront the international marketer considering pricing policy. The rest of this unit will consider these steps one by one and the major issues involved in setting the right price.

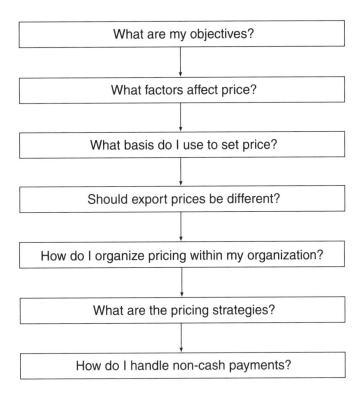

Figure 8.5
Setting the right price

Activity 8.5

How are prices determined in your organization:

- For the domestic market?
- For international markets?

Are they the same or are different methods employed? Why?

Pricing objectives

Before we can decide what price or prices the organization should be charging for its products and services in an overseas market or markets we need to understand clearly the objectives behind the pricing policy that will meet the organization's needs. Some of the objectives which may be relevant to the organization are as follows:

- *Rate of return* Often useful for setting minimum price levels. What is the required internal rate of return that the organization needs to justify the investment in the overseas market in the first instance?
- *Market stabilization* Keeping prices relatively constant and secure over the long term against competition so as not to provoke retaliation
- *Demand-led pricing* Where prices are adjusted to meet changes in customer demand. These may be caused by seasonality or other market changes
- *Competition-led pricing* Where prices are kept closely tagged to the competition and thereby maximize profit and profitability for all players
- *Product differentiation* Pricing the product or service on offer differently to add to the sense and imagery surrounding the differentiated nature of the product
- *Market skimming* Pricing to attract the very top end of any market at premium price levels, thereby also controlling distribution and sales and stocking levels
- *Market penetration* The opposite of market skimming whereby the organization prices to maximize sales and normally operates at relatively low margins
- *Early cash recovery* If the organization, for whatever reasons, requires fast recovery and cash in its balances to price the product or service accordingly to generate a fast response from the marketplace
- *To prevent competitive entry* Often a lower price is used as a barrier to prevent other organizations from entering into a market by making it unprofitable to do so.

Factors affecting prices

The second stage in the pricing process is to identify all those factors that are likely to affect the price that the organization sets. Factors affecting pricing can be broken down into three broad areas as follows:

- *Company and product factors* Would include corporate and marketing objectives as well as the market position held by the organization and the product. The product or service being priced also has a position in the product range and on the life cycle and faces certain types of competition from the market in which it is to be placed. Cost structures within the organization as well as inventory and transportation costs will be major factors which will influence the final price level
- *Market factors* Primarily centred around customers and their expectations and perceptions of the product or service which the organization is offering. Exactly what price level is the market willing to pay? The local market situation in terms of distribution channels and accepted practice in discounting procedures as well as market growth and elasticity of demand will also affect the price potential. The extent to which the organization has had to adapt or modify the product or service and the level to which the market requires service around the core product will also affect cost and will have some influence on pricing
- *Environmental factors* Factors beyond the customer that will affect the prices charged will include competition (their objectives, strategies and relative strengths) as well as government and legislative influences (currency fluctuations, recession, business cycle stage, inflation, etc.).

All these factors will need to be analysed and assessed on a market-by-market basis to produce a pricing policy that is both profitable and acceptable to the local marketplace. At the same time, the international marketer must balance the local requirements and interests against the organization's aspirations on a broader international/global basis. While factors may push price levels in one direction for a given market, a close or neighbouring market may be influenced differently. Although, as we will see later, standardization of prices is not necessarily an objective that the organization should follow, neither should prices in neighbouring or comparative markets be too far out of line.

Setting prices

There are a number of ways in which the organization might decide to fix its prices in its international markets. These are briefly described as follows:

- *Cost based* The process by which prices are based on costs of production (and may include costs of distribution too) and then are normally marked up by a predetermined margin level. The cost-based approach to pricing is likely to produce price levels that appear inconsistent from a customer or market point of view. At the same time, this approach can be useful in order to stimulate a fast return of cash from the marketplace and/or inhibit the entry of the competition into that marketplace.
- *Market based pricing* The customers' willingness to pay. This approach needs to be based on market research or a good understanding of the competition's pricing approach and can be a useful method of extracting the maximum profitability from the marketplace.
- *Competition based pricing* Involves using the competition as a benchmark for fixing prices. Competition either in direct or substitutional form allows the organization to position its product or service relative to the competition in the customers' eyes and to establish a differentiated offer in the competitive range. This method can also be used as a way of creating barriers to entry with low prices preventing competitive entry to particular international markets.

Export pricing

When marketing internationally through exports (from domestic production) there is the question of what price to set relative to the domestic price. Generally, costs are slightly higher for export than for domestic operations because markets are often smaller and transportation costs tend to be higher. Prices could be higher to cover these additional costs but, at the same time, if they are too high they are likely to encourage parallel importing. Another question to consider in export pricing is the currency of quotation. Some organizations quote export prices in domestic currency and some in foreign currency. One of the two parties, the buyer or the seller, will eventually need to carry the transaction risk associated with currency fluctuations in international markets. The longer the period between quotation and invoice payment, the greater that transaction risk will be.

Incoterms

Transportation and insurance costs are also an export consideration adding to the total price of a product. Students need to be familiar with the appropriate terms of reference, free on board (FOB), carriage insurance freight (CIF) and a number of others, so that they fully understand the choices that are available and how they impact on the revenue to the exporting company. The recommended textbooks will contain details. This coursebook is written from the strategic rather than a tactical perspective.

A final point in terms of export pricing, typically of interest to smaller organizations, is the possibility for export credit or payment guarantees offered by many governments throughout the world. Under this method (which in the UK is run by the ECGD), and subject to certain conditions, the governments, in order to promote export sales, offers insurance against non-payment of export orders.

Transfer pricing (internal)

Another pricing question which affects many international and multinational organizations is how to arrange the pricing between two subsidiaries of the same organization in different foreign markets. The three approaches open to the organization in this instance are as follows:

- *At cost* The producing subsidiary supplies to the marketing subsidiary at cost. In this event the producing subsidiary is treated as a cost base and the profits are accumulated at the point-of-sale (the marketing subsidiary)
- *At cost plus* Through this approach the profits are either shared between the two subsidiaries or, at the extreme, superprofits can be made at the producing subsidiary while losses can be incurred at the marketing subsidiary
- *At arms length* Under this approach the producing subsidiary treats the marketing subsidiary as it would any other customer and deals on a straight and strict commercial basis with the other part of the organization.

With transfer pricing international and multinational organizations have some degree of control about where profits are created in the organization as well as how funds might be moved among the various subsidiaries of the business. However, where profits are made is also where taxes are payable, and tax authorities on a worldwide basis are increasingly interested in how multinational organizations arrange pricing between subsidiaries. Penalties for misuse of the transfer pricing system are extremely high in many countries and the multinational organizations have only limited power to manipulate margins and the accumulation of profits on a global scale.

> ### Exam Hint
>
> Questions on pricing and pricing strategy are regular in the examinations. Experience, however, has shown that candidates' grasp of the factors which influence pricing is shaky. Make sure you understand:
>
> - The role of pricing in marketing strategy
> - The special challenges in pricing for international markets.

Pricing strategies

When considering international pricing strategy international marketers have two broad extremes open to them. The organization can attempt to standardize its prices throughout all the markets in which it operates or it can opt to adapt them to local conditions on a market-by-market basis.

The arguments for standardization and for adaptation have been well outlined in the section on product policy. The same arguments apply in terms of pricing policy for international markets.

The optimum approach, as ever, will depend upon the market and the organization's characteristics. Generally, a balance between the two extremes will be the most profitable and most logical route for the organization to follow. Some degree of standardization or conformity on pricing is required, certainly among markets or groups of markets which are geographically close. On the other hand, the number of factors that drive prices are likely to vary to such an extent as to make standardized pricing an impractical proposition for most organizations.

Non-cash payment

In some international marketing situations the case may arise where payment is offered but not in normal cash terms. This is often the case with business from less developed countries (LDCs) and former Eastern bloc markets which may not have access to foreign currency or whose own local currency is not acceptable to the marketing organization. In these instances it is often wiser not simply to discard the transaction out of hand but to look at other still profitable ways of concluding the business. There are two broad areas in which such non-cash payments can be acceptable. These are:

- *Leasing* This can be used as an alternative to straight purchase in markets where currency or capital is simply not available to the purchasing organization. Leasing can be attractive to both the buyer since it enables use of a product or service which otherwise would not be available to them and to the seller since a sale is made and purchase price is staggered (possibly including full service and maintenance) over a longer period of time
- *Counter-trade* This is a term used to cover a range of arrangements where some or all of the payment for the products or service is in the form of other products or services rather than in cash. Estimates vary as to the proportion of world trade which is covered by counter-trade measures but the proportion is significant. Arrangements included under the heading of counter-trade include items such as barter (a straight swap or transfer of goods) through to switch deals often including a third party which disposes of the bartered goods in exchange for currency through to buy-back arrangements whereby some or all of the cost of purchase is paid for through the production generated by the purchase items.

Activity 8.7

In your organization (or one that you know well), how important is non-cash payment? Have offers of non-cash payment been refused in the past? How might a Western company be made aware of the potential for deals of this type?

Although Western marketers have a natural inclination to concentrate on arrangements which involve the transfer of cash, counter-trade should not be ignored. Not only does it open up markets which otherwise would remain closed for many years, it also, surprisingly enough, offers the opportunity for even greater profits than might be achievable through a straightforward cash transaction.

Activity 8.8

Have you heard of the 'Big Mac Index' as a method of assessing and comparing markets? Find out what it is and who might use it.

International marketing and the internet

E-marketing

Let's suppose that e-customers are not cave-dwelling, wired geeks but are people as normal(?) as you and us. Let's also suppose that e-businesses will (eventually) have to make real profits in order to survive. Surprisingly enough, e-marketing and marketing share the same components and challenges:

E-goods/services

Disintermediation is one of the latest buzzwords that seems as if it has been invented by the internet. Disintermediation simply means cutting out the middleman and it has been going on for years – supermarkets cut out the grocery wholesalers thirty years ago and Direct Line started cutting out the insurance broker fifteen years ago. It will always happen where the intermediary stops adding value to the product or service.

The internet can add value in a number of areas and we can expect some changes to the traditional retailing of audio and visual products. In other areas the fight is going to be around more than the convenience of not leaving home! Where the internet could score heavily is by re-defining the categories. Most retail outlets are driven to offer as complete a range as possible within a 'product' category, such as shoes, books or PCs. E-businesses could pull together different product lines under a single lifestyle or market segment – but that would mean thinking in customer rather than product terms.

E-industry

It's that old favourite, what business are we in? Organizations who think they are in the 'e-business', 'internet' or 'web' business are, far from breaking paradigms, falling into the same old traps as the businesses they hope to replace. To recap, the business you are in:

- Is defined by the customer, not the products you sell
- Focuses the organization on needs satisfied (customers)
- Establishes directions for growth
- Establishes boundaries for effort
- Determines real competitors, as opposed to industry 'competitors'
- Establishes the markets to be served, and allows segmentation.

If the e-business thinks that it is in the same business as the traditional business it is trying to replace it will do no more than make the same old mistakes all over again. If it really is an e-revolution, this is where it has to start.

E-market

The e-market is no more than a collective noun for e-customers. E-customers are not a new breed of people previously undiscovered by traditional businesses – they are people who appear to be switching some of their purchasing on-line. E-customers, despite how it might appear from the way that e-businesses are approaching them, are not dumb acceptors of anything that turns up on the web but are very sophisticated buyers – and getting smarter every day.

Despite e-protestations to the contrary, e-customers make decisions based on emotions more often than logic, have their own lives offline and spend much of their time seeking maximum value in what they decide to buy. Maximum value does not mean lowest price – e-customers have already been there, done that offline!

Even more important, e-customers are not all the same. Market segments are alive and well in e-markets as everywhere else. We used to be able to accept the argument that the internet is so 'new' so it would attract mainly 'innovators' and 'early adopters' (innovation diffusion theory) but no longer. Internet penetration figures in Europe, the Far East as well as the USA already show this argument to be false.

E-communications

Now this is an area where e-profits can be soaked up at great speed. New arrivals on the e-scene have discovered that just putting a site up is no good if potential customers don't know where it is. Mainstream advertising is expensive and, apart from the web address, needs to give potential visitors some good reason for going there. Now that's when it starts to fall apart. The recent collapse of the e-retailer boo.com is evidence for this.

Any form of communication, e-communication included, must be integrated if the strategic aim, building the brand, is to be achieved. Integration means consistency. And consistency must be built in to all the e-communications. Not only does on-line and off-line communication needs to be consistent, but this also needs to be consistent with all the other forms of business communications. The product or service marketed, the price, the people involved, the distribution system and the service, surround, all communicate a message – it needs to be the same message.

For a fascinating example of how British Airways uses brand advertising online visit website www.channelseven.com/adinsight/case studies/2000/british.shtml

Questions

As a check on your understanding of what has been covered in pricing, consider the following questions:

Question 8.2

1. How does pricing policy interact with other elements of the marketing mix?
2. What might affect an organization's pricing objectives?
3. What factors affect a final price?
4. How might an organization go about setting the price for its product/service in an international market?
5. How are the domestic and export prices linked?
6. What are the three methods of transfer pricing?
7. What is meant by 'non-cash payment'?
8. Give examples of 'counter-trade'.

International marketing communications and physical evidence policy

Communicating in a multi-country setting is particularly difficult. The process involves dealing with language, culture, political and social constraints and local regulations. Customers differ, so how we address their needs requires careful consideration. Customers rarely buy features, they buy perceived benefits that reflect on their needs, motivations and behaviour. Applying a domestic SRC is of little use in international marketing. The subject of international marketing communication is a challenge.

The management of international marketing communications (Marcom)

Marketing communications (Marcom) is the most culturally sensitive area of international marketing. Cultural barriers abound and the SRC must be avoided.

We have discussed in depth the issues of culture. Perhaps we can redefine it again in simple terms: 'It's the way we do things round here'. Failure to recognize the difference and plan to take account of this will invite disaster. Remember, customers do not buy products but the benefits that accrue from them. These benefits are often mostly intangible. Marcom must ensure that all aspects of communication are compatible with the expectation and desires of the customer. Figure 8.6 indicates the potential 'break' in the flow of communication that can occur due to the cultural environment being different.

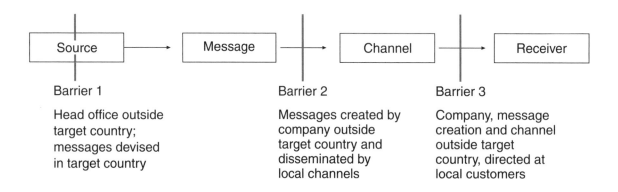

Figure 8.6
Barriers in the multi-country communications process (Source: Jeannet and Hennessey, 1994)

The danger, of course, when faced with cultural barriers is to fall back on one's own SRC not just at the tactical level but at the strategic and management decision level. The textbooks abound with examples and case studies of companies who have failed to accommodate cultural differences in their Marcom planning and execution.

It is quoted that convergence and modernity is minimizing cultural differences and as such fosters the spread of globalization. But even such global giants as Marlboro, Coca-Cola, McDonald's, Sony and others take great care and fine tune their Marcom to meet local requirements. In purist terminology there is no such thing as a global brand, i.e. one that communicates with 'one sight, one sound, one sell'. All companies have some adaptation in their mix.

The international marketing communications mix

It is assumed that the reader is familiar with the tools of Marcom and their roles in persuading customers to buy (Further detail can be obtained from the Integrated Marketing Communications syllabus of the Diploma). As markets differ, so must strategies. The first strategic consideration is whether to adapt a push versus a pull strategy. Figure 8.7 indicates how the tools of Marcom relate to their strategic decision.

Push strategy is less familiar in Westernized countries and is usually employed when:

1. The consumer culture is less 'Westernized'
2. Wages are low and it is cheaper to employ sales people than advertise

A variety of languages, ethnic and racial groupings are present

There is limited media availability

Channels are short and direct

6. The culture dictates its use (e.g. business etiquette)

7. The market is varied, i.e. split between urban and rural.

Pull strategy is familiar to the UK audience and is used when:

1. Advertising has great leverage in the consumer culture

2. There is wide media choice together with the wide availability of other Marcom tools

3. Marcom budgets are high

4. Self-service predominates, i.e. supermarket culture

5. The trade is influenced by advertising.

Figure 8.7
International and global promotion strategies (Source: Jeanette and Hennessy, 1994)

Profile strategy is also an important consideration as many international companies need to create a corporate identity that takes account of the needs of its international stakeholders and also positions the company within its international community. For example, having a single national identity, e.g. being seen as German, French, American, etc., versus being positioned as nationality-less, i.e. with no national allegiance or even being positioned as an insider (to quote Kenichi Ohmae). Whatever the choice, organizations are bound by their identity; it's rather like a badge, the company can choose its own badge or select it's shape, colours, etc., but then it needs to stand by it or risk confusing stakeholders ranging from customers, suppliers, distributors, management and workers through to national and international governments and pressure groups.

Having decided the appropriate Marcom strategy, push or pull and profile strategy, the next decision is which Marcom tools are appropriate to the task and what difficulties arise in the international sphere.

Personal selling

This generally forms the major thrust in international Marcom when:

- *Wages are low* Mitsubishi's Thailand subsidiary selling mainly air-conditioning units has 80 sales people in Bangkok. Philip Morris in Venezuela employs 300 sales people and assistants.

143

- *Linguistic pluralism exists* (multi-language) There are two points to be made, contradictory in essence. The first is that there is a trend to spoken English in business-to-business markets. The second and more important point is that knowledge and understanding of the local language is essential. Never forget, it is the buyer who chooses the language, not the seller. In situations where linguistic pluralization exists (e.g. India) it is essential that personal selling plays a major role in Marcom – particularly when it is also the case that literacy is low and alternative Marcom tools are not relevant in the situation.
- *Business etiquette* Success in selling can only be achieved if there is a relationship between buyer and seller. Few products are so unique that there are no alternatives or substitutes. Understanding and relating to the buyer's culture is a prerequisite of making the sale. Consider some examples. Lateness is inexcusable in Hong Kong – but expected in India; the performance of business introductions in Japan with the elaborate ritual of exchanging business cards; the banquets and frequent toasts in China; the lengthy process of familiarization between buyer and seller in Japan. These and many other examples make it clear that Western etiquette is at odds with many cultures. Even in Europe business etiquette varies considerably, e.g. meetings start early morning in northern Europe, not so in southern Europe. Incidentally, whoever invented breakfast meetings?

Negotiation strategies

Following on, it is apparent that negotiations and bargaining varies by culture. The Americans prefer confrontation with short exchanges and early decisions on the big issues leaving the details to later or to less senior management. The Japanese and the Chinese take the opposite view: great attention to detail, consensus within the group, long protracted negotiations. Before entering negotiations it is essential to understand the mindset of the other party. Being unprepared is a guarantee of failure. Other considerations are also important. For example:

- Location and space – where are the negotiations being held, how big is the room/office, seating arrangements (too close or not close enough)?
- Friendship – is it important to know your customer in terms of their family details?
- Agreements – are these rigid or flexible? (The Americans prefer rigid agreements, the Greek ones that are open to some interpretation and flexibility.)

Staffing the sales force

Increasingly, the trend is towards using local employees as opposed to expatriates. They are closer to the customers in culture and behaviour. They allow the company to position itself as an 'insider', reducing the risk of conveying a feeling of cultural imperialism. They subvert local restrictions on employing non-nationals. However, there are occasions when 'the person from HQ' syndrome still has a value.

Training or deployment of expatriates

Besides basic training in the PEST factors relating to a particular country it is sensible for the individual to acquire at least a basic understanding of the language. Having done that, an 'immersion' in the local culture prior to taking up a post is equally important. Toyne and Walters (1993) outline a programme shown in Table 8.2.

There is often the knock-on effect of how to deploy the expatriate sales person after the period of overseas activity and reintegrating him or her back into the company. Additionally, sending an expatriate overseas is increasingly expensive. Dependent on the 'attractiveness' of the location and the 'local' cost of living, it costs upwards of three times domestic salary to deploy someone overseas. The 'total' cost of employing a salesperson within the UK is currently put at around £60,000. Transferring the person overseas could easily exceed £150,000 p.a. and in some cases exceed £250,000 p.a.

Table 8.2 Approaches to implementation	
Initial training	
Length of training	Less than one week
Main objectives	Knowledge of key country facts and key cultural differences; some words of the (main) country language
Training activities	Area briefings; cultural briefings; distance-learning kits of books, video and audio tapes; survival language training
Location and timing	Before departure to assigned country
Follow-up training	
Length of training	One to four weeks
Main objectives	Development of a more sophisticated knowledge of culture and language; attitudes and beliefs need to be considered and perhaps adjusted
Training activities	Cultural assimilation training; role playing; handling critical incidents; case studies; stress-reduction training; moderate language training
Location and timing	Preferably before departure to the assigned country
Immersion training	
Length of training	More than one month
Main objectives	To develop appropriate competencies to manage in a culturally sensitive way and be functionally efficient and effective
Training activities	Assessment centre; field experiences; simulations; sensitivity training; extensive language training
Location and timing	In the assigned country during the work assignment, preferably front-load the activities
Source: Toyne and Walters (1993)	

Recruitment, training, motivation – control of local sales force

The employment of a local sales force implies a single country and maybe even a single culture sales force. Briefly, the critical issues are:

- *Recruitment* Finding suitable sales representatives may be problematical, e.g. where qualified candidates are in short supply or because of the low status associated with selling. Selling may conflict with the culture. Local requirements may favour certain ethnic groups (not suited to selling characteristics). Tribal differences may forbid cross-cultural selling.
- *Training* Once trained loyalty may diminish if the culture is entrepreneurial or, alternatively staff may be 'head-hunted'. Who does the training? Are the trainers acculturalized with both company culture and local culture? Training of this nature is expensive in time and money.

- *Motivation* This may be more of a challenge than in the domestic market where money is the appropriate method. Titles, overseas trips, the size of office, entertainment allowances may all improve self-image which may be more important than monetary rewards, especially where selling is not held in high esteem.
- *Control and evaluation* Utilizing the commission method of reward control is easier than using straight salary. But the conventional rules of sales territory, call frequencies, quotas and strict reporting procedures may have little effect in some situations. Freedom to negotiate (failure means loss of face) may be paramount. Comparison among the sales team may also be culturally negative. So the conventional methods may well require modification although those basic principles should apply.

Further discussion on the 'people' element is given in the next unit. In addition, an examination question at the end of Unit 8, is a very useful practice for the examination.

Personal selling through intermediaries

Many companies sell indirect, via their distributors or licensees. Success increases if they think of the distributor's sales force as their own, keeping them motivated, abreast of domestic/global developments within the organization, mailing them regularly with information, involving them in the company, making them feel part of a far bigger organization, rewarding them as part of the organization. Run a sales conference for them. Invite successful sales persons to a pan-distributors conference. Make them feel important – they are important!

Government sponsored trade missions

The DTI regularly sponsors trade missions for which there is financial support as well as technical and other advisory services. This is a vitally important avenue for selling overseas and is particularly relevant to the smaller firms. The DTI publishes a monthly update on what is available and when. It is worth recording that in 1994 the US government supported export promotion to the tune of 25 cents for every $1000 of GDP (Source: US Department of Commerce). France came second with approximately 18 cents. Japan spent over 12 cents while the UK spent less then 3 cents. What is more, over 20 per cent of UK diplomats abroad are engaged in full-time commercial work.

International trade fairs

These can be generalized or industry-specific and over 1500 international trade fairs occur annually. They play an important role in bringing buyers and sellers together in a way that would normally not be feasible – particularly for the 'missionary' firm wishing to enter a sub-continent or a region. The Hanover Fair, held annually, attracts 5000 exhibitors from around the world. Its origins were to make the link between East and West Europe but its scope and attractiveness is now global.

Trade fairs have many advantages:

- There is the interface between buyers and sellers
- Potential licensees or joint-venture partners may be discovered
- Products can be tested for interest
- Competitors' activities can be assessed
- They may be the only point of contact between buyers and sellers especially with former Communist bloc countries
- They are ideal for business-to-business organizations who often concentrate their Marcom budget around trade fairs
- Sometimes government assistance is available to fund the exercise. Contact the DTI for advice
- As such, trade fairs require careful planning, specialist advice and involvement, especially in language interpretation.

Consortium selling

This is usually associated with large-scale projects (airports, hospitals, hydroelectric plants, etc.). Partner selection is the crucial point here as is good to excellent relations with the host government.

Sales promotion

This is more common ground and most of us have familiarity with this area of Marcom. But beware, it is very culturally loaded. Sales promotions have a local focus both in terms of the offer and also from a legal perspective:

- *The offer* Airmiles are a great success in the UK but may have no relevance in most of Africa. Prosperity statuettes are popular in Chinese culture but would they work in the UK?
- *Cooperation from intermediaries* Retailers may be adept at processing coupons, handling oddly shaped premiums, creating displays, etc. – or they may not. Assuming that a French pharmacist is the same as a UK chemist would be a mistake. A country with small retailers may be difficult to contact (no phone, poor or non-existent postal service) and difficult to control.
- *Regulations* Laws relating to sales promotion differ virtually everywhere. The UK and the USA, for example, have few restrictions, other countries (e.g. Germany, Sweden, Japan) have many. What you can offer, where, when, how depends on the laws of each country. As of this moment there is no agreement within the 15 members of the EU. Table 8.3 shows the European practice.
- *Bribery* Again a cultural reference – the way we do things round here! It is difficult and presumptuous to comment on practices in a specific country, simply to say corporate hospitality is an important customer motivator that while bribery is a 'taboo' in the UK.

Getting it wrong on the international sales promotion front can have implications more severe than the Hoover debacle of the early 1990s in the UK, when several executives lost their jobs in a miscalculated promotion. Pepsi-Cola mounted a lottery promotion in the Philippines but it announced a wrong winning number resulting in 800,000 families demanding the $40,000 prize – that's a 32 thousand million dollar pay out! In trying to back out Pepsi found its offices fire-bombed and the executives escorted to safety to the USA accompanied to the airport by an armoured guard.

Table 8.3 Does you does or does you don't . . . ?

	UK	IRL	Spa	Ger	F	Den	Bel	NL	POL	Ita	Gre	Lux	Aus	Fin	Nor	Swe	Swi	Rus	Hun	Cz
On-pack price cut	Y	Y	Y	Y	Y	Y	Y	Y	Y	Y	Y	Y	Y	Y	Y	Y	Y	Y	Y	Y
Branded offers	Y	Y	Y	?	Y	?	N	Y	Y	Y	Y	N	?	?	?	?	N	Y	Y	Y
In-pack premiums	Y	Y	Y	?	?	?	Y	?	Y	Y	Y	N	?	Y	N	?	N	Y	Y	Y
Multi-buy offers	Y	Y	Y	?	Y	?	?	Y	Y	Y	Y	N	?	?	Y	?	N	?	Y	Y

Extra product	Y	Y	Y	?	Y	Y	?	?	Y	Y	Y	Y	?	Y	?	?	?	Y	Y	Y
Free product	Y	Y	Y	Y	Y	Y	?	Y	Y	Y	Y	Y	Y	Y	Y	Y	Y	Y	Y	Y
Re-use product	Y	Y	Y	Y	Y	Y	Y	Y	Y	Y	Y	Y	?	Y	Y	Y	Y	Y	Y	Y
Free mail-ins	Y	Y	Y	N	Y	?	Y	Y	Y	Y	Y	?	N	Y	Y	N	N	Y	Y	Y
With-purchase	Y	Y	Y	?	Y	?	?	?	Y	Y	Y	N	?	Y	?	?	N	Y	Y	Y
X-product offers	Y	Y	Y	?	Y	?	N	?	Y	Y	Y	N	?	?	N	?	N	Y	Y	Y
Collector devices	Y	Y	Y	?	?	?	?	?	Y	Y	Y	N	N	?	N	N	N	Y	Y	Y
Competitions	Y	Y	Y	?	?	?	Y	?	Y	Y	Y	?	?	Y	?	Y	Y	Y	Y	Y
Self-liquidators	Y	Y	Y	Y	Y	Y	Y	?	Y	Y	Y	N	Y	Y	Y	Y	N	Y	Y	Y
Free draws	Y	Y	Y	N	Y	N	N	N	Y	Y	Y	N	N	Y	N	N	N	Y	?	Y
Shareouts	Y	Y	Y	N	?	N	N	N	Y	?	Y	N	N	?	?	N	N	Y	Y	Y
Sweep/lottery	Y	?	?	?	?	N	?	?	?	?	?	N	?	Y	N	N	N	Y	?	?
Cash-off vouchers	Y	Y	Y	N	Y	?	Y	Y	Y	?	Y	?	?	?	N	?	N	Y	Y	Y
Cash-off purchase	Y	Y	Y	N	Y	N	Y	Y	Y	?	Y	N	N	?	N	N	N	Y	Y	Y
Cash back	Y	Y	Y	?	Y	Y	Y	Y	Y	N	Y	N	?	?	?	Y	N	Y	Y	Y
In-store demos	Y	Y	Y	Y	Y	Y	Y	Y	Y	Y	Y	Y	Y	Y	Y	Y	Y	Y	?	Y

Y permitted, N not permitted, ? may be permitted with certain conditions

Source: Institute of Sales Promotion

Sponsorship

This is growing in importance on the international front as global sports events proliferate. Coca-Cola, Mars, Gillette, Nike and other transnational organizations are busy building international awareness and identities via events such as the Olympic Games, World Cup Football, world tennis and golf, etc. Global media and communication will greatly expand and accelerate this trend – but it is only for the few companies that are capable of capturing mass-market international customers. Sponsorship is nowadays considered to be very important globally.

Activity 8.10

You should develop examples of local, regional and global sponsorship in anticipation of examination questions in this area.

Direct marketing/database marketing

This is well established in Western cultures and growing in importance. It is also expanding in countries like Hong Kong and Singapore – but has made, as yet, little impact in Eastern Europe and South America, most of Asia or Africa. It is culturally bound and limited by the dynamics of communication and distribution. Additionally, it is constrained by legislation, playing a low key role in Germany, for example.

Telemarketing, like direct marketing is booming in the USA, growing in the UK but constrained for similar reasons elsewhere, particularly those of infrastructure. Having said that, 0800 marketing looks like being one of the major Marcom tools of the 1990s. Colleagues of mine regularly phone the USA to order computer equipment, pay by credit card and get delivery within 2 weeks. Dell computers have their pan-European help-line based in Ireland contacted by 0800 local rate calls and ICL's equivalent is in Delhi.

Door-to-door marketing is again dependent on the cultural reference. The concept is not well received everywhere and Amway and Tupper Ware are hardly household names in every country. However, it is well received in Japan where even stocks and shares are sold door to door – and incidentally the technique has a place in the selling of motor cars. It was suggested that one of the reasons the Japanese stock market bounced back from a major fall in 1987 was the confidence gained from door-to-door sales persons exhorting customers to 'buy now, shares are cheap'!

Direct mail again is growing. It is increasingly sophisticated in its targeting and its creative delivery but again is limited in its development by cultural inhibitions and infrastructure. Recently Fiat had to apologize publicly in Spain for offence caused by a direct mail letter sent to females implying a romantic affair. It was to launch a new car but many were offended by its flirtatious tone.

Activity 8.11

Can you think of any instance of receiving any direct marketing communication from overseas? Will a fair proportion of the material you receive be postmarked Amsterdam? Can you explain why?

Public relations

Strictly speaking, the remit of PR extends beyond the scope of marketing to embrace corporate issues. Positioning the company within the host country is a corporate task. Being seen as an 'insider' is regarded as increasingly important – political links, employee relations and communicating with the wide spectrum of target markets such as the media, influencers, the general public, financial markets, local community, etc. The list is extensive. Foreign firms have a particularly sensitive role to consider in portraying themselves. We do not propose to cover the range of PR tactics but simply state the importance of PR in marketing the organization in overseas markets.

On a more tactical level (i.e. product level marketing) PR can be important where the market is both sophisticated or the opposite. In sophisticated Western markets PR agencies are employed in familiar terms of reference. In the case of developing markets PR is most important in spreading the message by word of mouth. Travelling exhibitions visiting small towns and villages, staging plays, sponsored by company X are frequently employed. In such an environment word-of-mouth communication has high believability.

The development and management of international advertising

This is by far the most culturally sensitive of Marcom tools. Correspondingly no other aspect of international Marcom has been examined so critically. The textbooks abound with examples of international advertising misinterpreted and misused.

International advertising

Putting it simply, any advertisement is 'a message sent in code'. It is encoded by the sender and decoded by the receiver. Some messages are easy to decode (e.g. 'Harrod's Sale Starts Friday'!). Others are complex. But each message is designed to appeal to a targeted group and is invariably surrounded by its cultural reference. Since culture differs by country (and frequently within countries), decoding the message internationally becomes more difficult, is wrongly decoded or is irrelevant. Try explaining a Silk Cut cigarette advertisement to anyone who isn't British. So it is hardly surprising that sometimes controversy rages over international advertising. Perhaps Benetton is a good example here. It has variously offended cultural, ethnic and racial norms in several countries – occasionally its advertisements have been 'pulled' from a market. However, it is Benetton's aim to shock and to challenge accepted wisdom – and in this they have succeeded. Their message is probably 'if you're a non-traditionalist and a mould breaker by nature then Benetton reflects your mood'. Awareness of the campaign and the company is extremely high in all the countries it operates and, to date, sales appear to have benefited from the campaign. Other companies have not been so lucky.

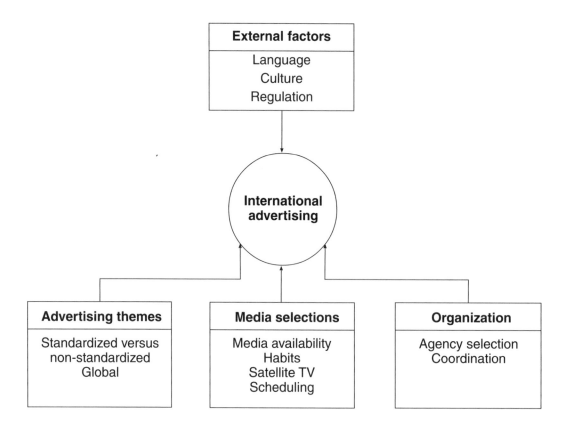

Figure 8.8
International and global advertising Source: Jeannet and Hennessey, 1994

So the three central issues in developing international advertising are:

- *Message* What do we need to change in our advertising (from our domestic campaign) in order that foreign customers can decode the message? Alternatively, do we need to construct a totally different message?
- *Media* Having solved that specific question we have then to decide what is the appropriate medium to communicate the message.
- *Control* Finally, will we coordinate the various activities across countries?

Influence of external factors (culture, language and regulation)

Culture

It is apparent to all that culture is the most difficult aspect to master. The question 'What is culture?' has already been dealt with in Unit 2 together with the pitfalls that surround it. The article from *The Times* encapsulates the influence of culture on advertising in Russia.

Ronald McDonald is not liked in Japan. His 'white' face is synonymous with death – white being the funereal colour in most of the Far East.

Perhaps a major faux pas of the late 1990s was Benetton's highly controversial advertising involving AIDS victims and, in a later campaign, body parts. In the USA the AIDS advertisements were not that well accepted, resulting in some Benetton franchisees refusing to sell the products. Benetton's attempts to raise social issues were not seen as a retailing function!

Language

Pepsi-Cola's campaign of 'Come alive with Pepsi' translated into 'Pepsi will bring your relatives back from the grave' is only one of many faux pas. The critical factor here is to transpose the language, not simply translate it. The textbooks abound with examples. The slogan 'Hertz puts you in the driving seat' can mean you are a chauffeur rather than a go-ahead business person.

Regulation

Each country has its own rules, laws and codes of practice. The Marlboro cowboy cannot run in the UK. There is a ban on cigarette advertising in France. What you can say, when you can say it, where you can say it and how you can say it varies across national boundaries. Muslim countries forbid campaigns showing scantily clad females or consumption of alcohol (although this varies by country). Advertising to children is another culturally sensitive area. Some countries do not allow commercials concerned with 'violent' toys and Power Rangers have been banished from Swedish television. Others forbid the use of children in commercials; others permit their employment but restrict them to certain categories of products. The list is formidable. Even now the EU has no harmonization proposals in place.

The role of advertising in society

Although a sub-sector of culture, governments occasionally take a standpoint on this issue. Recently Singapore and Malaysia have declared their opposition to advertising campaigns that are not consistent with the culture of the country – banning campaigns they consider excessively detrimental to the development of 'good behaviour characteristics' particularly among the young and adolescent. Good behaviour is defined as respectful to parents, religious values and authority.

Frequently the tone of voice of advertising reflects the culture of the society. German advertising is far more matter of fact and informative than its UK equivalent which relies more on humour. For the record, the most 'subtle' campaigns come from Japan, where talking about the product is considered bad taste. (For further elaboration on this point you should refer to textbooks commenting on low-context and high-context cultures.)

Insight – 'Fifteen years ago there were no adverts and no products to advertise. A soft drink was a soft drink and there was only one word for it – water'

Happy milkmaids, fields of corn, golden light and lots of old men vaguely modelled on Leo Tolstoy. This is the surreal image of Russia presented in television ads. Quite how anybody expects people who actually live here to believe that there are robust, rosy-cheeked girls in embroidered shirts happily slopping milk from one pail to the next in some pastoral idyll outside the ring road, I cannot imagine.

Fifteen years ago there was none of this drivel. No adverts, no products to advertise, no spin. Cheese was cheese (in fact there were two sorts – yellow and white), and a soft drink was a soft drink. There was only one word for it – water. Anything nonalcoholic came under this name. You knew where you were.

Then, in 1990, a billboard went up in Pushkin Square. It was huge. On it was a little line-drawing of a man holding a can. The caption, a ludicrously literal translation of the English, read: '7UP. More a jar of water than a way of life.' People stood before it, squinting up in a desperate attempt to extract meaning. This was the start of advertising in Russia.

For at least two years, direct translations of foreign advertisements baffled the Russian populace. 'Bounty – the enjoyment of paradise' did not disclose that there was something to eat beyond the palm-tree wrapper and not a sex aid, as the words suggested. But eventually the economic colonists got the hang of things and started running faintly 1950s style ads of the 'buy this, it does this and is better than that' type. This went down much better and Russians began to believe that there were differences between cans of drink, and the ways of life that went with them. They were not quite as convinced as their Western counterparts, perhaps – Russians in general have a more finely

developed sense of irony than we do – but they managed to have a Coke versus Pepsi war nonetheless.

Today, however, it's a new ball game. While the nightmarish 'Papa? Nicole!' might not yet be appreciated, Westernstyle coffee ads are. Nowadays, the idea is to show affluent Russians enjoying the finer things in life. There is a fantastic one in which a girl lets a waiting lover leave messages asking where she is, as she enjoys her delicious cup of coffee in a faintly sexual way.

The thing is, where is she? She cannot be shown in some awful Brezhnev high-rise, but the beautiful pre-Revolutionary apartments here are not yet fashionable because old people are still dying in them. So this gorgeous woman lives in a ground-floor place that overlooks a forest and is always bathed in golden light. If by some amazing chance such a place exists, she would need bars on the windows and an armed guard nearby.

But best of all, there are now Russian companies running sophisticated ad campaigns. The trouble is, they have a Russian product to sell to Russians. This means that they cannot use beautiful Russian youngsters, looking Westernized and standing in a basketball court saying 'I can chew it all day and it never loses its taste', because that is still selling the West to Russia. They have to sell Russia.

The results are hilarious. This surreal twilight zone country has emerged – happy peasants in fields of gold meet affluent new Russians with cars and country houses. The most toe-curling of these involves a little boy on in-line skates, gliding along a pristine riverbank (no such thing around these parts and anyway, he would fall down a pothole in the pavement and do himself an injury), hand in hand with his grandpa. I think the boy is wearing a Walkman around his neck and if not, he ought to be.

Grandpa has a long, grey beard and is wearing a belted peasant shirt and shoes made out of reeds. Presumably his son eschewed his simple way of life and became a contract killer or similar (in-line skates are expensive). Anyway, Grandpa is droning on about how the cathedrals are the heart of Russia (how he came out of Communism looking so well with such stringent religious beliefs is anyone's guess). The boy looks convinced.

Source: Anna Bundy (1999), The Times, April

The strangest, though, is *Milaya Mila* (sweet Lyudmilla), a pretty, buxom mother who goes out into the pale morning light, skips through the dew to her healthy, happy cows and comes home with pails of fresh milk for her eager, early-rising family.

What is so interesting about all these ads is that, without exception, they carefully omit the past 75 years. It is as though Russia leapt straight from Tolstoyan paradise to American dream without a glitch. Would that were true – and perhaps, with a carton of milk, a stick of chewing gum and an aromatic cup of coffee, it might just be.

comment@the-times.co.uk

Advertising themes (standard versus non-standard)

The advantage of a standardized theme is obvious. It gives economies of scale and allows the creation of pan-regional or even global brands. But such campaigns are rare. The first requirement is a standardized product (or virtually standardized) with a standardized name. Such do exist (Kodak, Fuji, BMW). But the facts are that these are exceptions, not the rule, and there are few examples of successful standardized themes on the contextual content of the advertisement. The actors, their clothes, the situation in which the advertisement is set are all culturally loaded and open to different decoding. One successful campaign is for 7-Up, a soft drink which utilizes a certain character Fido-Dido. The product is always pronounced in English and the character remains unchanged – appealing to the 'one-world youth culture'. Campaigns for major international brands invariably differ by country/region (e.g. Levi have adjusted its 'Launderette' and 'Refrigerator' advertisement to meet the cultural requirement). However, what is important is that the theme of youth remains constant – it is the interpretation of it that varies (i.e. decoding of the message is unchanged). The danger of going down the route of a standardized campaign, creating advertising that has 'some' meaning in every country, is that it motivates no-one anywhere. Euro advertising campaigns occasionally appear on UK television mainly to the annoyance of all. At the very least, they appear irrelevant. See if you can identify some.

Exam Hint

Create examples of companies/products/services adopting a global positioning. You will find this of invaluable assistance when you're in the examination room. Examples of practical knowledge are always rewarded. But do think beyond Coca-Cola, please!

There is relatively little global advertising, although global positioning is on the increase. Recognition of the growing importance and significance of global positioning is critical both from a professional and a student perspective. Coca-Cola's approach is to make a 'batch' of commercials which portray a similar positioning of the brand image and then discuss with country managers which commercials are most appropriate to their culture and environment. McDonald's adopt a broadly similar approach, taking a global position. Within Europe, Nescafés positioned as the premier instant coffee with 'best beans, best blend, best taste' and uses as its icon the red mug. The transposition of 'best, best, best' is left to local marketers as coffee and instant coffee specifically has vastly different perceptions across the European marketplace.

Summarizing, standardized advertising requires similar consumers, with similar lifestyles and aspirations seeking similar rewards. Such clusters exist, e.g. business travellers, senior business executives, etc., and it often seems that the inhabitants of Upper East Side, Manhattan have more in common with their counterparts in Kensington, London than they do with their neighbours a block away. How else would you explain the success of Hugo Boss suits, Rolex watches and other designer type products, Armani, Versace, etc.?

Media selection (media availability, satellite TV, scheduling)

Media availability

Setting aside regulations on advertising themes, the choice of media to carry messages varies enormously. The UK has abundant choice in newsprint with six or seven national newspapers. Nowhere else has this breadth of choice. Newsprint in most European countries is largely regional, although Germany has the Continent's biggest circulation paper with *Bild Zeitung*, selling about 5 million copies per day. Circulation for the No. 2 newspaper *FAZ* is little more than 500,000. France is dominated by a regional press, with *Ouest France's* circulation being double that of *Le Figaro* or *Le Monde*.

It is impossible to cover the subject of media availability in depth: it is sufficient to acknowledge its wide variability in terms of type of media – and the degree of penetration and influence in the marketplace.

For the record, media consists of television, newspapers and magazines, outdoor, cinema and radio.

Exam Hint

It would be useful if students obtained a copy of the European Market and Media Fact Book if they are serious about international (in their case European) media.

Satellite TV

This is a recent development but one that has grown into enormous proportions. Europe and the Far East are in the forefront of its current development phase with the creation of Sky Channel and CNN. Satellite, with its multi-country footprints, is becoming more prominent. Besides the language difficulties (i.e. transmitting in multi-languages) the beneficiaries of satellite are likely to be the major pan-regional advertisers. Satellite transmissions are being focused on by national governments as they frequently breach country regulations. Singapore and Malaysia have recently banned Star TV to protect their population from 'foreign values'. Elsewhere in the Far East, Star TV, a Hong Kong-based satellite company, owned by Richard Murdoch's corporation, overtook CNN as India's favourite foreign programme. It and others' growth potential in the Far East is colossal. Satellite will be a huge communication medium in the next century as technology advances.

Exam Question 8.3

The growth of satellite broadcasting has brought a whole new dimension to regional and global advertising. With reference to specific examples evaluate the strategic and tactical advantages of such a development on an organization's global communications strategy.

(June 1999, Question 3)

Go to www.marketingonline.co.uk or www.bh.com/marketing to access specimen Answers and Senior Examiner's advice for this exam question.

Scheduling media

The timing of the delivery of the message is decided by the demand of the audience. Most products have a cyclical sales demand peaking seasonally or in line with religious festivals and national holidays. Obviously, these differ by country/region (the Southern Hemisphere's Christmas is in their Summer). But holidays are also key purchasing moments and since holidays vary, media must be scheduled accordingly. In France most of the country closes down in July–August. The Germans stagger their summer holidays by *ländes* (provinces). In some Muslim countries advertising is restricted, or banned, during Ramadan. Winters and summers vary in duration and intensity across the globe. Thus seasonal products such as de-icing equipment or air-conditioning units will be advertised at different times. The international marketing company needs to take account of differences in scheduling (and budgets).

Exam Hint

Tutors and students studying the revisions to the syllabus (see appendices) will observe the Senior Examiner places increasing emphasis on the importance of the internet as a communications tool. References to the internet and its rapidly evolving contribution to the development of international marketing are incorporated in many of the units, e.g. CRM in Unit 6. Students are advised to build a base of examples from their own experiences of professional practice and their own country as it is anticipated the Senior Examiner will be asking questions relating to international marketing via the internet. It may even be that future mini case studies will involve marketing via the internet.

Exam Hint

Give serious thought to collecting examples of companies who utilize all the tools of marketing communications internationally. It might be useful to select a major multinational (not a UK company) and examine its Marcom plans in the UK. IBM is just such an organization, American, yet deeply entrenched in the UK. What are its advertising, PR, sales promotion, direct marketing and sales programmes?

Organizing and coordinating the advertising effort

Time and effort spent organizing and coordinating the advertizing effort is at least as important as time spent crafting the message and the media. The basic choices facing the multi-country international advertiser are:

1. *Domestic agency* It is most common that advertisers use their domestic agencies when first expanding overseas, for reasons of familiarity, relationship, trust and knowledge of their business (all the normal reasons for choosing an agency in the first place). But many smaller domestic agencies have no international experience themselves but form a liaison and association with similar-sized agencies overseas and service the advertiser's account by proxy. This generally is a stage-one operation.

2. *Appointing local agencies* This is generally a step taken by advertisers who recognize the need for a differentiated campaign. Local agencies understand local cultures, have the relevant contacts among the media and can create or adopt campaigns to meet the local requirements. Jaguar found, to its cost, when advertising in the Middle East that Arab headwear differed in detail from country to country. Locals easily spotted the difference and ridiculed the campaign, which was attempting to appeal to all suitably wealthy males. Nestlé adopt a roster approach, appointing from an approved shortlist of advertising agencies, thus getting benefits of acculturalization by market and minimizing the degree of control to a few agencies.

3. *Centralizing the effort* The 1980s in particular saw the spread of major agencies into the global arena. Many of the US majors were already established servicing global clients such as Esso, Coca-Cola, etc. But it was Saatchi & Saatchi who really began the trend towards global advertising, exploiting the theories of Levitt regarding globalization and persuading major multinational corporations to develop world advertising (e.g. British Airways and Mars). It was Saatchi who coined, or at least popularized, the phrase 'one sight, one sound, one sell' – global communication. The advantages of such a campaign are apparent and have been discussed extensively in the textbooks. Similarly, the advantages of central creativity and global servicing through a single agency are equally obvious. However, although global agencies are still a growing trend they have been shown to have limitations in that the global advertisement has been elusive. To many it is seen as a shimmering oasis that appears wonderful but impossibly difficult to grasp or achieve. Having said that, IBM in 1994 has placed all its Marcom through Ogilvy & Mather in an attempt to speak to all its customers with one corporate voice. It remains to be seen whether customers will respond to this positively. For decades McCann-Erickson (an Inter-public group agency) played the role of guardian of the universal brand values for Esso ensuring consistency of corporate logo and brand communication. Until recently another Inter-public group agency fulfilled the same task for Coca-Cola.

Activity 8.13

Who are the major advertising agencies in the UK? How many of them are international? Get a feel for what the structure of the advertising industry is like. How many international agencies have international clients?

Coordination

Whatever the strategic choice, domestic, local or central, international advertising has to be controlled both in terms of the message and in budgetary terms. This requires management expertise at the marketing headquarters (usually at the domestic base). While decentralization has its distinct advantages – the locals are closer to the customers – the danger is fragmentation, with country managers pursuing their own agendas frequently to the overall detriment to international brand values – imperceptibly at first but, over time, shifting consumer recognition and understanding away from the corporate goals. Decentralization requires very careful handling and control in terms of guidelines relating to advertising claims, tone of voice, logo, colours, etc. and in terms of scale of the budget and scheduling of the campaign. Conversely, heavy-handed centralized control can be equally destructive, stifling creativity if over-prescribed. Creative personnel, with the talent for differentiating your product offer from competition, dislike working within rigid guidelines. Essentially, the way (the style) through which international advertising is administered is at least as important as the company procedures employed.

Questions

As a check on your understanding of what has been covered in this unit, consider the following questions:

Question 8.4

1. Explain the greater importance often attached to personal selling in overseas markets.
2. What are the problems and difficulties in establishing a local sales force?
3. Specify some of the issues involved with sales promotions overseas. How might the deployment of a local rather than a domestic sales promotions agency assist in overcoming problems?
4. What factors influence the development of push or pull strategies in international marketing communications?
5. Specify the conditions under which a company might employ a local versus a home-based sales effort.
6. What patterns do you observe in the use of sales promotion across Europe?
7. What type of companies sponsor Formula 1 motor racing (apart from the oil giants)? What benefits do you think they gain?
8. Is global advertising for the few, or do you see it developing as a major force?
9. How should the advertising industry respond to the new technological trends in mass media communication (e.g. cable, satellite, internet, etc.)?
10. Why are some global advertising campaigns successful while others fail?

Case Study

International Pricing: The case of the exchange rate nightmare

Every international marketer's nightmare is unexpected changes in the exchange rate A, good example of this is Zimbabwe, whose currency has declined dramatically in recent months. In order to account for changes in exchange rates, exporters can employ a variety of methods including invoicing in a hard currency e.g. pounds sterling; invoicing in foreign currency having fixed the rate in advance with the bank; invoicing in foreign currency having fixed the exchange rate on the invoice; borrow foreign currency from a bank, sell in sterling and repay the loan with proceeds from the sale and offset imports in one country with exports in the same currency so avoiding the need to change currency. Another way is by selling the expected currency forward. Where credit terms have been given and goods have been sold at a price expressed in foreign currency, the risk of changes in the exchange rate can be covered by selling the expected currency forward. The following is a case of a UK exporter selling goods to Malaysia.

The exporter has sold the goods to Malaysia on 90 days terms and wishes to cover forward on 26th August. The rate quoted by the bank will be calculated as follows:

The bank rates on 26th August are 6.0025–6.0125 Ringgit. (Malaysian currency to the pound sterling).

I month forward is 1.75–1.25 cents premium

3 months forward is 4.50–4.00 cents premium

The exporter will be selling Ringgit to the bank, therefore the bank will apply its buying rate based on spot 6.0125 Ringgit.

The payment is expected in three months so the bank will calculate on the basis of three months forward rate 4.50–4.00 cents premium. The forward rate is at a premium i.e. dearer in the future, so the rate will be lower and the premium deducted from the Spot rate. However, the bank is buying, so it will wish to keep the rate as high as possible and will, therefore, deduct the smaller premium i.e. 4.00 cents.

The forward rate quoted would, therefore, be 6.0125 Ringgit less 4.00 cents = 5.9725 Ringgit.

If, on the other hand, the exporter is expecting payment sometime during September/October and wishes to cover forward, he will cover one month fixed, option one further month. The one month fixed takes him to 26th September and he can receive the benefit of the one month premium, but as payment may be received any time between 26th September and 25th October, he cannot receive the benefit of any extra premium for the second month and so the rate will be 6.0125 less 1.25 cents = 6.00 Ringgit.

This example shows the necessity to carefully plan for exchange rate fluctuations in pricing goods and services for international operations. Of course, as 11th September has shown, not all possible risks can be accounted for but, at least, some can.

Source: Based on the manual *Training Manual on Cotton Trading Operations*. International Trade Centre UNCTAD/ GATT, Geneva 1989

Extending knowledge

For a more detailed analysis and explanation of managing the international marketing mix, read: *International Marketing Strategy*, I. Doole and R. Lowe, 3rd Edition, Thomson, 2001. Chapters 9, 10 and 12, pp. 291–370 and 408–440.

International Marketing, S.J. Paliwoda and M.J. Thomas, 3rd Edition, Butterworth-Heinemann, 1999, Chapters 5,6 and 8, pp. 188–286 and 313–351.

Global Marketing Strategies, J-P. Jeannet and H.D. Hennessey, 5th Edition, Houghton Mifflin, 2001, Chapters 10, 11, 12, 13 and 14, pp. 396–594.

Summary

In this unit we have seen that the primary question in international product policy is that of product standardization. The argument over standardization-adaptation is a very important one because:

- The economies of scale which can be obtained through a standardized approach to international markets are considerable.
- The reasons for an organization to adapt or modify its product/service offering to each separate international market are also compelling. At the end of the day, the primary consideration must be for long-term profitability and the candidate will be required to assess this objective against any situations presented in the questions or the case study. Remember also that profitability is not the same thing as sales maximization, nor is it driven out by economies of scale on their own. A balance needs to be struck between the needs of the organization and those of the marketplace.
- Product policy is a key area in international marketing and decisions here will affect the entire marketing mix which follows. Customer considerations must always be top of mind for the marketer – domestic or international, and the role of market research in uncovering market needs cannot be overestimated in the international market situation.
- In this section we have considered the array of factors which influence and should help the international marketer to determine international pricing policy. Pricing is probably one of the most complicated areas of international marketing strategy but has major impact upon the financial performance of the organization. Pricing also plays a major role in supporting product strategy (differentiation and positioning) as well as communication strategy where it has a major impact on perceived quality.
- We have seen that in order to arrive at sensible prices the international marketer needs to understand the objectives behind the pricing approach as well as the factors which are often different from market to market. Standardized pricing approaches for international markets are not always necessary although some degree of coordination between markets may be desirable if only to stop the possibility of parallel importing.
- Pricing is treated by many marketers as a tactical activity. In this unit you should have understood that pricing policy has a major strategic influence on the organization and should not be relegated to purely tactical decision making at a lower level.
- Marketing communication is probably the most discussed area of international marketing. Not only is it rarely out of the news (it invites controversy) but the majority of us have exposure to it. What makes it so interesting is that it is culturally loaded. Everyone has a view. The challenge for the future is increasingly to internationalize the communicative mix. World consumers, world competitors, world advertising agencies lead to a consolidation in strategic terms of the marketing effort. Yet the paradox exists. Consumers though seeking global benefits remain doggedly local in their outlook. While strategy can take the global view, marketing must balance the benefits of 'one sight, one sound, one sell' with local needs. Issues such as cost, coordination and control also require careful consideration before any decisions are taken.

Objectives

This unit is a continuing discussion of the international marketing mix stated in the previous unit. A long-held traditional approach to the marketing mix has been that of the '4Ps', however in recent years, the mix has been extended to include the vital '3Ps', physical evidence, people and process. We have already dealt with physical evidence in the last unit so this unit concerns itself with people and process. Without people to plan, implement and control the international marketing plan then nothing will happen. This means that they need good human resource management also, for without proper motivation as well as control, staff will be ineffective and inefficient. Staffing issues concern the use of both internal, expatriate and local staff. Similarly, process management is all about production, maketing and operations management. This involves issues of customer contact and quality control standards. It must always be remembered that international operations are all about people engaging with people, hence the importance of people and process. In this unit you will study:

- The international people mix

  See syllabus section 2.3.7.

- The international process mix

  See syllabus section 2.3.6.

On completing the unit you will be able to:

- Understand the importance of people and process in international operations
- Develop the people and process elements of international operations.

International people and process policy

International people policy

It has been argued that the more technology makes products 'the same', the more personal service becomes the differentiator – for both products and services. Personal service is about people. The practised marketer will not need to be told about the key effects of choosing the right (and the wrong) people can have. Internationally, the problem may be exacerbated by cultural and other environmental issues that have already been discussed.

International staff

Traditionally, the nature of the staff employed to manage international marketing operations was driven by the stage of development of the market, the international operation and the level of involvement. These rules have broken down over recent years and a much more pragmatic approach is employed by most organizations.

Each approach has advantages and disadvantages and the key alternatives are:

- *The expatriate* Nationals employed from the home country ensures a good understanding of the culture of the parent company and requirements of any set plans and targets. It also ensures that top managers are 'groomed' for the most important positions in a wide range of company activities. On the negative side it tends to be expensive and may not be well advised where culture is sensitive and the need is for staff that understand the intricacies of dealing with customers with different needs and customs. This method tends to be unpopular with the host country and, of course, there are some countries where it is difficult to recruit expatriates.

- *The local national* Appears to be a commonsense approach to the problem. In this case the management of the international operation is in the hands of a member of the local culture. Not all as straightforward as it might seem, however, there may be some cultural misunderstandings with the parent organization and even cultural problems within the host market if they are dealing with a multicultural situation. Some training and development is also normally required out of the country to ensure that the local manager is aware of the parent culture and demands upon the subsidiary.
- *The third-country national* Started originally by chance but now a set pattern in the world of the global organization. In this case the local manager can be from another country within the organization's activity. An able manager can now be promoted and developed anywhere within the global operation. Bureaucratic problems can still exist but tend to be less severe with third country managers – the sense of 'imperialism' is diminished.
- *Internationals* A relatively new phenomenon with the advent of global corporations trying to create and develop a cadre of professional managers who are more at home working in the international environment than in the domestic. Much has been written about the new international managers but it remains to be proven whether this elite really exists or is just the mobile third-country manager doing what comes naturally. Most importantly, there is little evidence that a sense of personal identity and culture is replaced by an 'international culture'.

Whatever the approach used by the organization, it is clear that the number of staff affected by these decisions is likely to be very small and will affect management only. Far and away the most important aspect of international staff lies below the management level and here the local employee reigns supreme. Local employment is always a key political factor in allowing global and international organizations to enter host countries and the cultural abilities of locals to deal with locals is undenied.

International customers

The perception of local customers to the international organization will be determined, to a large part, by the perceptions of the people who work for them. Service quality, a key differentiator in more and more competitive markets is determined by a number of factors:

- The attitudes of the organization's staff
- Perceived internal relations
- The observable behaviour of staff
- The level of service-mindedness in the organization
- The consistency of appearance of staff
- The accessibility of the staff
- Customer-customer contacts.

It will be immediately seen that all these criteria are themselves culturally driven.

Customer-customer interaction is also a key factor in the people mix. Many products and services are effectively marketed and repeat purchased by the quality of the customer–customer interaction. Restaurants, theatres and motor cars are examples. Managing such customer–customer interaction requires a very sensitive touch and one which rarely exists outside the culture.

Just think how often you have been abroad and found yourself in a situation which you found uncomfortable but which the locals were obviously enjoying to the full. A Greek restaurant and a Chinese restaurant, both in London, will feel very different from each other (expressing the culture of the foods) and different from similar restaurants in either Greece or China (expressing the culture of the host country – the UK – and what behaviour is deemed acceptable).

Customer–staff interaction

Probably the most culture-bound activity in the entire marketing process, where the buyer and seller come together in an interpersonal relationship. Customer satisfaction and retention are the objective here. Whether the organization succeeds will depend on the cultural and environmental aspects of the interaction as well as the simple 'mechanics' of the process.

As has already been seen, international marketing communications is a cultural minefield for the unwary. Customer–staff interaction contains as many pitfalls.

Customer service

This is another cultural activity. Acceptable customer service cannot be standardized. Cultural norms preclude a global standard of customer service with what is deemed good service in one culture being seen as threatening and invasive in another. Customer service is always relative with organizations competing on a market-by-market basis according to what is required by the local culture.

Customer service initiatives also need to be supported by other elements in the marketing mix and by service level agreements with internal and external suppliers.

International process policy

Process policy is all about production and operations management. If we define operations as the means by which resource inputs are combined, reformed, transformed or separated to create useful outputs (i.e. benefits) then we can start to see the application of operations management as a concept in service as well as physical product organizations.

There are two aspects to the 'process' element of the mix which have an international marketing dimension, these are:

1. Degree of customer contact
2. Quality control standards.

Degree of contact

The managers responsible for the efficient and effective running of the operations management function in the organization will be working, quite properly, to a set of pre-determined performance criteria. These criteria are normally concentrated in areas such as output and costing – internal measures. The marketing strategy, on the other hand, has as its primary focus the customer and the marketplace. Bringing these two foci of attention together, the point at which a seamless partnership needs to be fused is where the customer comes into contact with the production system.

In international terms, we have issues with:

- Setting the pre-determined performance criteria – are they acceptable and/or understandable within the culture?
- The customer needs – are they well understood? Are they different from the parent company culture? Are they to be standardized? Must they be adapted?

Any production/operations system can be seen as a series of interrelated operations or jobs which ultimately end in the creation of either a product or a service; but in any case a package of benefits which the target customer will want to purchase. Since the managers responsible for operations will be motivated by internal, structured performance measures, they will concentrate on allocating resources to those areas of the operations process which are more delicate or more important in an operations sense.

Internationally, there are obvious pitfalls in developing the internal performance measures and then motivating personnel to meet those requirements.

First-line resources will be dedicated to ensuring that these 'critical' points in the production process work most efficiently and that the production flow is smooth and uninterrupted. The marketer, on the other hand, will, or should, be more concerned in ensuring that the operations process works cleanly and efficiently at those points where there is direct customer contact. Naturally enough, these points of high customer contact may not necessarily be the most critical point in terms of technical production flow.

It is specifically at these points of high customer contact that the 'process' element of the marketing mix needs to be managed most carefully. The customer should be able to see an overall logic and consistency to the organization's operations. At high contact points in the operations process, the organization should be asking itself whether the steps in the process are arranged in a logical manner from the customer's point of view. We should also be asking ourselves whether these steps are all necessary or whether any steps can be eliminated, combined or, at least, balanced. Finally, we should be asking ourselves whether the high contact steps in the operations process are employing the 'right' level of automation. In operations, there is always a trade-off between people and systems. Automation may remove the high cost element (people) but may, at the same time, produce problems in staff motivation. More dangerously, customers, faced with more and more technology can become dissatisfied – be careful that automation is not introduced at the expense of personal service. All these aspects of contract are, of course, culturally sensitive. Many aspects of automation (internet payment, voicemail, phonepad response) are normal in North America but deemed less acceptable by European customers.

Quality control standards

Quality control standards can, and should, be set for service operations in the same way as for manufacturing. Service quality standards may, however, be more qualitative than the quantitative standards set in manufacturing. As we have already seen, there is an area of potential conflict between operations management and marketing management when it comes to agreeing and setting quality standards. Standards should always be driven by the marketplace (represented in the organization by marketing) and should not be set by internal production-led benchmarks or, even more dangerously, by what we are able to achieve.

The process element of the marketing mix is, increasingly, an essential ingredient in the organization's battle in the marketplace. These aspects of the organization's activity are far too important to ignore and must be integrated into the overall marketing mix at a strategic level if the organization is to appear logical in market and marketing terms.

The following is a case study example showing an organization which exemplifies the international marketing mix in operation.

Exam Question 9.1

'International control methods ignore the "people" element.' Critically discuss this statement citing relevant examples to illustrate your answer. (December 2000, Question 7)

Go to www.marketingonline.co.uk or www.bh.com/marketing to access specimen Answers and Senior Examiner's advice for this exam question.

Exam Question 9.2

In international services, 'physical evidence', 'people', and 'process' are the major ways to evidence service benefits. As a Consultant to a global bank, suggest ways in which these elements can be used within the marketing mix to gain competitive advantage.

Go to www.marketingonline.co.uk or www.bh.com/marketing to access specimen Answers and Senior Examiner's advice for this exam question.

Exam Question 9.3

What differences, if any, are there in marketing products and/or services from:

1. A developed to another developed country?
2. A developed to a less developed country?

How might these differences be overcome? Illustrate your answer by choosing a product or service of your choice. (December 1999, Question 2)

Go to www.marketingonline.co.uk or www.bh.com/marketing to access specimen Answers and Senior Examiner's advice for this exam question.

Case Study

Rolls-Royce plc: A case of global expansion through organic growth and collaboration.

By any standards, Rolls-Royce, based in the UK, is a global operator. Since the dark days of 1971, when the company went bankrupt, it has risen to become a household name, particularly in aerospace technology. With a £10 billion order book, over £4 billion in annual turnover, a workforce of 40,000 people, more than 80 licensees and collaboration agreements worldwide and customers in 135 countries (80 percent of sales are overseas), it is a truly global player.

Rolls-Royce has three major divisions-aerospace, energy and marine power, all glued together by gas turbine technology and R & D. Aerospace is the biggest Division. Rolls-Royce manufactures aircraft engines for 300 airlines, 130 armed forces and 2,400 executive and utility operators. It has some 53,000 engines in service, growing all the time, in over 50 aircraft applications, based on its unique three shaft technology. Its main competitors: General Electric, and Pratt and Whitney, both US based. Until recently Rolls-Royce were number 3 in the league but now they are a clear number 2 and, in some areas, pushing number 1. In the 1980s Rolls-Royce had 7 per cent of civil engine business, now it is up to 35 per cent market share. Today the company manufactures in 20 different countries, although it biggest workforce and plant is based in Derby, UK. In the early 80s Rolls-Royce powered just four civil aircraft, now it is 32 and can be seen powering such giants as British Airways and Singapore Airlines. It has high hopes of powering the next generation of super Airbus in large numbers.

The Energy Division manufactures marine and industrial power applications. It specializes in power generation up to 150MW and has the world's most efficient and powerful gas turbine engine in the industrial Trent engine, a derivative of the civil aircraft engine. Rolls-Royce pumps half the world's gas and oil pipelines.

The Marine Power Division is a pioneer in the use of gas turbines for surface marine propulsion and nuclear power for Royal Navy submarines. The Division is the world's major player in integrated full propulsion systems and more than 30 navies use Rolls-Royce propulsion systems. As well as manufacturing marine engines, the division also offers a range of skills and management to support naval platforms, e.g. navy base facilities. Throughout the three divisions, standardized gas turbine technology underpins its operations although certain product adjustments have to be made to suit the different applications.

The company's growth has been supported by a huge R & D expenditure – about £700 million per annum. Developing a new aero-engine calls for enormous capital and 'risk and revenue' deals may be one of the ways of offsetting the inevitable risk attached. About £200 million is written off to the profit and loss account each year. The resultant acceleration of products from this R & D has led to increased market share. Not by any means is R & D limited to Britain, although most of it takes place in Derby in aero-engines, but also takes place in the USA and Canada. In fact R & D funding has declined in Britain and increased in Canada, where the Government is very interested in attracting R & D and provides grants to so do.

While market share is growing, fierce competition is forcing Rolls-Royce into greater efficiencies. Even with a growing order book which is necessary to maintain the business at its current size, modern production methods sometimes put pressure on the workforce.

However, the positive side of a growing order book raises the prospect of a very rosy future, especially in the future value of spare parts for aero-engines. Spares give a much higher margin than the original equipment, so the company could envisage a future where the aftermarket might dominate. The company spares position today comes from a past era of some 200 civil engine deliveries per annum. Today Rolls-Royce delivers some 1,100 engines per annum so the multiplier effect for the future is potentially enormous. The optimism could be blunted by competitors General Electric and Pratt and Whitney who are positioning to muscle in on the lucrative after market, so, incidentally, could Rolls-Royce on theirs.

Rolls-Royce manages it 'environmentals' in many ways. While still an independent company, it could be the target of a takeover. To help avert this it has built in all sorts of protections like a limit on foreign ownership, a limit of 15 per cent for one foreign shareholder and a golden share. A lot of R & D goes on making engines more efficient, cleaner and quieter, thus protecting the environment. The company is spared from the consequencies of the euro/sterling debate, as it deals in US dollars in what is, afterall, a US dollar industry. It has, consequently, to watch the US dollar/pound exchange rate. Changes in oil prices can be both a benefit and a problem. When the price of oil goes up, Rolls-Royce sells more industrial machines but fewer aero-engines if airlines fly less. The massive collapse in the Asian Tiger economies in 1997 resulted in the cancellation of options on orders for Rolls-Royce aero-engines by some of the Asian carriers.

Aero-engines are sold and marketed in a process involving the airline, airframe manufacturer (like Boeing) and the aero-engine manufacturer. They are not sold *per se* via agents or distributors but involves a sometimes complicated bidding process with the interested parties and 'influencers', e.g. current users. Once the order is obtained, the airframe manufacturer, carrier and engine manufacturer will work closely together, often, literally, on each others' premises. Relationship marketing and 'supply chain management' are key conceptual issues in action! Once fitted and in service, the engines need regular maintenance as specified not only by the manufacturer, but by the stringent safety codes laid down by regulatory bodies. Safety is key in the airline business. While Rolls-Royce will have its own fleet of engineers (creating a business in its own right), it is inevitable that other engine servicing outfits are able to maintain the original equipment and they do. So once sold, there is no guarantee of a permanent engine service contract. Similarly, Rolls-Royce may service engines originally manufactured by other companies. Wherever a aircraft touches down or takes off, it must be able to get speedy access to service and parts. No carrier can afford to have an aircraft idle on the ground for long.

Rolls-Royce is a classic global player of enviable reputation, experiencing organic growth with selected licensees and collaboration agreements, e.g. BMW. Its reputation has been built on a standardized technology, high quality product and service underpinned by massive R & D, a highly trained workforce and a management alert to global environmental opportunities, changes and trends.

Sources: www.rolls-royce.com/compi/compioo4.htm; Forkin, J. (2000). 'Sir Ralph on Derby, Rolls-Royce plc and the World.' *Business Matters*, South Derbyshire Chamber of Commerce, Nov/Dec., pp 4, 5.

Extending knowledge

For a more detailed analysis and explanation of managing the international marketing mix, read:

International Marketing Strategy, I. Doole and R. Lowe, 3rd Edition, Thomson, 2001, Chapter 9, pp. 292–294.

Global Marketing Strategies, J-P. Jeannet and H.D. Hennessey, 5th Edition, Houghton Mifflin 2001, Chapter 15, pp. 595–632.

Summary

In this unit we have considered the vital marketing mix elements of people and process and looked at a case study of a global operator, utilizing the international marketing mix. International operations would not take place without either of these elements. In considering people we have to look closely at the engagement of local people versus expatriates. Equally we have to carefully manage our own employees both effectively and efficiently.

The degree of customer contact and quality control standards are other vital issues. It is the whole essence of marketing that customers are delighted every time that they come in contact with an organization. On a global scale this is extremely important but difficult to accomplish. People are a vital part of this process.

Product policy is a key area in international marketing and decisions here will affect the entire marketing mix which follows. Customer considerations must always be paramount in the mind of the marketer – domestic or international, and the role of market research in uncovering market needs cannot be overestimated in the international market situation.

In this section we have considered the array of factors which influence and should help the international marketer to determine international pricing policy. Pricing is probably one of the most complicated areas of international marketing strategy but has major impact upon the financial performance of the organization. Pricing also plays a major role in supporting product strategy (differentiation and positioning) as well as communication strategy where it has a major impact on perceived quality.

We have seen that in order to arrive at sensible prices the international marketer needs to understand the objectives behind the pricing approach as well as the factors which are often different from market to market. Standardized pricing approaches for international markets are not always necessary although some degree of coordination between markets may be desirable if only to stop the possibility of parallel importing.

Pricing is treated by many marketers as a tactical activity. In this unit you should have understood that pricing policy has a major strategic influence on the organization and should not be relegated to purely tactical decision making at a lower level.

Marketing communication is probably the most discussed area of international marketing. Not only is it rarely out of the news (it invites controversy) but the majority of us have exposure to it. What makes it so interesting is that it is culturally loaded. Everyone has a view. The challenge for the future is increasingly to internationalize the communicative mix. World consumers, world competitors, world advertising agencies lead to a consolidation in strategic terms of the marketing effort. Yet the paradox exists. Consumers though seeking global benefits remain doggedly local in their outlook. While strategy can take the global view, marketing must balance the benefits of 'one sight, one sound, one sell' with local needs. Issues such as cost, coordination and control also require careful consideration before any decisions are taken.

Objectives

Distribution and logistics are fast becoming critical factors in international marketing. Speed or time is increasingly the critical differential linked to costs. Getting the product or service delivered to the customer when it is needed and responding flexibly to marketplace demands has now assumed paramount importance. Federal Express is the world's sixth largest airline, succeeding by fast delivery worldwide. Customerization and groupage are again logistic advances. In the field of distribution things are equally dynamic with technology and modernity changing old-established routes to the customer (e.g. garage forecourts have become a major competitor in grocery retailing terms in the past five years). The financial implications of international marketing are too often ignored or are placed in a less important role by modern marketers. Finance and marketing are inextricably linked. Marketing is the primary source of revenue to any organization (interfacing as it does with the customer). Whether revenue produces profits, the lifeblood of the organization, depends on the ability of marketing and finance to work together. In this unit you will:

- Study the factors important in developing distribution strategies
- Recognize the cost implications of logistics
- Be aware that service levels are a very important marketing tool
- Consider the management aspects of distribution
- Study new trends for the future
- Review the role of capital in international marketing operations
- Understand and be able to assess the risk involved in international operations
- Consider how profits are repatriated to the home organization. Having completed this unit you will be able to:
    i. Understand the financial implications of different international marketing strategies
    ii. Evaluate suitable marketing strategies from any financial viewpoint.

    See syllabus sections 2.3.4 and 2.3.5.

On completing the unit you will be able to:

- Explain the basis of a distribution strategy
- Identify the step-by-step approach and the impact each step might have on the overall delivery
- Review the impact of cost versus service and the management implication emanating from service-level decisions
- Evaluate the changing patterns in distribution and predict trends in what is happening (or likely to happen) in the future.

Study guide

This unit sets out to guide the reader through the balance of satisfying customers and making profits. Both are essential to commercial success. No business succeeds by totally putting one at the forefront.

> rnational distribution and logistics is fast becoming the difference between
> cess and failure. Customers will no longer wait on your terms. Your organization
> has to match their requirements or face the consequences.

The management of distribution and logistics

Getting the goods ready and available for purchase by foreign customers is an integral part of the marketing mix. It is not the remit of this text to cover the transport of goods via Incoterms such as Free On Board (FOB), Carriage Insurance Freight (CIF), etc. These are essential tactical issues of export implementation and important though they are, are not essentially a strategic issue and therefore outside the scope of this text. However, all students and practitioners of international marketing must be aware of Incoterms. Both the business environment and the cultural frame of reference vary by country – so therefore must the distribution and logistics underpinning it. The number of retail outlets per head of population varies enormously, as do the range and variety of intermediaries. The degree of government control over them also varies. What they sell, how they sell it and everything that goes along with effective 'delivery' of the offer is ultimately dependent upon one thing – the consumer. What we offer has to be available on terms that are compatible with the customers' needs and wants and match or exceed competitors' performance.

If this is so, then the company's distribution strategy is one part of the marketing mix and it needs to be consistent with other aspects of the marketing strategy namely product, price and communications. Furthermore, Stern and El-Ansary (1982) make the point that the marketing channel (distribution) is a continuation of interdependent operations in the process of making the product available for use or consumption. As such, the distribution channel is different in that it is largely managed rather than controlled. The management of channels within the chosen market is a combination of:

1. The culture, business environment and customer expectation
2. The objectives of the company, its resources, the availability of suitable channels and the ability of the company to service the channel appropriately.

Factors in developing the distribution strategy

Jeannet and Hennessey highlight four distribution decisions within the marketing mix, making the connection that distribution must be consistent with the rest of the mix (Figure 10.1).

The four decision points are:

1. *Distribution density* What is the ideal number of sales outlets required in order to service the customer? Remember, to be successful we need to be available where the customer expects it, so the critical factor is the consumer's shopping/buying behaviour. In general, fast-moving consumer goods are expected to be in extensive distribution and if that means every 'Mom and Pop' store then so be it. If the culture is to sell the product in single units (e.g. one cigarette or one sweet via street hawkers) then the company has to respond. The opposite is true in selling speciality and up-market branded goods where exclusive distribution may be required. Similarly, the purchase of industrial or business-to-business goods varies by country, from selling direct to end users, on the one hand, to recognized government suppliers/intermediaries, on the other. But throughout it is the buyer/customer who decides.

2. *Channel length* Put simply, this is the number of intermediaries involved in connecting the company, its product and the end buyer/user. Again, this is mainly determined culturally and varies by country. Japan, the leading high-tech country, has an exceedingly low-tech distribution system with many intermediaries connected via keiretsu agreements. This makes distribution slow, wearisome and very expensive as each

intermediary takes their 'cut'. Few Western companies have broken this internal mechanism and sell direct to customers.

3. Increasingly, in Western societies channel length is shrinking, making it at once easier and more difficult to break into a market. The UK grocery market is dominated by five major multiples, accounting for 62 per cent of total sales. In Germany five firms account for 80 per cent of total grocery sales.

4. *Channel alignment* This concerns the effective management of the various intermediaries in its distribution chain. For a company with no direct involvement in a foreign market this is a most difficult task. Distance seriously hampers coordination. Generally, one of the participants in the distribution chain stands out as the dominant member – major retailers in the UK; wholesalers in the USA; distributors (often the only importers) in emerging countries. The company has to recognize the dominant channel member country by country and align itself accordingly. Relationships are crucial, for the channel intermediaries are not and never will be in the control of the company. The skill is in managing the relationship.

5. *Distribution logistics* Physical distribution management (PDM) is described by Kotler as concerning the planning, implementation and control of physical flows of materials and final goods from points of origin to points of use in order to meet customers' requirements. However, in this context we will limit ourselves to the logistical aspect, i.e. to view the process from the perspective of the customer and to work our way backwards towards the factory. We recognize, in passing, the very important point of cost, for it is the balancing between customer needs and costs that is the basis for profit. Drucker, some while ago, dwelt on the balance between efficiency (doing things right) and effectiveness (doing the right things). A combination of the two is the ideal – but the realities of international distribution logistics mean there is always a trade-off.

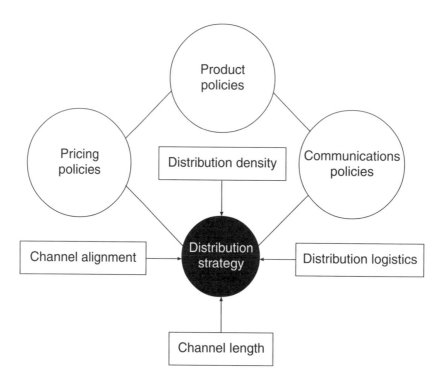

Figure 10.1
Distribution policies

High costs in international logistics

Moving goods from country to country is expensive. Up to 35 per cent of the cost of goods can be accounted for by distribution (varying by distance and other visible/invisible barriers). Additional impediments include:

- Delivery scheduling
- Just-in-time (JIT)
- Inventory holding levels
- Zero defect delivery
- Emergency need systems.

Intermediaries

Customers the world over are becoming increasingly demanding – the field of distribution logistics is increasingly competitive, internationalized and dominated by major players. As mentioned earlier, Federal Express has the sixth largest fleet of aircraft in the world, yet flies no passengers – dealing only with the shipment of goods.

The total distribution cost approach

Doole and Lowe (1999) explain how and why international logistics not only incurs additional costs but is more complicated. The formula they propose is:

$$D = T + W + I + O + P + S$$

$D =$ total distribution costs

$T =$ transport cost

$W =$ warehousing

$I =$ inventory costs

$O =$ order processing and documentation

$P =$ packaging

$S =$ total cost of lost sales resulting in failure to meet customers' performance standards.

The extra costs in international logistics

1. Distance from customers means increased:
   - Transport time
   - Inventory
   - Cashflow
   - Insurance.

2. Additional variables include:
   - Transport: sea, air, land
   - Documentation
   - Robust packaging (resistant to damage/pilfering).

3. Greater complexity:
   - The dimension of culture
   - Language
   - More documentation
   - The management of additional transport modes.

Activity 10.3

In the introductory Unit we identified macro factors influencing world trade. Can you relate some of these to the micro environment of distribution (e.g. the impact of urbanization)? Furthermore, examine the material towards the end of the unit dealing with global trends. Try bringing it all together.

Service levels

A few years ago successful businesses would have identified information technology (IT) as being the competitive differential. Today having IT means you can 'take part in the game', i.e. it is an essential prerequisite. The focus of competitive advantage has shifted to service.

Costs accelerate rapidly in response to increase in customer demands for availability and delivery. Near-perfect service (customer defined not company defined) is becoming the critical differentiator in the world marketplace as products become increasingly similar and it is difficult to distinguish one from another. Christopher (1987) identified the key discrimination as:

- Delivery response time to order
- Consistency and reliability of delivery
- Inventory availability
- Flexibility
- Ordering convenience
- Simplification of documentation
- Claims procedures
- Condition of goods on arrival
- Order status updates
- After-sales support.

These factors are difficult enough to deal with effectively on home territory. Problems magnify with physical and cultural differences. But remember, service standards will not be the same everywhere and the company, in order to succeed (profitably), must adjust its logistic to the needs of the customer and the marketplace. For example, in the UK, The Body Shop dictates a 2-hour delivery window on a designated date. Failure to comply means that its trucking company gets paid only certifiable costs and therefore delivers for free. Such demanding service levels are not universal, therefore why attempt to meet them? Deliver when the customer demands.

The subject of logistics is extremely complex. The international manager needs to be fully abreast of development in this field. However, the remit of this text is to remain strategic.

Managing, selecting and controlling the distribution channel

Unless it sets up its own distribution channel, the firm is in part, or wholly, in the hands of intermediaries. Managing rather than controlling the channel(s) is critical to success in the marketplace. Here the dangers of SRC become apparent. Doole and Lowe express this diagrammatically in Figure 10.2.

The management and control aspect of distribution will inevitably be influenced by the channels selected and the number of intermediaries employed. The methods of selection have been distilled by various authors to a number of 'Cs' (Table 10.1). The factors that combine to deliver the critical balance between efficiency and effectiveness become immediately apparent. The first six in both lists are essentially concerned with efficiency, the remainder with effectiveness. If there is to be a trade-off then effectiveness must dominate and efficiency is judged subjectively by the customer, culture and competition in the marketplace.

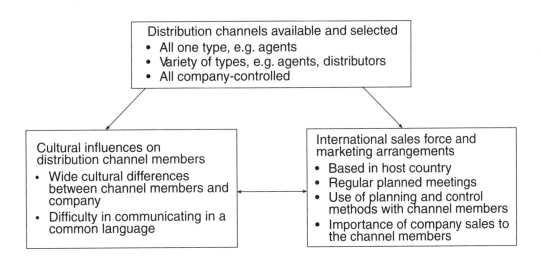

Figure 10.2
Distribution channels, cultural influences and their management (Source: Doole and Lowe 1999)

Table 10.1 Different C methods for selecting distribution channels			
Cateora	**Czinkota and Ronkainen**	**Usunier**	
Cost Capital Control Coverage Character Continuity	Cost Capital Control Coverage Character Continuity	Cost Capital Control Coverage Character Continuity	Efficiency
	PLUS Customer characteristics* Culture* Competition* Company objectives Communication	PLUS Customers and their characteristics* Culture*	Effectiveness
* External factors			

Activity 10.4

Study your own organization, even if it is a domestic-only one. Examine the balance between the efficiency factors versus the effective ones. Be critical. My guess is that 80 per cent of your company's effort is not behind being effective (from the customer's viewpoint). If you can't do it in your domestic base, what chance overseas?

Selecting the intermediaries

These may be self-selecting where there is little alternative on offer. Where choice is available selection might be based on:

- Compatibility with customer requirements
- Sales potential
- Geographic coverage
- Breadth of coverage – present and future (always think ahead)
- Financial strength
- Managerial competence
- Service-mindedness, self-motivation
- Synergy with company goals and management.

For example, while the manufacturer of Rolex watches has a wide range of potential distributors to choose from, the watch's high quality image and price would dictate the intermediary being chosen on the basis of sales potential and synergy with company goals and customer requirements. On the other hand, the distributor of a popular daily newspaper, would look for geographical coverage, and breadth of coverage. Daewoo, the South Korean car manufacturer surprised the car industry with a completely different distribution strategy. It chose Halfords in the UK as a distributor link as Halfords provided geographic coverage, opportunities for sales, financial strength, service mindedness and compatibility with customer requirements, i.e. service.

Occasionally quite different intermediaries might be necessary within a single country – dependent upon ethnic and racial differences, and the urban-rural split.

Motivation of intermediaries

Cateora (1993) identifies five key categories:

- Financial rewards
- Psychological rewards
- Communications
- Company support
- Corporate rapport.

Money is not always the right reward mechanism, although it is a powerful motivator everywhere. In the USA individual rewards work best, likewise in South-East Asia. In many countries, e.g. India, the ethics of non-confrontation clearly clashes with performance-led reviews. An additional point worth remembering is that a product with poor sales potential is hardly likely to enthuse intermediaries.

A feeling of belonging, participating in success, partnership bonding all go a long way to bring the company and its intermediaries closer. Relationship building through communication, support and feeling a part of the company add the value that brings success, especially if the product is only a small part of the intermediary's wider portfolio.

Control

This is generally reduced or limited when dealing with intermediaries and sometimes objective performance cannot be implemented. However, a contractual agreement may be arrived at although this may not be binding, more a statement of intent. The Western practice is to create written legal agreements – the Eastern practice often takes the form of obligation and working together. Care needs to be employed in introducing the Western SRC of formalizing control via mechanistic methodology.

Finally, the termination of an agreement may not be simple or straightforward. Exit distribution strategies can be extremely costly in some parts of the world where agents can demand up to five times the annual gross profit, plus other penalties to account for goodwill, the cost of laying off employees, etc.

Global trends in distribution

Jeannet and Hennessey identify six major shifts in world distribution patterns:

1. *The internationalization of retailing* IKEA, Pizza Hut, KFC, Toys'R'Us, McDonald's, The Body Shop, Benetton and others have all migrated around the world. Encouraged by its success in the late 1990s, Lidol, the cut price German retailer is set for rapid expansion in the UK.
2. McDonald's, the world's largest fast food chain, is expanding its outlets throughout the world by an average of 4.2 per day. Since 1995 they have grown from 14,000 outlets in 70 countries to over 23,000 in 120 countries, with much of the growth in Eastern Europe and India. They bring with them world standards and systems, suppliers and financing and in doing so simplify the marketing environment.
3. *Large-scale retailing* This is a corollary of the above – the inevitable trend is towards large-scale retailers. The small retailer is in decline everywhere – even in developing countries as consumer mobility increases. There are serious implications for employment and dislocation to traditional cultural patterns of shopping. Wal-Mart's purchase of Asda in the UK is making European retailers very nervous.

4. *Direct marketing* This is restricted to countries with sophisticated infrastructure, nonetheless this field of distribution is expected to grow rapidly. Changing life-styles, the growth of women in employment, mobile phones and home PCs will fuel this growth.

5. *Discounting* Lower distribution costs bring suppliers, distributors and customers closer, forcing down prices worldwide; just about everybody now lives in a 'deal culture' with few wanting to pay top price. A direct result of points 1–3 has generated international competition with a driving down of prices. A further factor is the growth of regionalism, the removal of barriers, the ease and speed of distribution within the region – all serving to direct customers to bargain deals.

6. *Information technology* Suppliers source the world and so do distribution chains. The development of Just-in-time inventory management means that products are delivered from all over the world, in a matter of days in some cases, broadening customer choice. In doing so they will simultaneously impair local customs and culture yet at the same time create world niche markets for products that otherwise might be restricted to a tiny corner of the world – an interesting paradox.

7. *Growth of own-label brands and development of retailer Eurobrands.* Everywhere in the developed world manufactured brands are under challenge. The growth of major retailers has limited the power of the manufacturers to both develop and maintain their brands (e.g. Coca-Cola is under threat from Sainsbury's Classic Cola in the UK). As Sainsbury's and others internationalize (by acquisition or natural growth) so will the retailers' power place increasing pressure on manufacturers' brands. Whether this will be of long-term benefit to customers remains an open question. That it will happen is not in doubt. Eventually there may be greater overlap and vertical integration between manufacturers and retailers globally.

8. *The internet* Throughout the text we have commented on the relevance of this channel in creating a new interface between supplier and customer. For many product categories and particularly many service areas the internet is becoming the channel of first choice. The growth of dot.com businesses is still phenomenal, despite recent failures, and it places suppliers in direct contact with customers in a way previously unimagined. Financial retail products account for 35 per cent of the UK internet shopping business, but, it should be noted, that shopping over the internet has declined 25 per cent in the USA in 2000. Consumers have simply lost faith in the medium. Small as well as large companies can leapfrog barriers to entry in many product categories. One recent example springs to mind of a small-scale operation, working entirely from home, yet marketing and delivering seeds for flowers on demand anywhere in the world. One of the authors of this text purchased his car via the internet and in fact 1 in 10 new car buyers use the internet at some point in the purchasing decision process.

It is absolutely imperative that students build up a dossier on developments in internet marketing not just simply from an examination but from a business/commercial viewpoint.

Questions

As a check on your understanding of what has been covered, consider the following questions.

Question 10.1

1. Outline the key factors in developing distribution strategy.
2. Put in charge of exporting JCB constructional equipment, what issues do you need to consider in entering the Kuwait market following the termination of the Gulf War?
3. Having considered the dynamics of fashion retailing, what distribution strategies would you recommend for a worldwide manufacture of designer footwear (e.g. the Timberland range of shoes)?
4. In what way might the element of an international logistics system be different from a domestic one?
5. As the marketing manager of a range of car polishes and equipment sold to car owners you have been asked to consider an appropriate distribution system. As an export organization what steps might you take before implementing any distribution system? What logistical concern do you have and what control mechanisms might you apply?

Financial implications of international marketing

The role of finance in marketing and international marketing strategy is a relatively recent addition to the syllabus but it is nevertheless essential for marketing management. The ultimate success of any marketing strategy must be judged on the profitability of the organization following the proposed strategy.

It is not always guaranteed that a question on the paper will be directed exclusively at the role of finance and financial implications of international marketing, However, it is clear from recent examiners' reports that answers to the mini case study which do not offer a clear perspective on the financial implications of proposed strategy will now be considered incomplete.

Prudent financial management is essential to the profitability and success of any organization, domestic or international. The major unique difference of an international organization is that the fund flows occur in a variety of currencies and in a variety of nations having distinct legal, political, social and cultural characteristics. These currency and national differences, in turn, create risks unique to international business. Additionally, a number of specialized international institutions and arrangements have developed because of these currency and national differences.

Activity 10.5

Who is responsible for international financial controls in your organization? How is responsibility split between finance and marketing? How is international marketing strategy affected by international financial considerations?

There are three principal aspects to the question of financial and international marketing strategy. This unit will consider these elements in order.

International capital

The organization embarking on international marketing must deal with a number of issues about its need for capital. Strategically the organization's capital requirements will depend largely upon the preferred method of market entry. In simple terms there are two forms of capital that will be needed:

- *Start-up or investment capital* is required to set-up the production, research and analysis, marketing, distribution and access processes before the sales process itself has started.
- *Working capital* is that cash required to finance the working transactions on a day-to-day basis. Working capital typically includes stock held and financing the debtor period between delivery and payment of invoice.

The international marketing organization's need for capital will be directly linked to its chosen method of market entry and level of involvement in international markets. For example, the organization exporting through agents or distributors will have fairly low capital requirements since it often has to produce few variations in product and only has to finance one or two deliveries at a time. If dealing through distributors, they will often take title to the goods and pay before they themselves have sold the goods on to the final users.

If an organization, for its own strategic reasons, has decided to enter a market through its own sales and marketing subsidiary, or even local manufacturing, it will require more capital to set up and establish the venture as well as additional levels of working capital to finance local stocks and wider product or service distribution in the target market.

Obviously, financial requirements may preclude smaller organizations from taking on levels of involvement that are beyond them. Larger organizations may consider that their capital may be more profitably employed in other markets and will evaluate different market opportunities accordingly.

Definition

Financial management

According to the finance textbooks the financial management of any organization, domestic or international, can be considered as having four separate tasks: 1) The acquisition of funds 2) The investing of funds in economically productive assets 3) The managing of those assets 4) The eventual reconversion of some (or all) of the productive assets into funds to return to the original investors, creditors, suppliers, employees and other interest groups.

International capital requirements will probably be higher (in relation to total business) than is normally acceptable in the home market. International business will likely involve the organization in travel costs, shipping costs, duties, start-up costs, higher inventories produced by delivery time lags and smaller fragmented markets, as well as trade and export credit facilities.

International financial risk

There are two types of financial risk unique to international business:

- Foreign exchange risk
- Political risk.

Foreign exchange risk

Foreign exchange risks arise from the need to operate in more than one currency. When an organization has assets or liabilities denominated in a foreign currency, or is doing business in a foreign currency, profitability will be influenced by changes in the value of that currency relative to the home or reported currency.

The most important foreign exchange risk is 'transaction exposure' which refers to gains and losses that arise from the settlement of transactions whose terms are stated in a foreign currency. Transaction exposure can be avoided, at a cost, by entering into forward contracts (this is a contract to buy or sell a given currency at an agreed price at an agreed future date). Some organizations simply ignore transaction exposure – and pay the price. Others, like the very large tour operators, have turned it into a separate business and actively manage their transaction operations as a distinct profit centre.

Activity 10.6

Take a market of your choice, or one that is particularly important to your organization.

- What is the history of currency movement over the past 12/24 months?
- What is the future prediction for movement?
- What are the prices of forward contracts being offered?

Political risk

Political risk is the term used to cover those risks arising from an array of legal, political, social and cultural differences in the target foreign market. Such risk normally produces losses where there is conflict between the goals of the organization and those of the host government.

The government controls the nation's financial rules and structure as well as a variety of non-financial instruments designed to help achieve society's economic, political, social, cultural and ideological goals. Also, since the relative importance of the foreign government's goals is likely to vary from time to time the organization may find itself unprepared and therefore paying extra taxes and able to repatriate fewer funds than previously. The organization may also find itself employing more local managers or paying higher wages to its labour force.

International financial risk is an integral part of carrying out business in the international arena. It therefore cannot be completely avoided but its effects can be lessened by careful planning and prediction of likely future events.

Repatriation of profits

In financial terms any project, including the decision to move into an international market, can be financially assessed according to the amount of investment required and the estimated funds which flow from the project. Internationally, of course, the organization will only take into account the funds which can be successfully repatriated from the foreign market in its assessment of the project.

Although the same theoretical financial framework applies to international as well as domestic projects, the calculation of returns is made more complex due to the special factors which influence international marketing. These factors include differing tax systems and legislation which affect the repatriated flows as well as differential inflation rates which can change competitive positions and hence cash flows, over time. Nevertheless, in the long run the international investment project must be judged on repatriated cash flows.

The organizations employing discounted cash flow methods of analysis (DCF) can assess competing domestic and international projects by building an additional amount into the discount factor to allow for the increased level of uncertainty in dealing in foreign markets.

Activity 10.7

Do you understand DCF methodology? Does your organization use DCF? What discount factors does it use for:

- Domestic operations?
- International operations?

How are these discount factors made up?

Conclusions

An understanding of the financial implications of any proposed international marketing strategy is essential for the international marketer if he or she hopes to get their project into the organization's list of priorities. Any organization exists to make a profit through satisfying its customers. International operations also need to be net providers of profit to the organization (see Table 10.2).

Table 10.2 Financial implications of international marketing

1 Capital requirements 　Investment capital 　Working capital
2 Financial risk 　Exchange risk 　Political risk
3 Repatriation of profits 　Taxation 　Political factors

Having said that, there may also be non-financial reasons for the organization approaching certain international markets. Such reasons might include competitive defence of a major market through involvement in a minor foreign market, use of a particular foreign market as a test-bed for new product development or image and positioning reasons on a broader international basis.

This unit on financial implications needs to be read and understood alongside the section in Unit 7.

Questions

As a check on your understanding of what has been covered in financial implications, consider the following questions:

Question 10.2

1. What is the role of financial management in international operations?
2. What are the three principal financial aspects to international marketing strategy?
3. What are the two types of international capital that may be required?
4. What are the two types of international financial risk?
5. How can transaction exposure be avoided?
6. How can political risk be reduced?
7. What are the key problems associated with profit repatriation?

Case Study

Compass Group: The 'invisible' worldwide contract caterer

Talk about worldwide distribution and names like DHL and Coca-Cola spring to mind. But Compass Group? Compass provides 15 million meals a day worldwide, worth £11.25 billion annually, as the biggest player in the £293 billion contract catering market. The Compass empire embraces names like Little Chef, Upper Crust and airport Burger King and, until recently, the Le Meridian chain of hotels.

Yet Compass have fallen victim in the recent past to that nightmare for fast food distributors, a decline in margins affected by a fall in turnover. Shares in Compass fell sharply following the events of 11th September as investors feared that US business would suffer and airport trade declined due to fewer air passengers. Compass lost £5 million, including some outlets in the World Trade Centre and £250,000 spent on free meals for rescue workers, but Compass has bounced back with investors reassured by a sales growth of 8%.

Opportunities still abound in the world of contract catering. Asia remains a land of opportunity where 80% of companies do their own catering compared to the USA, where 47% is self operated and the rest is contract. Shored up by its experience in UK motorway services provision, Compass is considering Continental motorway services, 300 government run catering contracts, opportunities in Italy and Japan, healthcare markets and feeding peacekeeping forces in various global locations. Like the distribution opportunities available to franchising (witness McDonald's), contract catering equally opens up a world of distribution possibilities.

Sources: Based on company information and The Financial Mail on Sunday, 6th Jan. 2002

Extending knowledge

International Marketing Strategy, I. Doole and R. Lowe, 3rd Edition, Thomson, 2001, Chapter 11, pp. 371–407.

International Marketing, S. Paliwoda and M. Thomas, 3rd Edition, Butterworth-Heinemann, 1999 Chapter 7, pp. 287–312.

Global Marketing Strategies, J.-P. Jeannet and H.D. Hennessey, 5th Edition, Houghton-Mifflin, 2001, Chapter 15, pp. 595–633.

Because of the complex detail involved in fully comprehending distribution and logistics the following reference text is included as recommended reading:

Export Practice and Management, A. Branch, 4th Edition, Thomson Learning, 2000.

Summary

Distribution and logistics are the fastest-changing areas in international marketing. It is essential that companies monitor trends in international trade. Yesterday's methods can and are being outdated virtually overnight. Think how companies such as Direct Line have revolutionized the marketing of motor insurance in the UK and are now moving on to household insurance and mortgages.

Ideally, firms would like to deal direct with customers. It may happen in the UK but in overseas markets it may not be feasible. Political and other numerous factors prevent this. The firm would also like to use a similar distribution chain to its home market. Again it is extremely rare that distribution and logistical systems in one country is replicated elsewhere. There are too many variables. Whatever route(s) is chosen, care must be taken to plan and control the effort. Inefficiencies have to be minimized in order to succeed.

In this unit we have seen that every marketing strategy activity in foreign markets has financial implication for the organization. The international marketer must understand the financial implications of any proposed strategy and given a choice between alternative strategic choices the marketer should be able to bring an understanding of financial implications to bear on the eventual recommendations.

Financial implications of marketing to foreign markets comes under three separate headings:

- Capital requirement
- International financial risks
- The repatriation of profits.

Remember, business upon which we make no profit or for which we cannot repatriate the funds to the home office is business we can easily find in the domestic market!

Exam Question 10.1

Write briefing notes to the Chief Executive of a global consumer electronics manufacturer critically analysing the effect of the growth of e-commerce on global channels of distribution. Ilustrate your case with relevant example. (June 2001, Question 2)

Go to www.marketingonline.co.uk or www.bh.com/marketing to access specimen Answers and Senior Examiner's advice for this exam question.

Objectives

Evaluation and control methods are key issues in international marketing strategy. Nothing the international marketing manager can do can remove risk completely from business decisions that are made, but careful and proper evaluation of strategy before implementation, coupled with rigorous control methods during implementation itself, can reduce these risks to levels more acceptable in highly competitive situations. In this unit you will learn how to evaluate international marketing strategy and control strategic implementation. More specifically, you will:

- Review the objectives set for international marketing strategy
- Evaluate strategy against the set objectives
- Review the planning processes appropriate with the international business strategy
- Understand the control systems necessary to ensure proper implementations of international marketing plans.

See syllabus section 2.3.10.

Having completed this unit you will be able to:

- Evaluate the suitability of specific international marketing strategies
- Develop control systems for the implementation of international marketing strategy.

Study guide

It is an important fact in today's markets that no matter how elegant, sophisticated or quantified an international marketing plan might be, unless it is executed in an equally sophisticated manner it will remain simply a document on a manager's shelf. Implementation and control systems are now key features on all Diploma examination papers and you are urged to prepare this section fully and be able to explain various measures open to the organization in your examination answer. To underline the importance that the examiners place on this unit, they estimate that it should require 10 per cent of notional hours taught. That is twice the amount of time dedicated to any of the components of the international marketing mix.

In this section you should be able to work carefully to apply the knowledge you have acquired in domestic marketing strategy into the international marketing arena. The Planning and Control paper and the Analysis and Decision paper now cover this element of the syllabus in great detail.

After you have completed this unit you should also spend some time talking to managers in your organization as well as looking beyond your organization to other industries to discover the different criteria used and control systems which are employed in practice.

This unit should be studied in relation to other units in this coursebook. The activities in this unit are especially important. Evaluation and control methods are difficult to learn from a book and need to be seen in operation. Try hard to complete the activities before taking the examination.

Evaluating strategies

How do we evaluate international marketing strategy? Here the answer is relatively simple and straightforward. It is the extent to which the strategy is expected to or is seen to achieve the objectives set for the activity.

When looking at organizations' objectives for international marketing strategy we should refer back to the introduction section of this coursebook and specifically Figure 1.3. This diagram, which outlines the international business process, starts, quite properly, with two key inputs. These are: information on foreign market potential and the organization's objectives. A clear, concise and understandable definition of the organization's objectives is crucial to the development of any robust and practical international marketing strategy.

Exam Hint

Examination questions on evaluation and control have been rare in the past but more questions are expected on this topic in the future. Also, a number of questions contain an evaluation or control element. The mini-case study is an area where control systems are important. The major case study (Analysis and Decision) paper has taken to making evaluation and control of international operations a major element to the questions!

Set against the background of a clear, concise and understandable objective for the organization, the evaluation of the marketing strategy becomes a relatively straightforward operation. As we can see from Figure 11.1, the strategic process as followed by all papers in the Diploma set of examinations essentially follows four steps. Stage 1 involves an audit of the organization's current situation, Stage 2 involves setting clear, concise objectives for the future development of the organization, Stage 3 involves strategic options and Stage 4 involves choice and control systems. For the international organization, having proceeded from Stage 1 through to 2 the next question is what are the various routes by which the organization might achieve its international objectives. Stage 4 (the section with which we are concerned in this unit) is about how we choose among the alternative strategic options and how we control implementation. However, as we saw in Unit 5 on international planning, as there are different approaches to planning, so there are to evaluation and control. Broadly, the techniques can be classified as 'traditional' and 'less traditional' types, the latter recent additions to control measures as finance and marketing people strive to find more relevant and appropriate ways to measure and control complex operations. These areas follows:

Traditional	Less traditional
Strategic control	Best practice/benchmarking
Efficiency control	Self-assessment
Annual plan control	Double loop learning
Profit control	Balanced scorecard
Brand equity metrics	
Stakeholder value	

This list is not meant to be exhaustive, but covers many types.

Traditional types

Strategic control

The prime responsibility for this lies with top management. The purpose is to ascertain if planned results have been achieved and involves techniques like the Marketing Audit.

Efficiency control

The prime responsibility for this lies with line and staff management. As the title suggests it is used to examine ways of improving the efficiency of marketing and involves techniques like sales force efficiency measures and advertising efficiency measures.

Annual plan control

The prime responsibility for this lies with top and/or middle management. As with strategic control techniques its purpose is to examine if planned results are being achieved on an annual basis.

Profit control

The prime responsibility for this lies with the marketing manager. The purpose is to see where the company is making or losing money and involves techniques like product profitability, channel profitability and ABC or Pareto analysis (the 80/20 rule).

For further detail of these techniques see the Planning and Control syllabus of the Diploma section 3.5.2.

Brand equity metrics

The responsibility for these lies with various members of management depending on the level of the task. Their purpose is to ascertain the 'equity' invested in the brand as measured by a variety of techniques including consumer and end user metrics, innovation metrics and trade customer/ retailer metrics. Much has been written recently about brand valuation as a balance sheet tangible. Brand equity metrics contibute to that debate.

For further details on these techniques see Ambler, T., and Styles C. (2000) The Silk Road to International Marketing, Financial Times, Prentice-Hall.

Stakeholder Value

The responsibility for this lies with top management. Its purpose is to increase stakeholder returns and involves a number of techniques including the Balanced Scorecard.

For further details on this see Doyle, P. (2000), *Value Based Marketing*, Wiley.

Evaluation of strategic options is never simple since nothing in the commercial world is guaranteed. We are never sure which strategic options are likely to work within the competitive environment and which ones, although looking very good, will not produce the results required.

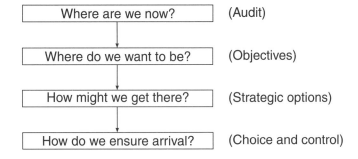

Figure 11.1

Typically, evaluation of strategic options falls under a number of concise categories. These are as follows:

Less traditional types

Best practice/benchmarking

The purpose of this technioque is to measure the organization against that of the 'best in the business'. Basically it assumes that what is best for the industry must be a good average to aim at. Above the norm would be deemed as undesirable, below it, exceptional.

Self-assessment

Many efforts have been made recently to develop self-assessment audits based on research into whole industry sectors, for example, retailing. By rating the organization on a numeric scale (usually 1 to 5) against a whole set of attributes, the organization can evaluate its performance viv-á-vis the 'perfect' score, say '5'. It can then see where improvements have to take place.

Double loop learning

Basically the technique allows the organization to 'learn from its past experience'. It is double loop because not only does it assimilate the feedback from its recent experience but it retains that learning for future reference. A good example of this is the 'Industry return average', for example, by virtue of many years' experience, a local omnibus operator in the UK will not survive if it is not making at least 17 per cent return on capital per annum.

The Balanced Scorecard

Since its introduction to the world in 1992 by Robert Kaplan and David Norton, this technique has had a profound effect on evaluation and control methodology. The technique centres on measures that drive performance. Much debate has raged over the shortcomings of financial and efficiency measures or whether one is better than the other. However, the debate should not be about managers choosing one or the other method, but using a balance of methods, hence the 'Balanced Scorecard'. The Balanced Scorecard addresses four elements-the financial perspective, the customer perspective, the internal business perspective and the innovation and learning perspective. Within each of these it addresses the goals and the measures to achieve them. For example, under the 'customer perspective' the goal might be to introduce new products. The corresponding measure of success is the percentage of sales from new products. Figure 11.2 summarizes the features of the Balanced Scorecard.

Figure 11.2
The Balanced Scorecard

The beauty-of the technique is that it is an effort to integrate many vital goals and measures against which to assess their achievement, rather than rely on one specific measure alone. For a more detailed discussion see Kaplan R.S. and Norton D.P., 'The Balanced Scorecard – measures that drive performance', *Harvard Business Review*, January to February 1992.

It is worth repeating that the control measures described above are not meant to be used in competition to each other but to give a more informed situational analysis than one or the other used in isolation. You would do well to learn about these different tecniques and how they can be used as they feature regularly in examination questions.

Short-versus long term

Strategy is about marshalling the gross resources of the organization to match the needs of the marketplaces and achieve the business objective, so this cannot be a short-term activity. Marketing, like other areas of management is full of managers who are driven solely by the short term. Not only is such short-termism inefficient, it can also be dangerous for the organization. Strategic decisions, like a general choosing his battleground, will have long-term implications and momentum has to be built up over a planned period of time.

On the other hand, like people who cannot exist for ever on a promise of 'jam tomorrow', so organizations need a constant flow of business, profits and cash to survive today so that they may live to see tomorrow! What is 'short term' and what is 'long term' will of course vary with the industry and the nature (and perceptions) of the target international markets. Like much in marketing, there is no 'right' answer. The Western financial markets, especially the USA and Great Britain, are often criticized for forcing organizations to concentrate on the shorter rather than the longer term. However, the recent collapse of the Asian markets has shown that having a 50-year view is no protection against a shortfall in today's profits!

Financial measures

The typical financial measures used in the evaluation of international marketing strategy will include:

- Profit
- Profitability
- Shareholder return
- Cash flow/liquidity
- Share price
- Earnings per share
- Return on net assets
- Return on sales.

It is worth noting that more and more business is being driven by one metric more than any other. *Return on net assets (RONA)* is the most important measure in international business at this time.

These are measures which will apply to any strategy for an organization in any situation, including international. The special aspect of international is that the strategy will normally be evaluated on repatriated cash flows in home rather than foreign currencies.

Activity 11.2

How are financial and non-financial measures of evaluation and control balanced in your organization? Do non-financial measures add an extra dimension to your organization's ability to control its international activity?

Non-financial measures

The non-financial measures of performance tend to measure external rather than internal performance of an organization and such measures may include:

- Market share
- Growth
- Competitive advantage
- Competitive position
- Sales volume
- Market penetration levels
- New product development
- Customer satisfaction
- Customer brand franchise
- Market image and awareness levels.

These measures, naturally, will vary from market to market in the international area and will need to be measured on a market and a global/international basis for the organization's international activities.

For a discussion of the use of financial versus non-financial measures and using multiple criteria, see the *Strategic Marketing Management 2001–2002* Coursebook (Meek, Meek and Ensor, 2001).

Extending knowledge

It is important that the student of international marketing strategy be aware, first and foremost, of the primary measures of marketing strategy in a domestic situation. For further understanding of the measures of performance and evaluating strategies, the student is directed towards the readings on the area within domestic marketing strategy such as:

Strategic Marketing Management, R.M.S. Wilson and C. Gilligan, Butterworth-Heinemann (1998).

Strategic Marketing Management 2001–2002, Meek, Meek and Ensor, Butterworth-Heinemann (2001).

International marketing and the internet

E-critical

E-marketing is one thing but e-strategy is another. The e-world seems to be full of impatient global e-entrepreneurs all desperate to get 'in there' and make a mark. But what is it all about? What exactly are the aims and objectives of the e-business? 'If you don't know where you're going, any road will take you there' is a well-worn quote – and one that e-business seems intent on making its own.

E-objective

An e-business, like any traditional business needs to have a reasonably clear idea of where it is going and what it is trying to achieve. To make uncountable millions of dollars for the founders is clear but not necessarily sufficient for the foundations of a business.

Developing a vision for an e-business is critical, especially if we hope to create real, rather than hypothetical value in the business.

E-strategy

Having agreed the e-objective, the next question must be, how are we going to do it? E-strategy is not easily agreed, but to try to do without a strategy seems foolhardy. In the most simple terms, the e-strategy will tell you what needs to be done (and what should not be done) as well as who is expected to do it, by when and with what results.

The e-alternative seems to be 'just get in there and do something'. That's fine if you have millions of dollars to play with and nobody really minds how much you lose – that sounds familiar though.

Evaluating international business planning

In international marketing, as with domestic marketing, the use of models in planning is a way of evaluating strategic options. A number of models have been used in international marketing that were developed primarily for domestic marketing purposes. These include the Boston Consulting Group matrix, the GEC/McKinsey approach and the Arthur D. Little method.

Although there has been much in the recent literature criticizing the use of models such as these, they are still a valid mechanism to test the *conceptual approach* to international marketing strategy. These models have been described in detail in the recommended texts as well as examples of organizations using them and the uses to which they have been put, so they will not be repeated here. The use of models such as these and others can be a helpful way of discriminating between likely strategic options and the results that they will bring in the market place when implemented.

Barriers to implementation

There are many barriers that stand in the way of successful implementation of international marketing strategy – some evident, some less so. The barriers fall broadly into three separate categories:

- Environmental barriers
- Organizational barriers
- Marketing department barriers.

Environmental or external barriers are focused around the 'SLEPT' methodology which we discussed in Unit 3. There are a number of factors under each of these headings which will work against the organization looking to develop or even start its international business. For example:

- Government restrictions on exports
- Product, communication or other laws
- Levels of economic activity in overseas markets etc.

Organizational barriers are inherent in areas such as leadership, organizational culture, organizational design, resources and control measures. For example:

- Top management sees itself as running a successful domestic company
- Senior management has experience in developing and satisfying domestic customer needs only
- Organization is designed for the efficient running of a domestic business and international operations are 'fit into' the existing system
- There is little or no specific international expertise
- There is little or no understanding of the special nature of international business
- Resources for international operations are dedicated only after domestic operations have been satisfied – the 'what is left' method
- Resources for international operations are considered 'high risk'
- Top and senior management are measured and rewarded according to domestic success only.

Marketing department barriers are often the most difficult to spot. If the marketing department is domestic market- and product- or sales-focused, there is little hope for internationalization.

For more background on barriers to strategic implementation, see the *Strategic Marketing Management 2001–2002* coursebook (Meek, Meek and Ensor, 2001).

Control systems

If planning is defined as 'deciding what to do' then control can be defined as 'ensuring that the desired results are obtained'. Planning without control is a purely intellectual exercise. Control systems are essential to make sure that an organization drives through the content of its international marketing plans and achieves its organization's objectives in the marketplace. Control systems are varied and selecting the right method of control will depend upon the nature of the international markets that the organization is addressing, the particular goals and objectives which the organization has set itself as well as the environments within which the organization has to operate internationally. In simple terms, a control process can be described as in Figure 11.3.

Control systems, then, if an organization uses traditional control methods, are a matter of balancing four primary issues:

1. Standard setting
2. Performance measurement
3. Performance diagnosis
4. Taking corrective action (if required).

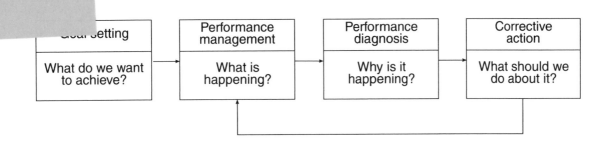

Goal setting	Performance management	Performance diagnosis	Corrective action
What do we want to achieve?	What is happening?	Why is it happening?	What should we do about it?

Figure 11.3
The control process

Activity 11.3

What control mechanisms are used in your organization? How, if at all, would you improve on them?

Setting standards

This is the role of the planning element of the process and the goals and objectives to which the organization's international marketing activity is directed. These activities are then translated into standards which, if met, will produce successful implementation of the international marketing strategy.

Performance standards tend to be measured in simple terms such as:

- *Quantity* How much was achieved? How much should have been achieved?
- *Quality* How good was that which was achieved? How good was it meant to be?
- *Cost* How much did the achievement cost? How much was it planned to cost?

Performance measurement

Typically, divergence from pre-set standards is normally picked up in the organization through a process of:

- *Regular auditing* of the organization's finance and marketing activities or
- *Budgets* – developing and identifying divergence from budgeted inflows and outflows or
- *Variance analysis* – falling out of the budgeting process, the detailed analysis of the variance (difference between actual and expected results) that arises from the organization's activities.

Performance diagnosis

Once the control system has been established and during the implementation phase of the international marketing plan, differences or deviations from the estimated (targeted) results can be highlighted. The international marketer's role is then to decide whether corrective action is required in one or more of the foreign markets and, if so, how to implement this action to bring the plan back on to target. The selection of corrective action depends to a large extent on the reasons behind the divergence from the planned results, and it is essential that the international marketer understands the reason for variances before simply setting off pre-planned contingency activities.

191

Models

There are a number of models that exist to aid the process of assessing and implementing control processes. These include:

* Benchmarking
* Balanced scorecard.

As well as being described earlier, a more detailed analysis of these approaches will be found in *Strategic Marketing Management 2001–2002* coursebook (Meek, Meek and Ensor, 2001).

Factors affecting international controls

There are a number of factors which affect the degree and effectiveness of a control system for international marketing strategy. Some of the most important are:

Activity 11.4

For an organization other than your own can you:

* Identify an occasion where problems in the international control system caused inappropriate marketing action to be taken
* Identify an occasion where control systems resulted in proper action being taken in an international market.

---

* *Communications* Control systems rely on effective communications (two-way) for their accuracy. The opportunities for breakdown of communication systems in the international organization are varied and the problems of both timely and accurate communications between head office and subsidiaries and/or agents and distributors have been well documented. Before any corrective action is taken it is important that the marketer understands the reasons for discrepancies against planned outcomes and the role that communications or miscommunications may have played in the process.
* *Data* The accuracy and flow of international data has always been a problem in international marketing situations. As international activity moves beyond the developed Western markets the availability and accuracy of international market/ product/industry data becomes increasingly less reliable. It is important to understand that control systems start off with data that may not be as reliable as in domestic marketing situations. In these instances greater degrees of latitude should be allowed in the control process before contingency plans are activated.
* *Environmental change* The diversity of environments within which the organization must operate internationally will undoubtedly affect control systems and the data used for their calculation. Currency values, legal structures, political systems and the inevitable cultural factors will all influence the development and control of marketing strategy. The issue of diversity of local environments must be reflected in the control system.
* *Organizational culture* The organization's culture and management philosophy about issues such as centralization or decentralization, internationalization or globalization will affect development of any control system. A highly centralized/global organization will likely require a control system that is detailed and all encompassing. Organizations where authority and decision making is devolved to the local unit level are likely to require a much less mechanistic approach to control systems.
* *Size of international operations* Depending on the nature of the international operation, the organization and the relative importance that international earnings play on the organization's balance sheet, the control system may be fundamental to the organization's reported profit levels. In the organization where international business

is a very small part of its day-to-day operations, control systems will be less rigorously applied and divergences from plan will be less closely scrutinized.

- *Faulty estimating* It may also be apparent from an analysis of the variances that the problem does not lie in the market nor in the organization's ability to deliver to a market's need but the original estimates set against which the plan was going to be judged. In this case the organization and the international marketer needs to re-estimate the rate at which the organization will achieve its strategic objectives.

Exam Hint

Faulty estimating is rarely cited as a problem in control systems – managers tend to believe figures. The mini-cases and the major case (analysis and decision) may contain suspect data – use your intuitive skills to assess whether the given targets are right in the first place.

Questions

As a check on your understanding of what has been covered in this unit, consider the following questions:

Question 11.1

1. What is the role of the control system in international marketing strategy?
2. What are the two categories by which strategy can be evaluated?
3. What are the types of measure that are included under the heading of 'financial measures'?
4. What are the types of measure that are included under the heading of 'non-financial measures'?
5. How can strategic models be used in evaluating international strategy?
6. What is a 'control system'? Give examples.
7. What are the four key issues in any control system?
8. By what methods can divergence from standards be picked up?
9. What are the special factors that affect the efficiency and effectiveness of control systems in international operations?

Exam Question 11.2

The Board of a South East Asian car manufacturer is considering changing its global planning and control process. It has, therefore, requested a report on the following: 'Benchmarking is a relatively new technique on which to base global marketing planning and control decisions'. Evaluate the technique in an international context, addressing particularly the proposition that it ignores 'the market'. As a Marketing Analyst in a Consultancy, prepare the report. (June 2001, Question 7)

Go to www.marketingonline.co.uk or www.bh.com/marketing to access specimen Answers and Senior Examiner's advice for this exam question.

Extending knowledge

For a more detailed analysis and explanation of evaluation and control methods for international marketing strategy, read:

International Marketing Strategy, I. Doole and R. Lowe, Thomson, 3rd Edition. 2001, Chapter 5, pp. 141–177.

International Marketing, S. Paliwoda and M. Thomas, 3rd Edition, Butterworth-Heinemann, 1999, Chapter 9, pp. 352–391.

Global Marketing Strategies, J-P Jeannet and D.H. Hennessey, 5th Edition, Houghton Mifflin. 2001, Chapter 17, pp. 669–698.

Summary

In this unit we have looked at the important stages of strategic evaluation and the control of implementation. First, we considered the problem of evaluating alternative strategies for international operations and deciding which strategic option offered the best chance of achieving the organization's objectives. Evaluation will be driven largely by the organization's objectives but can be measured both internally (financial measures), externally (non-financial measures) or, ideally, a combination of the two.

Second, we considered the control mechanisms that are necessary to ensure that the strategic plan is implemented in the foreign markets and the organization's objectives are achieved. We considered the range of analysis and control mechanisms which are used in different organizations including auditing, budgeting and variance analysis.

Finally, we considered the nature of the corrective action that can be taken by the marketer and the variables which affect the control mechanisms and the results that these give.

Objectives

A mini-case is a compulsory part of the examination and designed to provide you with an opportunity to apply your knowledge to a particular situation. The purpose of this unit is therefore:

- To help you understand how best to approach the mini-case study
- To highlight the sorts of mistakes that are commonly made
- To give you an opportunity to prepare a number of practice solutions.

By the end of this unit, you will:

- Be familiar with the sorts of mini-case studies that have been used over the past few years
- Have an understanding of the issues that they raise
- Have gained some practice at approaching these cases.

Study guide

Although with each of the previous units it has been a relatively straightforward exercise to identify how long you should spend working on the unit, it is far harder to do this with the mini-case. Instead, you should recognize that the more practice you get with the mini-case, the more likely it is that you will approach it in your examination with a degree of confidence and an understanding of what is required from you. You should, therefore, spend as much time as you can familiarizing yourself with the format of the mini-cases and the sorts of questions that are asked. Practise preparing solutions to the questions and then compare your answers with the solutions that we have included at the end of the unit.

Introduction

It needs to be recognized that the type of short case (popularly called the mini-case) set in the examinations cannot be treated in exactly the same way as the extremely long case set for the subject of *Strategic Marketing: Analysis and Decision.*

However, far too many students adopt a maxi-case approach, using a detailed marketing audit outline which is largely inappropriate to a case consisting of just two or three pages. Others use SWOT analysis and simply rewrite the case under the four headings of strengths, weaknesses, opportunities and threats.

Some students even go so far as to ignore the specific questions set and present a standard maxi-case analysis, including environmental reviews and contingency plans. Others adopt a vague and far too superficial approach. In each case, students are penalized. You should recognize therefore that the mini-case is simply an *outline* of a given situation whose purpose is to test whether candidates can apply their knowledge of marketing operations to the environment described in the scenario. For example, answers advocating retail audits as part of the marketing information system for a small industrial goods manufacturer confirm that the examinee has learned a given MkIS outline by rote and simply regurgitated this with complete disregard of the scenario. Such an approach cannot be passed. A more appropriate approach to the scenario involves a mental review of the areas covered by the question and the selection by the candidate of those particular parts of knowledge or techniques which apply to the case. This implies a rejection of those parts of the student's knowledge which clearly do not apply to the scenario.

All scenarios are based upon real-world companies and situations and are written with a full knowledge of how that organization operates in its planning environments. Often, the organization described in the scenario will not be a giant fast-moving consumer goods manufacturing and marketing company but is instead an innovative, small-or medium-sized firm faced with a particular problem or challenge. The cases are often, but not invariably, written from the viewpoint of a consultant and include an extract from a consultant's report.

The examination as a whole lasts for three hours. Including your reading time, you therefore have approximately one hour, fifteen minutes for the mini-case.

Note: The mini case represents 40 per cent of the marks in the examination. Budget your time to take account of this.

Exam Hint

On opening the examination paper, read the mini-case at your normal reading speed, highlighting any issues that appear to you to be particularly significant. Having done this, read the questions in Section 1 and then read the mini-case again, identifying and highlighting those issues which are particularly relevant to the questions posed. Remember that both questions in the section need to be answered and that the examination paper will indicate the split of marks. Allocate your time accordingly and do not make the mistake of spending much more than approximately one hour, fifteen minutes on the mini-case (Section 1).

The mistakes that candidates make

We have already touched upon some of the mistakes that candidates make in approaching the mini-case. We can, however, take these further with the list of the 13 most common errors that candidates make.

The thirteen most common mini-case errors

1. Ignoring the specific questions posed and providing instead a general treatment of the case.
2. Thinking that every mini-case study demands a SWOT analysis; it doesn't.
3. Not answering in the format asked for. You will normally be asked for a report, a memorandum or a marketing plan and should answer using one of these frameworks.
4. Making unrealistic assumptions about the extent to which organizations can change their working practices.
5. Assuming that unlimited financial resources will be available to you.
6. Failing to recognize the difficulties of implementation.
7. Introducing hypothetical data on costs.
8. Rewriting the case and ignoring the questions.
9. Failing to give full recognition to the implications of what is recommended.
10. Not spending sufficient time on the second of the two questions.
11. Not being strategic.
12. Not being international.
13. Not writing in report format.

In preparing the following schematic answer schemes reference has been made to two essential text books:

- *International Marketing Strategy* (Doole and Lowe), Thomson, 2001
- *International Marketing Strategy,* 1999–2000 (Fifield and Lewis), Butterworth-Heinemann, 1999.

To have any chance of doing well in this subject, candidates are advised to have studied both these texts. Top quality candidates must have read widely via accepted quality journals.

Another vital point here is that the writing of an an actual prescribed answer is often misleading. There is no single approach or answer that is correct (and which therefore makes all others wrong). At the Diploma level the CIM is seeking professional, logical solutions that are frequently underpinned by academic theories. It is therefore of more help and assistance to provide here guidelines and frameworks. We seek to communicate to you an 'approach' to each of the questions from the perspective of the examination, paying regard to the specific construct of each question.

Further study and examination preparation

Specimen exam paper: June 2001

Specimen exam paper December 2001

Appendix 1
Guidance on examination preparation

Preparing for your examination

You are now nearing the final phase of your studies and it is time to start the hard work of exam preparation.

During your period of study you will have become used to absorbing large amounts of information. You will have tried to understand and apply aspects of knowledge that may have been very new to you, while some of the information provided may have been more familiar. You may even have undertaken many of the activities that are positioned frequently throughout your Coursebook, which will have enabled you to apply your learning in practical situations. But whatever the state of your knowledge and understanding, do not allow yourself to fall into the trap of thinking that you know enough, you understand enough, or even worse, that you can just take it as it comes on the day.

Never underestimate the pressure of the CIM examination.

The whole point of preparing this text for you is to ensure that you never take the examination for granted, and that you do not go into the exam unprepared for what might come your way for three hours at a time.

One thing's for sure: there is no quick fix, no easy route, no waving a magic wand and finding you know it all.

Whether you have studied alone, in a CIM study centre, or through distance learning, you now need to ensure that this final phase of your learning process is tightly managed, highly structured and objective.

As a candidate in the examination, your role will be to convince the Senior Examiner for this subject that you have credibility. You need to demonstrate to the examiner that you can be trusted to undertake a range of challenges in the context of marketing, that you are able to capitalize on opportunities and manage your way through threats.

You should prove to the Senior Examiner that you are able to apply knowledge, make decisions, respond to situations and solve problems.

Very shortly we are going to look at a range of revision and exam preparation techniques, and at time management issues, and encourage you towards developing and implementing your own revision plan, but before that, let's look at the role of the Senior Examiner.

A bit about the Senior Examiners!

You might be quite shocked to read this, but while it might appear that the examiners are 'relentless question masters' they actually want you to be able to answer the questions and pass the exams! In fact, they would derive no satisfaction or benefits from failing candidates; quite the contrary, they develop the syllabus and exam papers in order that you can learn and then apply that learning effectively so as to pass your examinations. Many of the examiners have said in the past that it is indeed psychologically more difficult to fail students than pass them.

Many of the hints and tips you find within this Appendix have been suggested by the Senior Examiners and authors of the Coursebook series. Therefore you should consider them carefully and resolve to undertake as many of the elements suggested as possible.

The Chartered Institute of Marketing has a range of processes and systems in place within the Examinations Division to ensure that fairness and consistency prevail across the team of examiners, and that the academic and vocational standards that are set and defined are indeed maintained. In doing this, CIM ensures that those who gain the CIM Certificate, Advanced Certificate and Postgraduate Diploma, are worthy of the qualification and perceived as such in the view of employers, actual and potential.

Part of what you will need to do within the examination is be 'examiner friendly' – that means you have to make sure they get what they ask for. This will make life easier for you and for them.

Hints and tips for 'examiner friendly' actions are as follows:

- Show them that you understand the basis of the question, by answering *precisely* the question asked, and not including just about everything you can remember about the subject area.
- Read their needs – how many points is the question asking you to address?
- Respond to the question appropriately. Is the question asking you to take on a role? If so, take on the role and answer the question in respect of the role. For example, you could be positioned as follows:

  'You are working as a Marketing Assistant at Nike UK' or 'You are a Marketing Manager for an Engineering Company' or 'As Marketing Manager write a report to the Managing Partner'.

  These examples of role-playing requirements are taken from questions in past papers.
- Deliver the answer in the format requested. If the examiner asks for a memo, then provide a memo; likewise, if the examiner asks for a report, then write a report. If you do not do this, in some instances you will fail to gain the necessary marks required to pass.
- Take a business-like approach to your answers. This enhances your credibility. Badly ordered work, untidy work, lack of structure, headings and subheadings can be off-putting. This would be unacceptable in the work situation, likewise it will be unacceptable in the eyes of the Senior Examiners and their marking teams.
- Ensure the examiner has something to mark: give them substance, relevance, definitions, illustration and demonstration of your knowledge and understanding of the subject area.
- See the examiner as your potential employer, or ultimate consumer/customer. The whole purpose and culture of marketing is about meeting customers' needs. Try this approach – it works wonders.
- Provide a strong sense of enthusiasm and professionalism in your answers; support it with relevant up-to-date examples and apply them where appropriate.
- Try to do something that will make your exam paper a little bit different – make it stand out in the crowd.

All of these points might seem quite logical to you, but often in the panic of the examination they 'go out of the window'. Therefore it is beneficial to remind ourselves of the importance of the examiner. He/she is the 'ultimate customer' – and we all know customers hate to be disappointed.

As we move on, some of these points will be revisited and developed further.

About the examination

In all examinations, with the exception of Marketing in Practice at Certificate level and Analysis and Decision at Diploma level, the paper is divided into two parts.

- Part A – Mini-case study = 40 per cent of the marks
- Part B – Option choice questions (choice of three questions from seven) = 60 per cent of the marks

Let's look at the basis of each element.

The mini-case study

This is based on a mini-case or scenario with one question, possibly subdivided into between two and four points, but totalling 40 per cent of marks overall.

In essence, you, the candidate, are placed in a problem-solving role through the medium of a short scenario. On occasions, the scenario may consist of an article from a journal in relation to a well-known organization: for example, in the past Interflora, EasyJet and Philips, among others, have been used as the basis of the mini-case.

Alternatively, it will be based upon a fictional company, and the examiner will have prepared it in order that the right balance of knowledge, understanding, application and skills is used.

Approaches to the mini-case study

When undertaking the mini-case study there are a number of key areas you should consider.

Structure/content

The mini-case that you will be presented with will vary slightly from paper to paper, and of course from one examination to the next. Normally the scenario presented will be 400–500 words long and will centre on a particular organization and its problems or may even relate to a specific industry.

The length of the mini-case study means that usually only a brief outline is provided of the situation, the organization and its marketing problems, and you must therefore learn to cope with analysing information and preparing your answer on the basis of a very limited amount of detail.

Time management

There are many differing views on time management and the approaches you can take to managing your time within the examination. You must find an approach to suit your way of working, but always remember, whatever you do, you must ensure that you allow enough time to complete the examination. Unfinished exams mean lost marks.

A typical example of managing time is as follows:

Your paper is designed to assess you over a three-hour period. With 40 per cent of the marks being allocated to the mini-case, it means that you should dedicate somewhere around 75 minutes of your time to both read and write up the answer on this mini-case. Some students, however, will prefer to allocate nearer half of their time (90 minutes) on the mini-case, so that they can read and fully absorb the case and answer the questions in the context of it. This is also acceptable as long as you ensure that you work extremely 'SMART' for the remaining time in order to finish the examination.

Do not forget that while there is only one question within the mini-case, it can have a number of components. You must answer all the components in that question, which is where the balance of times comes into play.

Knowledge/skills tested

Throughout all the CIM papers, your knowledge, skills and ability to apply those skills will be tested. However, the mini-cases are used particularly to test application, i.e. your ability to take your knowledge and apply it in a structured way to a given scenario. The examiners will be looking at your decision-making ability, your analytical and communication skills and, depending on the level, your ability as a manager to solve particular marketing problems.

When the examiner is marking your paper, he/she will be looking to see how you differentiate yourself, looking at your own individual 'unique selling points'. The examiner will also want to can personally apply the knowledge or whether you are only able to repeat the materials.

t of answers

On any occasions, and within all examinations, you will most likely be given a particular communication method to use. If this is the case, you must ensure that you adhere to the requirements of the examiner. This is all part of meeting customer needs.

The likely communication tools you will be expected to use are as follows:

- Memorandum
- Memorandum/report
- Report
- Briefing notes
- Presentation
- Press release
- Advertisement
- Plan

Make sure that you familiarize yourself with these particular communication tools and practise using them to ensure that, on the day, you will be able to respond confidently to the communication requests of the examiner. Look back at the Customer Communications text at Certificate level to familiarize yourself with the potential requirements of these methods.

By the same token, while communication methods are important, so is meeting the specific requirements of the question. This means you must understand what is meant by the precise instruction given. **Note the following terms carefully:**

- **Identify** – select key issues, point out key learning points, establish clearly what the examiner expects you to identify.
- **Illustrate** – the examiner expects you to provide examples, scenarios and key concepts that illustrate your learning.
- **Compare and contrast** – look at the range of similarities between the two situations, contexts or even organizations. Then compare them, i.e. ascertain and list how activities, features, etc. agree or disagree. Contrasting means highlighting the differences between the two.
- **Discuss** – questions that have 'discuss' in them offer a tremendous opportunity for you to debate, argue, justify your approach or understanding of the subject area – *caution* it is not an opportunity to waffle.
- **Briefly explain** – this means being succinct, structured and concise in your explanation, within the answer. Make your points clear, transparent and relevant.
- **State** – present in a clear, brief format.
- **Interpret** – expound the meaning of, make clear and explicit what it is you see and understand within the data provided.
- **Outline** – provide the examiner with the main concepts and features being asked for and avoid minor technical details. Structure will be critical here, or else you could find it difficult to contain your answer.
- **Relate** – show how different aspects of the syllabus connect together.
- **Evaluate** – review and reflect upon an area of the syllabus, a particular practice, an article, etc., and consider its overall worth in respect of its use as a tool or a model and its overall effectiveness in the role it plays.

Source: Worsam, Mike, *How to Pass Marketing*, Croner, 1989.

Your approach to mini-cases

There is no one right way to approach and tackle a mini-case study, indeed it will be down to each individual to use their own creativity in tackling the tasks presented. You will have to use your initiative and discretion about how best to approach the mini-case. Having said this, however, there are some basic steps you can take.

- Ensure that you read through the case study at least twice before making any judgements, starting to analyse the information provided, or indeed writing the answers.
- On the third occasion read through the mini-case and, using a highlighter, start marking the essential and relevant information critical to the content and context. Then turn your attention to the question again, this time reading slowly and carefully to assess what it is you are expected to do. Note any instructions that the examiner gives you, and then start to plan how you might answer the question. Whatever the question, ensure the answer has a structure: a beginning, a structured central part of the answer and, finally, always a conclusion.
- Keep the context of the question continually in mind: that is, the specifics of the case and the role which you might be performing.
- Because there is limited material available, you will sometimes need to make assumptions. Don't be afraid to do this, it will show initiative on your part. Assumptions are an important part of dealing with case studies and can help you to be quite creative with your answer. However, do explain the basis of your assumptions within your answer so that the examiner understands the nature of them, and why you have arrived at your particular outcome. **Always ensure that your assumptions are realistic.**
- Only now are you approaching the stage where it is time to start writing your answer to the question, tackling the problems, making decisions and recommendations on the case scenario set before you. As mentioned previously, your points will often be best set out in a report or memo type format, particularly if the examiner does not specify a communication method.
- Ensure that your writing is succinct, avoids waffle and responds directly to the questions asked.

Part B

Again, with the exception of the Analysis and Decision case study, each Part B is comprised of six or seven more traditional questions, each worth 20 per cent. You will be expected to choose three of those questions, to make up the remaining 60 per cent of available marks.

Realistically, the same principles apply for these questions as in the case study. Communication formats, reading through the questions, structure, role-play, context, etc. – everything is the same.

Part B will cover a number of broader issues from within the syllabus and will be taken from any element of it. The examiner makes the choice, and no prior direction is given to students or tutors on what that might be.

As regards time management in this area, if you used about 75 minutes for the mini-case you should have around 105 minutes left. This provides you with around 30 minutes to plan and write a question and 5 minutes per question to review and revise your answers. Keep practising – use a cooker timer, alarm clock or mobile phone alarm as your timer and work hard at answering questions within the timeframe given.

Specimen examination papers and answers

To help you prepare and understand the nature of the paper, go to www.marketingonline.co.uk or www.bh.com/marketing to access Specimen Answers and Senior Examiner's advice for these exam questions. During your study, the author of your Coursebook may have on occasions asked you to refer to these papers and answer the questions. You should undertake these exercises and utilize every opportunity to practise meeting examination requirements.

The specimen answers are vital learning tools. They are not always perfect, as they are answers written by students and annotated by the Senior Examiners, but they will give you a good indication of the approaches you could take, and the examiners' annotations suggest how these answers might be improved. Please use them. You can also access this type of information through the Virtual Institute on the CIM website using your student registration number as an access code.

Other sources of information to support your learning through the Virtual Institute are 'Hot Topics'. These give you scope to undertake a range of associated activities related to the syllabus and study areas, and will also be very useful to you when you are revising.

Key elements of preparation

One Senior Examiner suggests the three elements involved in preparing for your examination can be summarized thus:

- Learning
- Memory
- Revision

Let's look at each point in turn.

Learning

Quite often students find it difficult to learn properly. You can passively read books, look at some of the materials, perhaps revise a little, and regurgitate it all in the examination. In the main, however, this is rather an unsatisfactory method of learning. It is meaningless, shallow and ultimately of little use in practice.

For learning to be truly effective it must be active and applied. You must involve yourself in the learning process by thinking about what you have read, testing it against your experience by reflecting on how you use particular aspects of marketing, and how you could perhaps improve your own performance by implementing particular aspects of your learning into your everyday life. You should adopt the old adage of 'learning by doing'. If you do, you will find that passive learning has no place in your study life.

Below are some suggestions that have been prepared to assist you with the learning pathway throughout your revision.

- Always make your own notes, in words you understand, and ensure that you combine all the sources of information and activities within them.
- Always try to relate your learning back to your own organization.
- Make sure you define key terms concisely, wherever possible.
- Do not try to memorize your ideas, but work on the basis of understanding and, most important, applying them.
- Think about the relevant and topical questions that might be set – use the questions and answers in your Coursebooks to identify typical questions that might be asked in the future.
- Attempt all of the questions within each of your Coursebooks since these are vital tests of your active learning and understanding.

Memory

If you are prepared to undertake an active learning programme then your knowledge will be considerably enhanced, as understanding and application of knowledge does tend to stay in your 'long-term' memory. It is likely that passive learning will only stay in your 'short-term' memory.

Do not try to memorize parrot fashion; it is not helpful and, even more important, examiners are experienced in identifying various memorizing techniques and therefore will spot them as such.

Having said this, it is quite useful to memorize various acronyms such as SWOT, PEST, PESTLE, STEEPLE, or indeed various models such as Ansoff, GE Matrix, Shell Directional, etc., as in some of the questions you may be required to use illustrations of these to assist your answer.

Revision

The third and final stage to consider is 'revision', which is what we will concentrate on in detail below. Here just a few key tips are offered.

Revision should be an ongoing process rather than a panic measure that you decide to undertake just before the examination. You should be preparing notes *throughout* your course, with the view to using them as part of your revision process. Therefore ensure that your notes are sufficiently comprehensive that you can reuse them successfully.

For each concept you learn about, you should identify, through your reading and your own personal experience, at least two or three examples that you could use; this then gives you some scope to broaden your perspective during the examination. It will, of course, help you gain some points for initiative with the examiners.

Knowledge is not something you will gain overnight – as we saw earlier, it is not a quick fix; it involves a process of learning that enables you to lay solid foundations upon which to build your long-term understanding and application. This will benefit you significantly in the future, not just in the examination.

In essence, you should ensure that you do the following in the period before the real intensive revision process begins.

- Keep your study file well organized, updated and full of newspaper and journal cuttings that may help you formulate examples in your mind for use during the examination.
- Practise defining key terms and acronyms from memory.
- Prepare topic outlines and essay answer plans.
- When you start your intensive revision, ensure it is planned and structured in the way described below. And then finally, read your concentrated notes the night before the examination.

Revision planning

You are now on a critical path – although hopefully not too critical at this time – with somewhere in the region of between four and six weeks to go to the examination. The following hints and tips will help you plan out your revision study.

- You will, as already explained, need to be very organized. Therefore, before doing anything else, put your files, examples, reading material etc. in good order, so that you are able to work with them in the future and, of course, make sense of them.
- Ensure that you have a quiet area within which to work. It is very easy to get distracted when preparing for an examination.
- Take out your file along with your syllabus and make a list of key topic areas that you have studied and which you now need to revise. You could use the basis of this book to do that, by taking each unit a step at a time.
- Plan the use of your time carefully. Ideally you should start your revision at least six weeks prior to the exam, so therefore work out how many spare hours you could give to the revision process and then start to allocate time in your diary, and do not double-book with anything else.
- Give up your social life for a short period of time. As the saying goes 'no pain – no gain'.

- Looking at each of the subject areas in turn, identify which are your strengths and which are your weaknesses. Which areas have you grasped and understood, and which are the areas that you have really struggled with? Split your page in two and make a list on each side. For example:

Planning and control	
Strengths	Weaknesses
Audit – PEST, SWOT, Models Portfolio analysis	Ratio analysis Market sensing Productivity analysis Trend extrapolation Forecasting

- Break down your list again and divide the points of weakness, giving priority in the first instance to your weakest areas and even prioritizing them by giving them a number. This will enable you to master the more difficult areas. Up to 60 per cent of your remaining revision time should be given over to that, as you may find you have to undertake a range of additional reading and also perhaps seeking tutor support, if you are studying at a CIM Accredited Study Centre.
- The rest of the time should be spent reinforcing your knowledge and understanding of the stronger areas, spending time testing yourself on how much you really know.
- Should you be taking two examinations or more at any one time, then the breakdown and managing of your time will be critical.
- Taking a subject at a time, work through your notes and start breaking them down into subsections of learning, and ultimately into key learning points, items that you can refer to time and time again, that are meaningful and that your mind will absorb. You yourself will know how you best remember key points. Some people try to develop acronyms, or flowcharts or matrices, mind maps, fishbone diagrams, etc., or various connection diagrams that help them recall certain aspects of models. You could also develop processes that enable you to remember approaches to various options. (But do remember what we said earlier about regurgitating stuff, parrot fashion.)

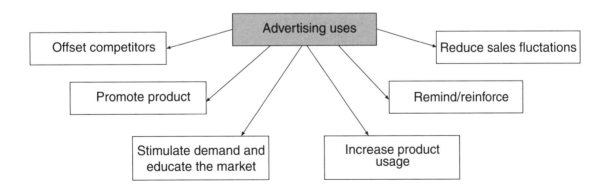

Figure A1.1
Use of a diagram to summarize key components of a concept (Source: Adapted from Dibb, Simkin, Pride & Ferrell, Marketing Concepts and Strategies, 4th edition, Houghton Mifflin, 2001)

Figure A1.1 is just a brief example of how you could use a 'bomb-burst' diagram (which, in this case, highlights the uses of advertising) as a very helpful approach to memorizing key elements of learning.

- Eventually you should reduce your key learning to bullet points. For example: imagine you were looking at the concept of Time Management – you could eventually reduce your key learning to a bullet list containing the following points in relation to 'Effective Prioritization:'

    - Organize
    - Take time
    - Delegate
    - Review

Each of these headings would then remind you of the elements you need to discuss associated with the subject area.

- Avoid getting involved in reading too many textbooks at this stage, as you may start to find that you are getting confused overall.
- Look at examination questions on previous papers, and start to observe closely the various roles and tasks they expect you to undertake, and importantly, the context in which they are set.
- Use the specimen exam papers and specimen answers to support your learning and see how you could actually improve upon them.
- Without exception, find an associated examination question for the areas that you have studied and revised, and undertake it (more than once if necessary).
- Without referring to notes or books, try to draft an answer plan with the key concepts, knowledge, models and information that are needed to successfully complete the answer. Then refer to the specimen answer to see how close you are to the actual outline presented. Planning your answer, and ensuring that key components are included, and that the question has a meaningful structure, is one of the most beneficial activities that you can undertake.
- Now write the answer out in full, time-constrained and written by hand, not with the use of IT. (At this stage, you are still expected to be the scribe for the examination and present handwritten work. Many of us find this increasingly difficult as we spend more and more time using our computers to present information. Do your best to be neat. Spidery handwriting is often offputting to the examiner.)
- When writing answers as part of your revision process, also be sure to practise the following essential examinations techniques:

    - **Identify and use the communication method** requested by the examiner.
    - **Always have three key parts to the answer** – an introduction, middle section that develops your answer in full, and a conclusion. Where appropriate, ensure that you have an introduction, main section, summary/conclusion and, if requested or helpful, recommendations.
    - **Always answer the question in the context or role set.**
    - **Always comply with the nature and terms of the question.**
    - **Leave white space.** Do not overcrowd your page; Leave space between paragraphs, and make sure your sentences do not merge into one blur. (Don't worry – there is always plenty of paper available to use in the examination.)
    - **Count** how many actions the question asks you to undertake and double-check at the end that you have met the full range of demands of the question.
    - **Use examples** – to demonstrate your knowledge and understanding of the particular syllabus area. These can be from journals, the Internet, the press, or your own experience.

- **Display your vigour and enthusiasm for marketing.** Remember to think of the Senior Examiner as your customer, or future employer, and do your best to deliver what is wanted to satisfy their needs. Impress them and show them how you are a 'cut above the rest'.
- Review all your practice answers critically, with the above points in mind.

Practical actions

The critical path is becoming even more critical now as the examination looms. The following are vital points.

- Have you registered with CIM?
- Do you know where you are taking your examination? CIM should let you know approximately one month in advance.
- Do you know where your examination centre is? If not find out, take a drive, time it – whatever you do don't be late!
- Make sure you have all the tools of the examination ready. A dictionary, calculator, pens, pencils, ruler, etc. Try not to use multiple shades of pens, but at the same time make your work look professional. *Avoid using red and green as these are the colours that will be used for marking.*

Summary

Above all you must remember that you personally have invested a tremendous amount of time, effort and money in studying for this programme and it is therefore imperative that you consider the suggestions given here as they will help to maximize your return on your investment.

Many of the hints and tips offered here are generic and will work across most of the CIM courses. We have tried to select those that will help you most in taking a sensible, planned approach to your study and revision.

The key to your success is being prepared to put in the time and effort required, planning your revision, and equally important, planning and answering your questions in a way that will ensure that you pass your examination on the day.

The advice offered here aims to guide you from a practical perspective. Guidance on syllabus content and developments associated with your learning will become clear to you as you work through this Coursebook. The authors of each Coursebook have given subject-specific guidance on the approach to the examination and on how to ensure that you meet the content requirements of the kind of question you will face. These considerations are in addition to the structuring issues we have been discussing throughout this Appendix.

Each of the authors and Senior Examiners will guide you on their preferred approach to questions and answers as they go. Therefore where you are presented with an opportunity to be involved in some activity or undertake an examination question either during or at the end of your study units, do take it. It not only prepares you for the examination, but helps you learn in the applied way we discussed above.

Here, then, is a last reminder:

- Ensure you make the most of your learning process throughout.
- Keep structured and orderly notes from which to revise.
- Plan your revision – don't let it just happen.
- Provide examples to enhance your answers.

- Practise your writing skills in order that you present your work well and your writing is readable.
- Take as many opportunities to test your knowledge and measure your progress as possible.
- Plan and structure your answers.
- Always do as the question asks you, especially with regard to context and communication method.
- **Do not leave it until the last minute!**

The writers would like to take this opportunity to wish you every success in your endeavours to study, to revise and to pass your examinations.

Karen Beamish
Academic Development Advisor

The answers that follow are indicative and are not intended to be complete. Some of the answers to the activities are embedded in the course materials, the essential text, in web sites or simply in the mind of the reader.

Unit 1

Debriefing Question 1.2

The principal factors that the organization must consider as it evolves from a domestic to a global operator are:

- Increasing risk from the effects of the 'environmental factors' e.g. political, social, competition, cultural, currency fluctuations, competition, technology etc. (see the Doole and Lowe text Chapters 1 and 3)
- The possibility of increasing lack of control over operations
- Market differences
- Cost escalation
- Need for more information
- Increase in resources – people, money, facilities
- Increasing complexity – in planning, marketing mix, implementation and control
- Need for organizational changes and training requirements.

Debriefing Question 1.3

Answers which discuss the 'domestic to global' evolution only are missing the point. It is the internal factors to the firm which have to be considered in the answer. Answers which include the Porter or Ohmae analysis are particularly good.

The factors to be considered are:

- Organizational: size, type
- Resources: financial, human, manufacturing or services, competencies, marketing and administrative skills
- Management: ability to grasp latent or actual opportunities, research ability, knowledge of international operations
- Product or service: ability to internationalize or standardize, pricing structures and to see necessary marketing mix decisions
- Supporting services: ability to obtain transactional service support, e.g. banks.

Debriefing Question 1.4

The organization is affected in its approach to customers overseas, raw material and component resourcing, in its financing requirements, in its domestic market through international competition and in its general business level affected by the trade cycle.

The organization's approach to international marketing strategy can be affected by the marketer's self-reference criterion. The four key questions in international marketing are: whether to go international, where to operate, what to market in the overseas environment and how to operate internationally.

The two key drivers to start off an entry into international marketing are saturation in the home market and market potential overseas.

'Level of involvement' means how deeply the organization wishes to get involved in overseas operations.

The strategic decision to enter foreign markets will have tactical effects on the market entry method, use of personnel, cost effects and organizational effects.

The three criteria for foreign market selection are: market potential, similarity to home or other foreign markets and market accessibility.

The special factors to be taken into account are; the marketing mix, the functional requirements, costs, financial considerations, human resources and risk.

An organization may go international bcause the home market is saturated, there is intense domestic competition, the organization has excess capacity, it has a comparative advantage in product, skill or technology, geographic diversification, product life-cycle differences and organizational and financial reasons.

Intense domestic competition may force the organization to go overseas so that it can compete on a more equal footing with its rival.

The organization may find that it can compete at different points of development in the industry or product life cycle overseas. It may export a product no longer used in its domestic market or place a more advanced one into an overseas market.

The two main forms of financial risk are foreign exchange and political risk.

The two management decisions informed by research are helping the organization decide whether to follow an international route by quantifying opportunities and to develop and implement suitable marketing strategies and programmes that will allow exploitation of the opportunities.

The two types of data that might be collected are feasibility data and operational data.

Unit 2

Debriefing Activity 2.1

In order to complete this exercise, list four international products or services.

Debriefing Activity 2.2

A good area to select would be digital technology, for example, television or mobile phones.

Sky, in television broadcasting, would be a good example of technological breakthrough. Work out how long it took On Digital, for example, to break into this digital technology. Why did it take On Digital the time it did to break into this area? What were the driving forces?

It took about a year. The driving forces were certainly market potential, potential long-term returns on investment and prospect of being 'first in' with all its advantages.

Debriefing Activity 2.3

In order to provide an answer this activity choose six main brands. Any text with a chapter on 'Globalization' or 'International Product Development', for example Doole and Lowe, will list the world's major brands, or at least, a lot of them.

Doole and Lowe provide an excellent description of brand values (including universal quality, reliability, instant recognition and continuous innovation) and valuation in their chapter on 'International Brand Development'. You will do well to read this chapter carefully.

Debriefing Exam Question 2.1

Candidates should explain what a World Bank inspired change from a 'command' to a 'market' economy is, i.e. it is an Economic Structural Adjustment Programme (ESAP) aimed at producing, (a) a market economy and (b) a non-government interventionalist economy (public enterprises, subsidiaries, etc.). The relevant theory should be explained.

Implications in terms of potential market channel development: ESAP usually produces a number of internal effects which create opportunities and problems as follows (these should be related to potential market and channel development):

Unit 3

Debriefing Activity 3.1

Select a manager or company involved in international operations.

Identify what elements of culture are known, e.g. language, religion, values and attitudes, education, technology, social organization, law and politics and aesthetics.

To see how well this information is used in international marketing planning, see how it is used, if at all, in the following areas:

1. Selection of marketing objectives
2. SWOT analysis
3. PEST analysis
4. Selection of strategic options
5. Selection of target markets
6. Selection of market entry method
7. Selection of the marketing mix
8. Organizational considerations, i.e. structures
9. Selection of resources
10. Selection of evaluation and control procedures.

You should evaluate the risks and opportunities involved at every stage of the planning process imposed by these cultural considerations.

Debriefing Activity 3.2

The World Bank classifies economies based on GNP per capita:

- Low income economies
- Middle income economies
- Upper middle income economies
- High income economies
- Other economies.

This tells you that, according to their classification, they will be either less developed, newly emerging, emergent or post-industrial economies and that they will import or export the appropriate goods and services accordingly. For example lesser developed countries will be mainly primary goods exporters where value is added elsewhere and finished goods importers. On the other hand emergent economies are likely to be exporters of technologically advanced goods and services and importers of high value goods and services. The political stance is likely to be more 'hands off', facilitative, accountable and tolerant as countries evolve through the lesser developed to post-industrial spectrum.

The implications to the international marketer are mainly in the areas of market potential, environmental, market and transactional risk, and transaction facilitation.

Debriefing Activity 3.3

The main features to look out for are:

- Country boundaries, i.e. size, neighbouring states
- Mountain ranges, deserts and river systems
- Location of country, major capital locations, nearness to developed countries
- Access to air, sea, rail and road routes.

These factors will affect the development and execution of marketing plans, for example distribution systems, access to markets, cost escalation for trans-shipment to landlocked countries, market potential, etc.

Debriefing Activity 3.4

For the current inflation rate look in government statistical tables or relevant source.

People manage with high prices by cutting down on consumption of all but essential goods, working harder or taking two jobs, operating in the parallel economy, postponing purchases or payments and substituting for cheaper goods. A symptom of high inflation can be rises in the crime rate!

It could affect exports in that there may be a drop in demand for the products or services, lengthening of the payment period and/or shortfalls in payment and you may be affected by subsitute sales.

Debriefing Activity 3.5

Different forms of competition are substitute (matches and lighters), like (Nike and Reebok) and form (gifts). These are a result of changes in technology, purchase occasion, consumer tastes, incomes and other socio/demographic factors.

Competition affects the development of international marketing plans in that it helps determine markets to operate in, the organization's competitive stance (or position), what strategy it will adopt, how it will compete in the market place (the marketing mix) and how it will deploy its resources (people, monetary and facilities) to maximum effect.

The five competitive forces are the threat of new entrants; macro forces, e.g. technological; micro forces, e.g. customers changing their needs and wants; the threat of substitute products; and 'the industry' itself, e.g. is it oligopolistic or highly competitive and how are the players jockeying for position?

Debriefing Question 3.1

Candidates should contextualize the answer by giving a brief description of what a collapse of some South-East Asian countries means in an international context, particularly the devaluation of local currencies against international currencies and its effect on the demand and supply of goods and services.

The answer requires two areas of discussion – the major consideration in pricing goods and services for the international market and the contingencies planned for currency collapses.

Major considerations:

- Pricing objectives – financial, marketing, competitive, product differentiation
- Level and type of demand and sensitivities
- Intensity and type of competition
- Cost
- Government restrictions and controls
- The distribution channel
- The quality/price connection
- Pricing strategies, policies and methods

- Risk, i.e. currency devaluation, lack of payment receipts
- 'Under' and 'over invoicing'.

Contingency planning:

First of all there should be a discussion on foreign exchange risk:

- Match receipts and payment, i.e. payment in like currencies
- Quotations and invoices in own currency
- Invoice in foreign currency with rate fixed in advance with a bank
- Invoice in foreign currency, fixing exchange rate on invoice
- Borrow foreign currency from a bank, sell in dollars or pounds and repay the loan with the proceeds of the exchange
- Offset imports in one currency with exports in the same currency
- Forward buying/hedging against inflation, future buying
- Spot trading
- Use a basket of currencies
- Pay in advance
- Countertrade.

Debriefing Question 3.3

1. The SLEPT factors – social/cultural, legal, competition, currency, technolgical, economic, political.
2. Language, religion, values and attitudes, education, social organization, technology and material culture, law and politics and aesthetics.
3. 'Language' will affect interpersonal relationships, promotional strategy, internal spoken and written communications, and transactional activities, e.g. market research.
4. 'Religion' will affect market demand potential for products and services and use of images and symbolism in communications.
5. 'Values and attitudes' will affect products offered, packaging, communications activities, motivation of personnel and planning deadlines.
6. 'Education' will affect labelling of products, communication messages and managerial issues.
7. 'Social organization' will affect marketing planning in its entirety.
8. 'Technology' will affect customer needs and wants, all elements of the marketing mix and evaluation and control activities.
9. 'Aesthetics' will affect product decisions, e.g. colours and size and communication decisions.
10. Governments either participate in or regulate economies. This affects the scope of operations in an economy, the rules of engagement and market accessability.
11. The main aspects are local domestic laws and international laws. These will affect the export of goods, the responsibility to respect and uphold laws in international operations and marketing mix decisions.
12. The main aspects are an international structure which affects marketing between nations and domestic economies of every nation in which the firm is attempting to market. It affects international operations in that it affects market demand and size, market opportunities, target markets and marketing mix decisions.
13. Models can aid in the development of international marketing strategy as they can act as a 'rough screen' for determining market potential and the extent of use and effectiveness of the marketing mix elements. They also help determine the extent of likely competition.
14. The main aspects of the international 'technology' environment are that it is not limited to national boundaries, it can be expensive and it can reduce barriers to entry. It affects international operations in that highly technological products can help the 'standardization' argument, but it may limit operations to markets which can afford it.

15. The main aspects of the international 'competitive' environment are: it is on the increase, its effect can be seen with the market entry of low cost operators, e.g. China; and global sourcing is being used as a means to achieve international competitive advantage. It is at the heart of all globalization decisions that is its main effect on international operations.

16. Business to business works in the international environment in that this market is the source of the international supply chain linking producers to consumers in all types of goods and services. Also it is the arena where 'added value' or 'added costs' can be found.

The three parametres by which we can prioritize and select foreign markets are 'market potential', 'similarity' and 'accessibility'.

Unit 5

Debriefing Activity 5.1

You should choose an appropriate commodity, product or service. Identify the major emphases in:

- Marketing objective setting
- Gathering SLEPT data and SWOT data
- Market data
- Customer data
- The marketing mix – product, price, promotion, distribution, physical evidence, people and processes
- Organizational and financial requirements
- Incoterms
- Evaluation and control techniques.

The change of emphases will be brought about through consideration of the product, market requirements, stage of country development, technology considerations, logistical considerations, trading bloc developments, etc.

Debriefing Table 5.5

Example: Avocados from Zimbabwe

- Should we go international? Selectively go international with a target Winter months selling window
- Competitors? South Africa, Israel, South America
- Where should we go? Sell to the UK supermarkets
- How should we get there? Choose an agent in the UK to import
- How should we sell? Sell loose packed product to supermarket specifications
- Market it through a contract to the 3 top supermarkets
- How do we organize? Fix marketing budget? Organize a contract with the agent and share marketing budget. Seal a contract with outgrowers in Zimbabwe, collection and packing shed, freight forwarder, uplift facility and UK supply chain
- Expected outcomes? Expect 10 per cent of retail price.

Debriefing Activity 5.6

Level of involvement means 'How close to the consumer need I be to succeed?'

To compare costs between a small firm and a mutinational consider factors like investment in plant and equipment, personnel, product variations, transactional costs, number of channels of distribution, marketing costs (marketing mix), evaluation and control expenses.

ing Activity 5.8

rganizations like the International Chamber of Commerce or the Society of Motor
urers and Traders.

Debriefing Activity 5.9

A plan for forging a positive relationship should include the following:

- A reward system seen fair by all
- Making the distributor feel part of the organization
- Developing a training programme
- Determining agreed targets and other performance standards
- Regular evaluation of performance standards
- Regular and effective communications
- Regular and timely payments and adherence to other elements of the contract.

Debriefing Activity 5.10

Examples are abundant in Quelch and Bartlett (op. cit.) and Doole and Lowe

Debriefing Activity 5.12

Mergers and takeovers include:

- Vodaphone and Mannesmann
- French Telecom and Orange
- Lloyds TSB and Scottish Widows
- AOL and TimeWarner
- Glaxo and Smith Kline
- BP and Amoco
- Astra and Zeneca
- NatWest and Bank of Scotland.

Benefits include:

- Economies of scale and scope
- Joint R & D and marketing
- Synergy
- Self-protection against predators
- Rationalization of costs, administration and production
- Market power
- Stakeholder returns.

Debriefing Question 5.3

1. Analysis, planning, implementation and evaluation and control.
2. Different local conditions, different ways of doing business, lack of communication, interpretation difficulties, misunderstanding, insufficient infrastructure and lack of training.
3. Depends on the severity. It should affect the decisions on where to compete, how to compete, with what to compete and when to compete.
4. Benefits are local knowledge, product/market variations respectively.
5. Control elements appropriate are establishing standards, measuring performance against them and correcting deviations.
6. Control systems are important so that the business activities can be measured. A good one allows measures what it is supposed to measure.
7. A marketing audit is an internal and external analysis. Its weakness is that it is a static snapshot in time, its advantages are that it allows a systematic approach to planning.

8. The BCG model gives a snapshot of an organization's current portfolio in terms of competitve position. It shows potential market possibilities.
9. Decisions on local staff recruitment, remuneration and administration.
10. Six characteristics: commitment from top management, good planning, good implementation, effective control techniques, good management and ample resources.
11. Alliances fail because management cannot agree, synergy could not be attained, the partners pursue different objectives, economies of scale and scope were not achieved and the organizational cultures were too different.

Unit 6

Debriefing Question 6.2

1. Globalization means 'the process of focusing an organization's resources on the selection and exploitation of global market opportunities consistent with and supportive of its short and long term strategic objectives and goals' (Toyne and Walters, 1989).
2. A pure globalization is not practical in every circumstance. There is, inevitably, an environmental factor which mitigates against pure globalization.
3. Factors actively promoting globalization are the international flow of information, the international spread of technology, size of investment required, emergence of global customers, relative world peace and reduction of trade barriers.
4. Factors inhibiting globalization are customers' tastes, culture, and local market conditions.
5. An organization can get close to planning a true global strategy provided it can gather and distil data on competition, market needs and business conditions and operations.

Unit 7

Debriefing Exam Question 7.1

This question is couched in a service context, so the answers should be suitably tailored to this situation. Answers should begin by contextualizing e-commerce development in the light of:

- An international strategy context
- A global communications context.

Candidates should give a brief description of the electronic facilities available and relevant to consultancy organizations, e.g. the internet.

Impact and opportunities should include:

- The opportunity to develop a global strategy rather than a 'marketing' opportunity
- A method of market entry
- Global communication possibilities
- Availability to build online/continuous consultancy capabilities relatively cheaply
- Product market development opportunities
- Interactive capabilities
- Offers 'twenty-four hour service'
- Inter-office linkages/customer lead follow up

Dangers of e-commerce include:

- Data security issues
- Data protection issues
- Competitor access
- System overload (too many competitors)
- System failure
- System corruption
- etc.

Debriefing Exam Question 7.4

A two-part question inviting a discussion on organizational and resource development and the implications on the host country.

Candidates should contextualize the answer and provide the relevant theoretical underpinning, e.g. Ohmae, and include the domestic, international, multinational, global spectrum.

Proposed changes in organizational form, resources and operations will be affected by:

- The size of the firm and business
- Number of foreign countries in which it operates
- Level of involvement
- The organization's overseas objectives for its foreign business
- Experience in international business
- Value and variety of products
- Nature of the marketing task.

Form may evolve from:

- Export department to international division to subsidiary to headquarters/ subsidiary arrangement (with centralization and decentralization argument and different organizational forms, e.g. matrix, product or brand).

Resources may evolve from:

- Expatriate to local staff issues
- Headquarters to subsidiary to local staff issues
- Expanded policies on recruitment, training, etc.
- Sources of finance – local bank to international banks
- Physical resources, i.e. local manufacturing to global manufacturing and marketing.

Operations may evolve:

- Ethno-centric to poly-centric or a combination
- Management (local to global) effectiveness (reference to models, e.g. Farmer-Richman)
- Transactional elements, e.g. global agencies
- Partnering and alliancing
- Marketing form development
- Social effects
- Cultural effects
- Economic effects, e.g. employment opportunities, standards of living
- Technological/skills/capabilities transfers
- Legal/tax implications and effect of 'expatriates' status
- Remittance of profits

Unit 8

Debriefing Activity 8.1

- Indirect exporting will require no product change
- Direct exporting will generally require no product change
- Marketing subsidiary may require local product development
- Licensing will require no product change
- Joint venture may require product change
- Wholly-owned operations may require product change.

Debriefing Activity 8.2

You should consider:

- The local, regional and international market trends, viz: tastes, distribution channels, prices and trade barriers
- The regional supply conditions in terms of technology, economies of scale and costs of involvement
- The local, regional and global competition.

The implications for marketing strategy should be considered:

- Objectives
- Choice of country and market
- Strategic stance
- Marketing mix considerations
- Evaluation and control.

Debriefing Activity 8.4

1. Packaged horticultural products from Kenya. The packaging includes cellophane and recyclable cardboard and the labelling includes weight, a description of contents and country of origin, bar code and sell by date. These elements have been made necessary by the demands of the supermarket for merchandising purposes and the packaging and phytosanitary regulations of the EU.
2. Packaged food ingredients from Korea. The package is recyclable and the labelling includes net weight, country of origin, nutrition information, ingredients, bar code, cooking instructions and best before date. These elements have been made nescessary by both EU and UK food packaging and labelling regulations.

Debriefing Question 8.1

1. Core component, e.g. physical elements, packaging component, e.g. design, support service component, e.g. locally available services. This helps develop international product policy because a consideration of all the components in the considered market will help determine any necessary product adaptions
2. Special aspects of services are that they are intangible, perishable, heterogenous, inseparable and not usually ownable
3. The five aspects of international product policy are standardization–adaption arguments, production–promotion mix decisions, image, branding and positioning, special aspects of packaging and portfolio considerations.
4. Observed trends in markets, supply and competition are national or regional, regional and regional respectively.
5. Benefits of a standardized approach to international markets are economies of scale, production, R & D and marketing, consumer mobility, spread and flow of technology, flow of information, cost of investment and reducing trade barriers.
6. Factors driving the company to adaption of product offerings are differing use conditions, government factors, culture and language, local market needs and tastes and company history and operations.
7. Meaning and importance of the product/promotion mix are the optimum combination of both product and promotion according to market conditions. Without this, markets can be created or destroyed very quickly.
8. Products are positioned in international markets through the product's perception in the actual or potential consumer's mind. It is based on the product's actual and psychological propositions.
9. Branding strategies are corporate umbrella branding, family umbrella names, range branding and individual brand names.

10. It is difficult to develop a truly global brand because of the many global cultural differences. It may be possible in 'image' building.
11. International packaging decisions are affected by local distribution considerations, climatic, geographical, economic and legal considerations.
12. Portfolio analysis can be used in international product policy but it has limitations: it is a snapshot in time, data is complex and difficult to analyse, there is a need to define the strategic business units, and the markets and competition are ever-moving.

Debriefing Activity 8.5

The issues here are price escalation and policy, for example, transfer pricing in international markets. As an answer to the question set consider the following case.

A manufacturer of standard engineering components is considering a potential large order from an overerseas enquirer. Locally the company sells the components for £10, basing the price on a competitive basis as there are many domestic suppliers. In considering the international order it has to consider channel margins, delivery, insurance and other forwarding costs. The enquirer is wishing to sell the product in his own market at £25.

The company calculates the following:

	£	
Target price in the foreign market		25
Less 40% retail margin on selling price	10	
Retailer cost		15
Less 15% importer/distributor mark up cost	1.96	
Distributor cost		13.04
Less 125 value added tax on landed value and duty	1.40	
CIF value plus duty		11.64
Less 9% duty on CIF value	0.96	
Landed CIF value		10.68
Less ocean freight and insurance	1.40	
Regional FOB price to reach target price		9.26

The calculation shows that by fulfilling the export order, the company would sell at a lesser price than in the domestic market. The decision to go ahead will depend on whether it is selling to production and demand capacity locally and whether the incremental sales overseas might lead to more orders (loss-leader policy) and/or it can renegotiate the price.

Debriefing Activity 8.6

Company factors should include: corporate and marketing objectives, market position, cost structures and inventory and transportation costs.

Market factors should include: what is the market willing to pay, local market situation vis á vis distribution channels, discounting procedures, market growth and elasticity of demand and the degree of product adaption or standardization.

Environment factors include: competition, government and other legislative issues, currency fluctuations, inflation, business cycles, etc.

Debriefing Question 8.2

1. Pricing policy interacts with other elements of the marketing mix in that it can signify product quality and/or image. For example Rolex watches are very highly priced. This not only sends a message about the quality of the product but enables a high quality marketing communications image dictating the type of media to be used and the exclusivity of distribution outlets.
2. An organization's pricing objectives may be affected by rate of return reqirements, competition, demand, market factors, product differentiation considerations and early cash recovery.
3. Factors affecting final prices are company and product factors, market factors and environmental factors.
4. Price setting may be done on a cost base, market base or competition base.
5. Domestic and export prices are linked in that there is the question of how export prices are to be set relative to domestic pices. Generally they will be higher because of cost escalation, e.g. insurance, freight, possible currency fluctuations and marketing margins.
6. Three Transfer pricing methods are at cost, at cost plus and at arm's length.
7. Non-cash payment is where payment is made on a non-cash basis, generally relevant to LDCs whose currencies are not acceptable or available. The usual methods are leasing and counter-trade.
8. Counter-trade can be barter, swaps, switch deals or transfer of goods.

Debriefing Activity 8.11

Ask yourself the questions:

- Is Amsterdam a mailing centre?
- Is it centrally located in Europe?
- Are there cost implications?
- Are cultural factors being addressed?
- Does the direct communication emanate from further afield?

Debriefing Activity 8.12

Examples include Mercedes Benz cars, Renault cars, Zurich Insurance, Sony, Emirates Airlines, IBM, Visit Malaysia, holidays in South Africa.

Debriefing Exam Question 8.3

Answers should begin with contextualizing satellite broadcasting in terms of:

- International strategy
- Communications strategy
- Media strategy

Particularly, candidates should express how the development enhances the 'adaptation' versus 'standardization' debate, especially in an international strategy context.

Strategic advantages:

- The use of satellite as an aid in the accomplishment of a 'global' and/or 'local' communications strategy
- Support to market entry strategy
- Cost and efficiency arguments
- Ability to cross-link with other broadcasters
- Ability to continue across media, i.e. radio and television.

Tactical advantages:

- Ability to reach segments at different times of the day/night
- Tactical segments globally, e.g. 'news segments'
- Use of media in continuation or irregularly

- Ease and speed of access to medium
- 'Virtual' shopping capabilities.

Debriefing Activity 8.13

In order to answer these questions contact the Institute of Practitioners in Advertising (IPA), UK, look in *Campaign* or contact The Institute of Marketing UK.

Debriefing Question 8.4

1. Personal selling has greater importance when wages are low, liguistic pluralism exists, business etiquette requires a personal visit, and the contract or product is of large value or complexity respectively.
2. Problems in establishing a local sales force include recruitment, training, motivation and control and evaluation.
3. Issues involved in sales promotion are the offer, cooperation from intermediaries, regulations and bribery. Local agencies will understand these issues.
4. Factors influencing push or pull strategies are push: culture, wages, language, media availability, length of channel and market variability; pull: advertising leverage power, wide media choice, high budgets, self-service predominates and the influence on the trade of advertising.
5. Patterns in sales promotion in Europe reveal UK, Ireland and Eastern Europe as the most frequent users.
6. Companies sponsoring Formula 1 include cigarettes (where possible), clothing, petroleum and tyres. They attain a 'share of mind', a co-branding position and an international awareness and identity.
7. With the internet, global advertising could be for the many.
8. The advertising industry should respond to e business and satellite development by offering clients more targeted market reach opportunities, more production capabilities and expertise and more segment possibilities.
9. Some global campaigns work but others fail due to insensitivity to cultural differences, poor scheduling and coordination of effort, lack of campaign integration, scale of budget, wrong choice or lack of media, poor agency selection, poor message choice, competition, insensitivity to market stage of development and poor training or lack of clarity of objectives and brief and communication to personnel involved.

Illustrate your answer by examples.

Unit 10

Debriefing Activity 10.1

Choose, for example, food retailing.

There are two processes, the functional and the physical distribution processes.

The functional distribution process (unless the manufacturer went direct) would be wholesaler to retailer to customer. The physical distribution process would be warehousing, transport and order processing.

The additional factors if servicing the same industry overseas are the culture, business environment, customer expectations, company objectives, resources, channel availability, channel monetery expectations and channel management issues.

Debriefing Activity 10.2

The changes taking place that affect logistics are inventory holding levels, the internet, convergence of distribution companies, consolidation of loads, etc.

Debriefing Activity 10.3

You should consider the following and their effect on the micro environment of distribution: increasing wealth, technological development and advances in communications, growth of multinational and transnational corporations, emerging global consumers, world brands, the one world marketplace, interdependence, WTO, the emergence of economic blocs, and global financial facilitators.

Debriefing Activity 10.4

Efficiency factors will be related to costs, capital, control, coverage, character and continuity.

Effectiveness factors will be related to customer characteristics, culture, competition, company objectives and communications.

Debriefing Question 10.1

The key factors in developing distribution strategy are costs, capital requirements, coverage by the channel, control issues, continuity, character, customer characteristics, culture, competition, company objectives, communications, channel length, channel and motivation requirements.

Issues to consider are channel availability, sales potential, geographic coverage, financial strength, service capabilities, breadth of coverage and the ability to meet the company's objectives.

The distribution strategy open to Timberland would be exclusivity via fashion retailers, own outlets or exclusive high price stores.

An international logistics system would differ from a domestic one in terms of complexity, (culture, language, documentation, management) costs (cashflow, insurance), transport time, mutimodal use and inventory requirements.

As a export organization you would consider all effectiveness and efficiency factors plus all the issues regarding the selection, management and control of distribution channels. The logistics elements would be very important as the products are relatively low value, face high competition and fast moving. Inventory levels and warehousing would be major concerns as would the possibility of theft.

Debriefing Activity 10.5

Identify the function or personnel concerned.

Which efficiency measures are they responsible for? What are they?

Identify how target market choice, market entry strategy and distribution is affected by financial considerations.

Debriefing Activity 10.6

To answer these questions you need to look at a source of currency movement information.

Debriefing Question 10.2

1. The role of financial management is to ensure prudence in operations to safeguard a return on investment from international operations.
2. The three principal financial aspects to international marketing strategy are to raise capital both start up and working, manage financial risk (foreign exchange) and safeguard the repatriation of profits.
3. The two types of international capital which may be required are start-up or investment capital and working capital.
4. The two types of international financial risk are foreign exchange risk and political risk.
5. Transaction exposure can be avoided by entering into forward contracts or hedging.

6. Political risk can be reduced by, as far as possible, aligning the organization's goals and objectives with that of the host governments.
7. The key problems associated with profit repatriation are different tax systems, legislation which affect repatriated flows, as well as differential inflation rates which can change competitive positions and hence, cash flows.

Unit 11

Debriefing Activity 11.4

Look for breakdown in communications, incomplete or incomparable data, changes in the environment (SLEPT) factors, clashes or changes in organizational culture, problems associated with changes in size and faulty forecasting or estimating.

Look for the above factors again, but this time in a positive way.

Debriefing Question 11.1

1. The role of the control system is to ensure that desired results are obtained from planning activity.
2. Strategy can be evaluated by the short term, e.g. profits and the long term, e.g. brand equity building.
3. Types of measures under financial measures include profit, profitability, shareholder return cash flow/liquidity, share price, earnings per share, return on net assets and return on sales.
4. Types of measures that are non-financial are market growth, growth, competitive advantage, competitive position, sales volume, market penetration levels, new product development, customer satisfaction, customer brand franchise and market image and awareness levels.
5. Strategic models, e.g. the Boston Matrix, can be used to test the conceptual approach to international marketing strategy.
6. A 'control system' is to ensure that an organization drives through the content of its international marketing plans and achieves its organizational objectives in the marketplace.
7. The four key issues in a control system are standard setting, performance measurement, performance diagnosis and taking corrective action if required.
8. Divergence from standards can be picked up by regular auditing of the organization's finance and marketing activities, developing and identifying divergence from budgeted inflows and outflows and through variance analysis, i.e. the difference between actual and expected results.
9. The special factors that affect the efficiency and effectiveness of control systems are the lack of, or poor, communications, incomplete or innacurate data, environmental changes, the organizational culture of centralization versus decentralization, the size of international operations and faulty estimating.

Syllabus

Aims and objectives

- To enable students to develop a thorough understanding of international marketing theory and key concepts.
- To develop a knowledge and understanding of vocabulary associated with international/ global marketing strategy in different types of economies, organizations and market situations.
- To appreciate the complexities of international and global marketing in a mix of economies.
- To create an awareness of processes, context and influences associated with international and global marketing strategies in a range of economies.
- To develop students' appreciation of strategies and plans for a mix of international and global economies.
- To develop an understanding of the implications for implementation, monitoring and control of the international marketing planning process.

Learning outcomes

On successful completion of this unit students will be able to:

- Demonstrate an understanding of the changing nature of the international trading environment, the major trends, strategic and contextual, affecting the global decision, and the different business and social/cultural conventions which affect buying behaviour and marketing approaches in international markets.
- Determine marketing strategies appropriate to industrialized, developing and lesser developed economies, and identify and explain the relevant sources of information and analysis necessary to support the appropriate strategy.
- Formulate strategies for export, international, multinational, transnational and global marketing operations and evaluate the relevant organizational changes as an organization moves through the export to global spectrum.
- Select and justify an appropriate marketing strategy, marketing mix and evaluate the financial, human resource, operational and logistical implications of different international strategies.
- Determine the appropriate control measures in international operations.

Indicative content and weighting

2.1 International Strategic Analysis (30%)

2.1.1 Identifying and analysing opportunities in the international trading environment.

- Changing patterns of trade globally and types of markets (product/service/commodity/ not for profit).

2.1.2 The strategic and contextual elements of global operations.

- Organizational and external. Global and multinational marketing as a strategic decision.
- Strategic networking and the international supply chain.

2.1.3 The changes in the world trading environment: Countries, world, regions (e.g. European Union ASEAN etc.) and trading blocs.

224

2.1.4 The SLEPT factors: Social/cultural, legal, economic, political, technological and ethical, green and other environmental considerations. The role and effect of pressure groups.

2.1.5 The 'C' factors: Countries, currency, competitors and their effect on international marketing planning.

2.1.6 Evaluating customers' buying behaviour (consumer, business, institutional) in different countries at different stages of economic and political development.

- Using marketing research to identify opportunities, similarities and differences.

2.1.7 Market Research Agency selection for international marketing support, the use of databases, intelligent and expert systems. Government initiatives and the importance of cross-cultural analysis.

2.1.8 The use of competitive/absolute/comparative analysis in international market appraisal.

2.1.9 The consequences of a more ethical responsibility approach including green and environmental issues and their effect on global corporate operations.

2.2 International Strategic Planning (30%)

2.2.1 Different approaches to International Marketing Planning; Transactional; Relational, and Knowledge Based Approaches between developed countries and Lesser Developed Countries (LDCs) and developing and emergent economies.

2.2.2 The organizational and management issues pertinent to the export to globalization spectrum decision, organizational structures, cultures, capabilities and the leveraging of core competencies and capabilities.

2.2.3 The globalization process-partnering, alliances, mergers and their effect on the structure of industry and the competitive environment.

2.2.4 The organization as a learning organization and non-linear approaches to planning, including expert and database system, emergent strategies and 'muddling through'.

2.2.5 The cross-cultural dimensions of global activity and cultural sensitivity.

2.2.6 The effect of market/economic transience on global operations and within the host country environment – social, supply chain, labour and economic factors.

2.2.7 Managing and controlling in-house and external resources. The expatriate, national and global staff.

2.2.8 Standardization and differentiation: the issues of globalization in international marketing.

2.2.9 The determination of market entry choices, selection and decision and the implications for strategy and sources of global finance to support entry strategies.

2.2.10 The determination of market entry choices, selection and decision and the implications for strategy.

2.2.11 Sources of global finance to support entry strategies.

2.3 International Strategy Implementation and Control (40%)

2.3.1 Identifying and selecting a product management strategy.

2.3.2 Determining pricing strategies for international markets: Skimming and penetration pricing; currency considerations in exporting and international marketing. Price escalation in the value chain, the futures market, hedging/forward buying, tendering and bartering. The meaning and specifics of Incoterms and specific pricing methods.

2.3.3 Determining international marketing communications issues relating to international positioning strategies. The importance of cultural differences and similarities.

2.3.4 The selection of a distribution and logistics strategy. Foreign channel management. Channel members' expectations and performance; customer service levels. The evolving forms of distribution, e.g. e-business.

2.3.5 Global technological developments and their strategic competitive effect e.g. e-commerce, Internet in general and global media.

2.3.6 The process and evidence of global operations – strategies, human and their physical transactional activities.

2.3.7 Assessing the people elements of global operations – cross/inter cultural dimensions and transaction activity and human involvement.

2.3.8 The role of a relationship marketing approach as complementary to a traditional marketing mix approach.

2.3.9 Implementing international/global marketing strategy across different countries and the strategic implications. The tactical and operational issues relevant to different countries and situations.

2.3.10 Establishing criteria for control and evaluation of marketing and other business functions including self-assessment, benchmarking, best practice, and the balanced scorecard. The strategic implications of differing rates of implementation across the developed and developing world.

Reading list

Core texts

Doole, I. and Lowe, R. (2001) *International Marketing Strategy: Analysis, development and implementation*. 3rd revised edition. London, Thomson Learning.

Usunier, J. (2000) *Marketing Across Cultures*. Harlow, FT/Prentice-Hall.

Paliwoda, S. and Thomas, M. (1998) *International Marketing*. 3rd revised edition. Oxford, CIM/Butterworth-Heinemann.

Ambler, T. and Styles, C. (2000) *The Silk Road to International Marketing*. London, FT/ Prentice-Hall.

Jeannet, J. and Hennessey, H. (2000) *Global Marketing Strategies*. 5th revised edition. US, Houghton Mifflin.

Syllabus guides

CIM (2002) *CIM Companion: International marketing strategy*. Cookham, Chartered Institute of Marketing.

BPP (2002) *International Marketing Strategy*. London, BPP Publishing.

Carter, S. (2002) *International Marketing Strategy Coursebook*. Oxford, Butterworth-Heinemann.

Supplementary

Bradley, F. (2001) *International Marketing Strategy*. 4th edition. Harlow, Pearson.

Chee, H. and Harris, R. (1997) *Global Marketing Strategy*. London, Pitman.

Czinkota, M. and Ronkainen, I. (2000) *International Marketing*. 6th revised edition. US, Harcourt Brace.

Grant, R.M. (2002) *Contemporary Strategy Analysis: Concepts, techniques, applications.* 4th revised edition. Oxford, Blackwell.

Keegan, W. and Schlegelmilch, B. (2000) *Global Marketing Management: A European Perspective.* Hemel Hempstead, Prentice-Hall.

Kotler, P. and Kartajaya, H. (2000) *Repositioning Asia: From bubble to sustainable economy.* Chichester, John Wiley.

Mead, R. (1998) *International Management: Cross cultural dimensions.* Oxford, Blackwell.

Terpstra, V. and Sarathy, R. (1999) *International Marketing.* 8th edition. US, Dryden.

BPP (2002) *International Marketing Practice and Revision Kits.* London, BPP Publishing.

International Marketing Strategy: Success Tape. Learning cassettes by BPP Publishing.

Index